Calling on the name of
the Lord

NEW STUDIES IN BIBLICAL THEOLOGY 38

Series editor: D. A. Carson

Calling on the name of the Lord

A BIBLICAL THEOLOGY OF PRAYER

J. Gary Millar

APOLLOS

INTERVARSITY PRESS
DOWNERS GROVE, ILLINOIS 60515

APOLLOS (an imprint of Inter-Varsity Press, England)
36 Causton Street
London SW1P 4ST, England
Website: www.ivpbooks.com
Email: ivp@ivpbooks.com

InterVarsity Press, USA
P.O. Box 1400
Downers Grove, IL 60515-1426, USA
Website: www.ivpress.com
Email: email@ivpress.com

First published 2016

Set in Monotype Times New Roman
Typeset in Great Britain by CRB Associates, Potterhanworth, Lincolnshire
Printed and bound in Great Britain by Ashford Colour Press Ltd, Gosport, Hampshire

USA ISBN 978-0-8308-2639-1 (print)
USA ISBN 978-0-8308-9398-0 (digital)
UK ISBN 978-1-78359-395-8

 As a member of Green Press Initiative, InterVarsity Press is committed to protecting the environment and to the responsible use of natural resources. To learn more, visit greenpressinitiative.org.

British Library Cataloguing in Publication Data
A catalogue record for this book is available from the British Library.

Library of Congress Cataloging-in-Publication Data
A catalog record for this book is available from the Library of Congress.

P   23 22 21 20 19 18 17 16 15 14 13 12 11 10 9 8 7 6 5 4 3 2 1
Y   35 34 33 32 31 30 29 28 27 26 25 24 23 22 21 20 19 18 17 16

For Lucy, Sophie and Rebekah
(the noisiest pray-ers I know)
praying that you will
call on the name of the Lord
for the rest of your lives

Contents

Series preface		9
Author's preface		11
Abbreviations		13
Introduction: prayer and the gospel		15
1 The day prayer began: prayer in the Pentateuch		19
The day prayer began		19
Calling on the name of Yahweh		22
Interim conclusions: the essential nature of biblical prayer		27
Prayer in the Pentateuch – a thesis tested		30
Conclusion		42
2 Big prayers and the movements of history:		
prayer in the Former Prophets		45
Prayer in the book of Joshua		45
Prayer in the book of Judges		47
Prayer in the books of Samuel		52
Prayer in the books of Kings		59
Conclusion		65
3 Praying in the light of the future:		
prayer in the Latter Prophets		67
Long prayers and large books		67
Short prayers and short(ish) books		91
Conclusion		106
4 Praying for a new covenant: prayer in the Writings		107
The wisdom of prayer		107
Praying through the exile		116
Praying for a new covenant (prayer in Ezra–Nehemiah		
and Chronicles)		120
Conclusion		136

5   The psalms, the Messiah and the church   137
    Are the psalms 'prayers'?   137
    Whose prayers are these?   140
    Does the psalter have a message?   163
    How does the psalter contribute to a biblical
        theology of prayer?   165

6   Jesus and prayer: prayer in the Gospels   167
    The birth of Jesus and prayer   168
    The teaching of Jesus and prayer   170
    The parables of Jesus and prayer   183
    The life of Jesus and prayer   185

7   The church at prayer: prayer in the book of Acts   191
    Prayer in Jerusalem   191
    Prayer in Judea and Samaria   195
    Prayer at the ends of the earth   199
    Conclusion   199

8   Church planting and prayer: prayer in Paul's letters 201
    Praying for others with Paul   201
    Paul's teaching on prayer   209
    Paul's exhortations to pray   212
    Conclusion   215

9   The end of prayer: prayer in the later New Testament 217
    Prayer and Hebrews   217
    Prayer and James   219
    Prayer and Peter   224
    Prayer and Jude   224
    Prayer and John   225
    Conclusion   229

Afterword: why this matters – (re)learning to pray big prayers 231
    Introduction   231
    Analysis: Whatever happened to evangelicals and prayer? 232
    Diagnosis: Why is the church praying less?   233
    Relearning to pray   236

Bibliography   241
Index of authors   251
Index of Scripture references   255

Series preface

New Studies in Biblical Theology is a series of monographs that address key issues in the discipline of biblical theology. Contributions to the series focus on one or more of three areas: (1) the nature and status of biblical theology, including its relations with other disciplines (e.g. historical theology, exegesis, systematic theology, historical criticism, narrative theology); (2) the articulation and exposition of the structure of thought of a particular biblical writer or corpus; and (3) the delineation of a biblical theme across all or part of the biblical corpora.

Above all, these monographs are creative attempts to help thinking Christians understand their Bibles better. The series aims simultaneously to instruct and to edify, to interact with the current literature and to point the way ahead. In God's universe, mind and heart should not be divorced: in this series we will try not to separate what God has joined together. While the notes interact with the best of scholarly literature, the text is uncluttered with untransliterated Greek and Hebrew, and tries to avoid too much technical jargon. The volumes are written within the framework of confessional evangelicalism, but there is always an attempt at thoughtful engagement with the sweep of the relevant literature.

Many books have been written on prayer. Not a few are of the 'how to' variety. Some are almost mystical. Others carefully work through biblical passages – the prayers of Paul, for instance, or of David. Still others survey the many different kinds of address to God found in the Bible. The approach of Dr Gary Millar, in this volume, is unique: he combs through the entire Bible to discover the *focus* of prayers in each book or corpus of the Bible: this is a biblical theology of prayer. At one level what he uncovers is scarcely surprising: the vast majority of biblical prayers are tied in one fashion or another to God's purposes across the sweep of redemptive history, culminating in Jesus and the gospel. At another level what he finds is revolutionary: a great deal of contemporary Christian praying is centred on individual anxieties, needs and preferences, and not on the purposes and promises of God.

This is not so much wicked (after all, Peter tells his readers, 'casting all your anxieties on him, because he cares for you', 1 Peter 5:7) as horribly imbalanced. In other words, Gary Millar's work not only informs us about prayer in the Bible, but also, rightly absorbed, drives us to prayer that is in line with God's saving purposes. And suddenly it becomes clearer what it means to pray in Jesus' name.

D. A. Carson
Trinity Evangelical Divinity School

Author's preface

All theology needs to be preached and lived. That is why writing an academic book on prayer is a deeply challenging experience, and it is why I am so grateful to Fiona, my wife, for her partnership in the gospel and all of life, and her constant encouragement to live out what I have been teaching and writing during the past couple of years. It is also why I gladly dedicate this book to my daughters Lucy, Sophie and Rebekah, who share with us (and create!) the unique delights and disasters of family prayer time, a daily reminder in our house of our need to call on the name of the Lord.

Thinking and writing about prayer, as well as seeking to grow in my own commitment to and enjoyment of prayer, has also lead me to reflect on and thank God for the people who have taught me most about prayer over the years. I am deeply thankful for my parents, John and Lorna Millar, for encouraging me to pray from my earliest days; for my youth fellowship leaders at my home church in Lisburn, Northern Ireland, who introduced me to praying with others; for my fellow students in the Christian Union groups at Queen's in Belfast and Aberdeen; for the unique and life-changing experience of congregational prayer modelled on Saturday nights by William Still and the church family at Gilcomston South, Aberdeen; for my in-laws, Warner and Sheena Hardie, who introduced me to the delights of praying for world mission around the breakfast table; and for the faithful 'prayer warriors' at Hamilton Road Presbyterian Church, Bangor. Our experience over twelve exciting years in Dublin heightened our commitment to pray for gospel faithfulness and gospel growth, and we will never forget the times of prayer we enjoyed in Howth, and Malahide Presbyterian Church in both good times and bad.

Writing this book has also deepened our gratitude for those precious people who have prayed for us so faithfully over many years – we need it more than ever, and hope they will be encouraged to pray on for God to do his work in and through us by the Spirit through reading these pages.

Since my move to Australia in 2012, many people have listened to me 'think out loud' about prayer, and helped me to sharpen that thinking. I am deeply grateful to those involved in the Tasmania Christian Convention, Ignite Conference in Brisbane, Coffs Harbour Presbyterian Church in New South Wales, the Ministry Training and Development Conference of the Anglican Diocese of Sydney, Queensland and Northern New South Wales Church Missionary Society Summer School and the churches of the central coast of New South Wales, who have all been exposed to the developing ideas in this book, and have helped make it better than it otherwise would have been.

I am also grateful to my colleagues at Queensland Theological College, who have listened to random extracts of the argument of the book (and often sharpened them), helped track down resources and set me free to write. The peerless Annette McGrath, our librarian, has been an immense help. A special word of thanks is also due to the students/graduates who helped in the latter stages of production – Kamina Wust, Katie Allan, Melinda Smith and Lorissa Achjian. It is a privilege to be part of a godly and supportive community like Queensland Theological College, which is committed to 'calling on the name of the Lord' to keep the promises he has made to us in the gospel.

Don Carson continues to be an example and an encouragement to me, and this book is much better than it would have been because of him. Philip Duce at Inter-Varsity Press has been a pleasure to work with, as always. My thanks go also to Eldo Barkhuizen, whose rigorous and gracious copy-editing brought new clarity to the argument.

My prayer is that even through this book our God and King will continue to glorify his name in all the earth, as he moves people like us to call on his name.

Gary Millar
August 2015

Abbreviations

AB	Anchor Bible
AcBib	Academia biblica
ANE	ancient Near East(ern)
AOTC	Apollos Old Testament Commentary
AYB	Anchor Yale Bible
BCOTWP	Baker Commentary on the Old Testament Wisdom and Psalms
BECNT	Baker Exegetical Commentary on the New Testament
BECOT	Baker Exegetical Commentary on the Old Testament
BTCB	Brazos Theological Commentary on the Bible
BZAW	Beihefte zur Zeitschrift für die alttestamentliche Wissenschaft
CC	Continental Commentaries
DCH	*Dictionary of Classical Hebrew*, ed. D. J. A. Clines, 6 vols., Sheffield: Sheffield Phoenix, 1993–2008
DOTP	*Dictionary of the Old Testament: Pentateuch*, ed. T. D. Alexander and D. W. Baker, Downers Grove: InterVarsity Press; Leicester: Inter-Varsity Press, 2003
EBC	The Expositor's Bible Commentary
ECC	Eerdmans Critical Commentary
FOTB	Focus on the Bible
FOTL	The Forms of the Old Testament Literature
GKC	*Gesenius' Hebrew Grammar*, ed. E. Kautzsch, rev. and tr. A. E. Cowley, Oxford: Clarendon, 1910
HALOT	*The Hebrew and Aramaic Lexicon of the Old Testament*, ed. L. Koehler and W. Baumgartner, tr. and ed. under the supervision of M. E. J. Richardson, 5 vols., Leiden: Brill, 1994–2000
HBT	*Horizons in Biblical Theology*
JSOTSup	Journal for the Study of the Old Testament, Supplement Series

LHB/OTS	Library of the Hebrew Bible / Old Testament Studies
MLBS	Mercer Library of Biblical Studies
MT	Masoretic Text
NAC	New American Commentary
NIBC	New International Biblical Commentary
NICNT	New International Commentary on the New Testament
NICOT	New International Commentary on the Old Testament
NIDOTTE	*New International Dictionary of Old Testament Theology and Exegesis*, ed. W. A. VanGemeren, 5 vols., Carlisle: Paternoster; Grand Rapids: Zondervan, 1997
NIGTC	New International Greek Testament Commentary
NIVAC	New International Version Application Commentary
NSBT	New Studies in Biblical Theology
NT	New Testament
NTS	*New Testament Studies*
OBT	Overtures to Biblical Theology
OT	Old Testament
OTL	Old Testament Library
PNTC	Pillar New Testament Commentary
PTW	Preaching the Word
SBET	*Scottish Bulletin of Evangelical Theology*
SBLDS	Society of Biblical Literature Dissertation Series
SHBC	Smyth & Helwys Bible Commentary
TynB	*Tyndale Bulletin*
THOTC	The Two Horizons Old Testament Commentary
TNTC	Tyndale New Testament Commentaries
TOTC	Tyndale Old Testament Commentaries
VT	*Vetus Testamentum*
WBC	Word Biblical Commentary
ZECNT	Zondervan Exegetical Commentary on the New Testament

Introduction:
prayer and the gospel

It is a difficult and formidable thing to write on prayer,
and one fears to touch the Ark. Perhaps no-one ought to
undertake it unless he has spent more toil in the practice of
prayer than on its principle. But perhaps also the effort to
look into its principle may be graciously regarded by him
who ever liveth to make intercession as itself a prayer to
know better how to pray.

(P. T. Forsyth, *The Soul of Prayer*)

For various reasons, including those expressed so beautifully by
P. T. Forsyth, I had no intention or ambition to write a book on
prayer. Over the past few years, however, several interrelated concerns
have driven me to this unexpected place! At the root of my interest
is simply a desire to pray more and more effectively as one who
belongs to, is called to and is enabled to pray by the Lord Jesus Christ.
To that is added a growing sense of disquiet at the marginalization
of prayer in local churches across the English-speaking world. In
the circles I move in there has clearly been a significant increase
in expository preaching, for which I thank God. Evangelism has
become more thoughtful, relational and clearly gospel-centred, which
is hugely encouraging. The quality of engagement with the biblical
text in small groups is, I think, significantly richer than was the case,
say, in the 1980s. All this is massively encouraging. But there is
another trend that often goes unnoticed – *the church in many places
has stopped praying.*[1]

I am not suggesting that this has been a policy decision, or the result
of a blatant declaration of self-reliance. In most cases, I suspect, it
has just happened – often as a result of the laudable goal of getting
more people engaged in the life of the local church. We have decen-
tralized, and the prayer gathering has been replaced by a small-group
programme. And the net result when it comes to prayer? All too often
prayer is relegated to that slot somewhere after 9.30 p.m., where the

---

[1] This analysis is developed more fully in the afterword.

group leader (of which I have often been a prime example) says something like 'Oh, I didn't realize it was so late. We'd better stop there and pray for a couple of minutes before we go.' The fact that the rushed prayers that follow are often dominated by concern for someone's next-door neighbour's grandmother who may or may not be a Christian and has been diagnosed with cancer (important though it is to pray for people like this) simply serves to highlight the lack of gospel depth in our view of prayer.

These twin concerns of personal growth, and a sense that prayer was slipping off the agenda of the church, were fuelled by the observation that books on prayer seemed at least to have lost their place in the pantheon of must-read Christian classics. So, for example, when I was a student from the late 1980s onwards, no respectable member of the Christian Union would ever have admitted to not having read Ole Hallesby's classic book *Prayer*[2] and would probably earnestly have been working through Don Carson's more recently published *A Call to Spiritual Reformation: Priorities from Paul and His Prayers*.[3] Even among theological students today I am struggling to think of a title on prayer from any generation or written at any level that commands such attention.[4] When I decided several years ago to plunge in at the deep end and give a series of five conference addresses on prayer, I struggled to find a book that simply dealt with the biblical material on prayer, beginning with Genesis and finishing with Revelation. There were helpful studies on the Lord's Prayer, and Paul's prayers, and some excellent books on the practice of prayer, but no single comprehensive treatment of the unfolding story of what the Bible says about prayer.[5]

---

[2] Hallesby 1931.

[3] Carson 1992.

[4] Paul Miller's marvellous *A Praying Life* (2009) is one exception, and during the time of writing of this volume the relative 'silence' has been broken by two extremely helpful Reformed evangelical books on prayer: see Keller 2014; Philip 2015.

[5] There was, of course, Graeme Goldsworthy's immensely stimulating *Prayer and the Knowledge of God* (2003). But unusually for Goldsworthy his approach is more systematic-theological than biblical-theological in its true sense. Further investigation did uncover some other excellent books on prayer in the Bible – Tim Chester's insightful *The Message of Prayer* (2003), while not strictly speaking a biblical theology, does cover much of the biblical material. *Teach Us to Pray* is a valuable collection of studies (see Carson 1990, and in particular, the chapter by Ed Clowney [Clowney 1990: 136–173]), as, at a more academic level, is *Into God's Presence*, edited by Richard Longenecker (Longenecker 2001). There are also several studies by critical scholars (see e.g. Clements 1985; P. D. Miller 1994), but it remains the case that there is no study of which I am aware that simply traces the unfolding biblical material on prayer.

As I continued to try to think through these rather disparate concerns, I came across these statements in Calvin's discussion of prayer in *The Institutes of the Christian Religion*, 3.20.1–3:

> Just as faith is born from the gospel, so through it our hearts are trained to call upon God's name [Rom. 10:14–17]. And this is precisely what [the apostle] had said a little before: the Spirit of adoption, who seals the witness of the gospel in our hearts [Rom. 8:16] raises up our spirits to dare to show forth to God their desires, to stir up unspeakable groanings [Rom. 8:26], and confidently cry, 'Abba! Father!' [Rom. 8:15].[6]

> So true is it that we dig up by prayer the treasures that were pointed out by the Lord's gospel, and which our faith has gazed upon.[7]

> But they . . . do not observe to what end the Lord has instructed his people to pray, for he ordained it not so much for his own sake as ours.[8]

For Calvin it is clear that there is an unbreakable link between prayer and the gospel. And with that simple, but compellingly profound, insight the trajectory of this study was set. What follows in these pages is an exposition of the fact that prayer in the Bible is intimately linked with the gospel – God's promised and provided solution to the problem of human rebellion against him and its consequences. The gospel shape of prayer is evident from the opening pages of the Bible – and in particular from the first mention of prayer in Genesis 4:26, when people first begin to 'call on the name of Yahweh' – right through to the end, when the church prays, 'Come, Lord Jesus!' (see Rev. 22:20).

This study will follow the contours of the Bible's teaching on prayer. After defining prayer as 'calling on the name of the Lord', my intention is simply to demonstrate how the biblical material builds on this basic understanding. As a result, more biblical text will be quoted than is normal in an NSBT volume. This is deliberate. Even careful readers of the Bible often overlook significant teaching on prayer because it is deeply embedded in passages of narrative or poetry where the

---

[6] Calvin 1960, 2: 850–851.
[7] Ibid. 851.
[8] Ibid. 852.

CALLING ON THE NAME OF THE LORD

main emphasis lies somewhere else. Prayer is an important biblical-theological 'thread' running through the Scriptures, but it is one that is easily missed in the tangle of other material. My hope is that this volume will make a small contribution to help the church rediscover the persistent biblical witness to the importance of prayer.

Initially the focus will be on showing how 'calling on the name of Yahweh', or *prayer that asks God to deliver on his covenantal promises*, is the foundation for all that the Old Testament says about prayer. On moving to the New Testament it will become apparent how *calling on the name of Yahweh* is redefined by Jesus himself, and how, after his death and resurrection, the apostles understood *praying in the name of Jesus* to be the new covenant expression of *calling on the name of Yahweh*. Prayer throughout the Bible, it will be argued, is to be primarily understood as asking God to come through on what he has already promised; as Calvin expressed it, 'through the Gospel our hearts are trained to call on God's name'.[9]

At the conclusion of this volume I have added an afterword. While not strictly following the logic of the argument, it is a vital part of the whole. This book is, at one level, an academic exercise. But at another it would be wholly disingenuous to undertake to write on prayer without both attempting to live out what is written and to apply it to the life of the church. The last word in this volume, then, is reserved for a brief attempt to apply the previous chapters' insights to the challenges we face as the church of Jesus Christ, calling on him in the middle of our broken world, as we await his return.

[9] Ibid. 850–851.

Chapter One

The day prayer began:
prayer in the Pentateuch

The day prayer began

The early chapters of Genesis are critical for any discussion of biblical theology. It is here – in creation, Eden and beyond – that the building blocks for understanding the storyline of the Bible are found. And it is here (not surprisingly) that *prayer begins*.

Where is the first prayer in the Bible? Sometimes it is suggested that the conversations between Adam, Eve and God in Eden are prayer. But the text does not present them in this way – they are described using the normal language of conversation.[1] In the same way that the relationship with God is not *explicitly* described as a 'covenant' because 'covenant' categories in the Old Testament are generally pressed into service when God is initiating steps to *restore a broken relationship*, these pre-fall, natural conversations are not described as 'prayer'.[2] Nor are any of the interactions surrounding Cain and Abel's sacrifices called prayer.[3] It is only when we come to the end of Genesis 4 that we find anything that looks unambiguously like prayer.

[1] This simple statement masks an important methodological point. As I will explain, in this study 'prayer' is taken to refer to the deliberate activity when human beings call on God *when he is not immediately present*. This is why the conversations between God and Adam (and God, Adam and Eve) in the Garden of Eden are not considered to be 'prayer'. Similarly, Abraham's conversation with Yahweh in Gen. 18 (when 'Abraham still stood before Yahweh . . . [and] drew near and said . . .' (18:22–23) does not, strictly speaking, belong to the category of prayer (contra many popular-level books, including e.g. Keller 2014: 26).

[2] I have no wish to enter the systematic theological debate at this point on the nature of the relationship between God and his newly created people. My point is not that it is inappropriate to describe pre-fall relationships as 'covenantal' in a systematic theological sense, but simply to point out that this is not how the text uses the language of covenant or how the language of prayer is used.

[3] Contra e.g. M. E. W. Thompson 1996: 12.

Genesis 4:25–26 states:

And Adam knew his wife again, and she bore a son and called his name Seth, for she said, 'God has appointed for me another offspring instead of Abel, for Cain killed him.' To Seth also a son was born, and he called his name Enosh. At that time people began to call upon the name of the LORD.[4]

This is the day that prayer began.

The key phrase is 'at that time, [men] began to call upon the name of Yahweh'. The construction emphasizes that this moment saw the definite beginning of something new.[5] However, in the flow of Genesis the most significant question is surely why this new beginning is signposted here. Why is the beginning of prayer triggered by the birth of Enosh? This is an intriguing question.

There seems to be no intrinsic significance attached to Enosh himself.[6] He plays no part in the unfolding narrative, and after this is mentioned only in the genealogies of Genesis 5 and 1 Chronicles 1. So we must look elsewhere for a rationale. Commentators have often noted the apparently inexplicable inclusion of this note after Cain's family tree in Genesis 4; so von Rad: 'The notice about the beginning of the Yahweh cult is strange and cannot be rightly explained.'[7] Those who have tried to explain the phrase have generally done so as a comment on the development of ancient religion (e.g. Wenham, Westermann et al.), although Calvin tried to trace it back to the godly

---

[4] Most books on prayer, even those with specific sections on the Pentateuch, make no comment on 'At that time people began to call upon the name of the LORD' (e.g. Clements 1985; Peskett in Carson 1990: 19–34; Balentine 1993; Chester 2003; however, Clowney, in Carson [1990: 138], without developing its significance does note the fact that prayer began at this point. Goldsworthy (2003: 72) also notes that prayer begins here but does not develop it, as does Verhoef 1997: 1062.

[5] See GKC 103c. According to GKC 144k, the passive is used here with an impersonal subject to denote an active. However, there are few parallels for this, and it may simply be an unusual way of focusing the reader's attention on the fact that *prayer begins*, rather than on the indeterminate identity of those who started this practice. So also Walton 2011: 279.

[6] No connection is made with etymological or aetiological possibilities flowing from the root.

[7] Von Rad 1972: 112–113. See also McKeown 2008: 44–45. This verse has been fertile ground for source-critical discussion, esp. in view of Exod. 3:13–14 and 6:3. However, this is not the place to mount a detailed defence of the early use of the name of Yahweh. For an overview of the discussion see e.g. Baker 2003: 359–368, as well as the slightly dated but nonetheless useful short treatment of the issue in Motyer 1959.

parenting of Seth.[8] On the whole, however, there has been little or no attempt to root this phrase in its theological context of the early chapters of Genesis.

In the immediate context I would argue that the focus of the unfolding narrative is fixed firmly on the importance of descendants – or, to be more exact, on *which descendant* would be the recipient of Yahweh's blessing. This dynamic is clearly present in the Cain and Abel narrative. However, I would go further and suggest that as early as 3:15 the search is on for one particular 'offspring' (*zera*').[9]

Within the narrative world of Genesis 1 – 11 it is likely that the fulfilment of promise of 3:15 is to be sought, in the first instance at least, in one of Adam and Eve's own children. The tension of the narrative at the beginning of chapter 4 is predicated on the fact that the reader wants to know if either Cain or Abel could be the 'serpent crusher' of 3:15. The shock factor, then, flows from the fact that Abel, the godly offspring, is terminated (thus instantly obviating any claim to be *the* offspring), while the murderous Cain remains. Given how the narrative unfolds in Genesis, it is conceivable that a murderer would be part of the line of promise – however, at this stage of the primeval history the emphasis is not on the universal sinfulness of humanity, but on the determination of God to keep his promise, which brings us back to 4:25–26.

After the Cainite genealogy 'closes off' the significance of this part of the family for the unfolding plan of God (in exactly the same way as the genealogies of Ishmael and Esau do later in the book), the birth of Seth in 4:25 instantly eases the tension. It is, however, extremely surprising that Seth receives no more attention in the narrative. His sole contribution to the developing story is to father Enosh. This strange omission is barely discussed in the literature.

The simplest explanation of the passing reference to Seth is that he is of limited significance to the flow of Genesis because (whether or not he is godly) he shows no sign of doing anything resembling crushing the head of the serpent. He comes, and he goes – however, he does produce a son, Enosh. And Enosh's contribution to the

---

[8] Calvin 1847: 223.

[9] I am, of course, aware of the controversy surrounding the reference of Gen. 3:15. Although I am personally convinced of the messianic implications of this verse, I would argue that the interpretation offered in Gen. 4:25–26 does not necessarily require such a reading. The growing preoccupation with the identity in each generation of the descendant through whom blessing will come (see e.g. Gen. 12, 22, 25, 38, 49–50) also makes it highly likely that the text should be read as messianic.

narrative? It is a case of like father like son, as he too simply comes and goes.

This means that, theologically speaking, the context of the innovation of 4:26 is one of salvation-historical anticlimax. There is a growing sense that the promise of 3:15 *may not be fulfilled immediately.* The expected offspring is clearly neither Cain, nor Abel, nor Seth, nor Enosh. It seems that at this point the realization begins to dawn on the Adamic community that the fulfilment of promise may take some time. In context this is the most natural explanation of the fact that Enosh's birth leads to people 'calling on the name of Yahweh'.

Calling on the name of Yahweh

At this point we do need to spend a little time teasing out the precise nuance of the phrase 'calling on the name of Yahweh'. One key lexicon suggests that this denotes 'entering into an intensive relationship as someone who calls'.[10] However, this seems to be overreaching slightly. On the other hand, Clowney reduces the significance of the phrase to 'calling his name aloud'.[11] This seems reductionist. So what is the import of this phrase?

The simple answer seems to be that it refers to crying out to God *in prayer*. The beginning of the post-Eden 'conversation' between humanity and God begins with 'crying out to God' (or 'calling on the name of Yahweh'). This, then, I would argue, provides us with a biblical-theological definition of prayer. This is supported by the other Old Testament occurrences of the phrase.[12]

There is substantial discussion on the significance of the slightly circumlocutory expression 'the name of Yahweh'. Essentially, 'the "name of the LORD" (*yhwh*) is metonymical for the nature of the Lord'.[13] However, the precise nuance of the use of this phrase has to be determined by biblical usage, rather than general Hebraic (or ANE) usage.

When this phrase is used in the Old Testament, it is asking God to intervene specifically to do one thing – to come through on his promises.[14] In Genesis 12:8 and 13:4 Abram 'calls on the name of

---

[10] *HALOT* 1130 9c (but cf. *DCH* 7: 294 (2)b.

[11] See his comment in Carson (1990: 138).

[12] See Gen. 12:8; 13:4; 21:33; 26:25; 1 Kgs 18:24; 2 Kgs 5:11; 1 Chr. 16:8; Pss 79:6; 80:18; 99:6; 105:1; 116:4, 13, 17; Isa. 12:4; 41:25; 64:7; Jer. 10:25; Lam. 3:55; Joel 2:32; Zeph. 3:9; Zech. 13:9.

[13] Ross 1997: 148. Ross's *NIDOTTE* article on *'šēm'* is excellent.

[14] See the comments of P. D. Miller (1994: 61).

Yahweh' at key moments in the narrative – modelling a 'faith response' to God's promises and showing that as he moves into the land he does so relying on Yahweh himself to do what he has said. Similarly in 21:33, at the climax of the agreement with Abimelech the Philistine (which leads both to Abraham's receiving the title to the well at Beersheba and the neutralizing of the Philistine threat to his 'occupation' of the land), Abraham plants a tamarisk tree and 'calls on the name of Yahweh'. In the only other occurrence in Genesis Isaac responds to Yahweh's reiteration of the covenant promises in 26:24 by building an altar at Beersheba and 'calling on the name of Yahweh'. To call on the name of Yahweh in Genesis, then, is to respond to God's promise-making initiative by asking him to act to fulfil his promises.

This is also the case in the rest of the Old Testament. Elijah's challenge to the prophets of Baal in 1 Kings 18:24 ('And you call upon the name of your god, and I will call upon the name of the LORD, and the God who answers by fire, he is God') fits neatly into this pattern. It is also clear that (1) Elijah understands this phrase as describing *prayer*, and (2) the prayer he prays revolves around God's promises to the patriarchs:

> And at the time of the offering of the oblation, Elijah the prophet came near and said, 'O LORD, God of Abraham, Isaac, and Israel, let it be known this day that you are God in Israel, and that I am your servant, and that I have done all these things at your word. Answer me, O LORD, answer me, that this people may know that you, O LORD, are God, and that you have turned their hearts back.' (1 Kgs 18:36–37)[15]

In the prophetic literature it is equally clear that 'calling on the name of Yahweh' is not a vague term to cover all kinds of interaction with the divine – it is intimately connected with Yahweh's declared plans to rescue his people and to act in judgment and salvation. Isaiah 12:3 sets the tone:

> With joy you will draw water from the wells of salvation. And you will say in that day:

---

[15] The only other occurrence of the phrase in the Former Prophets comes in 2 Kgs 5:11 on the lips of Naaman, who expects Elisha to 'call on the name of Yahweh his God' (although Elisha does not). Even though the prophet's actions are counter-intuitive, the Syrian's words add implicit support to my argument.

'Give thanks to the LORD,
   call upon his name,
make known his deeds among the peoples,
   proclaim that his name is exalted.'

In fact 'calling on the name of Yahweh' is the definitive mark of
the people of God. This can work negatively (see Jer. 10:25) or more
positively:

> And it shall come to pass that everyone who calls on the name of
> the LORD shall be saved. For in Mount Zion and in Jerusalem there
> shall be those who escape, as the LORD has said, and among the
> survivors shall be those whom the LORD calls. (Joel 2:32)

For at that time I will change the speech of the peoples
   to a pure speech,
that all of them may call upon the name of the LORD
   and serve him with one accord.
(Zeph. 3:9)

They will call upon my name,
   and I will answer them.
I will say, 'They are my people';
   and they will say, 'The LORD is my God.'
(Zech. 13:9)

In each case there is a clear connection between Yahweh's prior
covenantal commitment to save his people and 'calling on the name
of Yahweh'. If anything, this becomes clearer in the final prophetic
example, where the servant of the Lord (here depicted as a Ps. 2 kind
of figure of divine judgment) turns out to be the one who definitively
'calls on Yahweh':

I stirred up one from the north, and he has come,
   from the rising of the sun, and he shall call upon my name;
he shall trample on rulers as on mortar,
   as the potter treads clay.
(Isa. 41:25)

Behold my servant, whom I uphold,
   my chosen, in whom my soul delights;

24

> I have put my Spirit upon him;
> he will bring forth justice to the nations.
>
> (Isa. 42:1)

It seems increasingly clear that the phrase 'calling on the name of Yahweh' is used to depict prayer, but not simply in a generic sense. Rather, the idea of calling on the name of Yahweh is intrinsically related to God's commitment to rescue his people and deliver on his promises. This is borne out in the way in which the phrase is used in both Chronicles and Psalms.

The phrase occurs only once in Chronicles, but it does so at a highly significant moment in the narrative. As the chronicler's insistence that Israel both desperately needs atonement and that God has already put the 'building blocks' of a decisive act of forgiveness in place begins to emerge, David recommissions a version of the tabernacle (1 Chr. 16:1–7). At this point Chronicles records an intense burst of Davidic (psalmic) praise, which starts with the call

> Oh give thanks to the LORD, call upon his name;
> make known his deeds among the peoples!
>
> (1 Chr. 16:8)[16]

The context is explicitly covenantal (see e.g. 1 Chr. 16:15–18), and the prayer is based on God's keeping his promises.

As we might expect by now, this pattern is replicated in Psalms, even though the phrase occurs surprisingly few times. It is used to demarcate those who trust in Yahweh from those who do not:

> Pour out your anger on the nations
> that do not know you,
> and on the kingdoms
> that do not call upon your name!
>
> (Ps. 79:6)

> Then we shall not turn back from you;
> give us life, and we will call upon your name!
>
> (Ps. 80:18)

---

[16] The chronicler is quoting Ps. 105:1.

Those who call on the name of Yahweh are those who have tasted his salvation, and are enjoying his covenant blessings. This is made clear by Psalm 116, which is virtually a meditation on what it means to 'call on the name of Yahweh':

> I love the LORD, because he has heard
> my voice and my pleas for mercy.
> Because he inclined his ear to me,
> therefore I will call on him as long as I live.
> The snares of death encompassed me;
> the pangs of Sheol laid hold on me;
> I suffered distress and anguish.
> Then I called on the name of the LORD:
> 'O LORD, I pray, deliver my soul!' . . .
>
> What shall I render to the LORD
> for all his benefits to me?
> I will lift up the cup of salvation
> *and call on the name of the LORD* . . .
>
> I will offer to you the sacrifice of thanksgiving
> and *call on the name of the LORD.*
> (Ps. 116:1–4, 12–13, 17)

It is clear, then, that as the Old Testament unfolds, to 'call on the name of Yahweh' is not simply to 'pray' in any generic sense. To call on the name of Yahweh is to cry to God to come through on his promises, and specifically to rescue and give life to his covenant people. It is a prayer for salvation, or an expression of the fact that one is relying on God *for* salvation. To put it anachronistically, 'calling on the name of Yahweh' in the Old Testament denotes 'gospel-shaped prayer'.

This conviction finds somewhat unexpected support in two seminal passages in the New Testament. Both Peter, preaching on the Day of Pentecost in Acts 2, and Paul, in the middle of his discourse on how the promises of God relate to Israel in Romans 9 – 11, draw on Joel 2:32 in summing up the requisite response to the grace of God long promised and revealed in the Lord Jesus Christ.[17]

---

[17] See Acts 2:17–21 and Rom. 10:12–13. As we will see later, the New Testament simply substitutes *kyrios* for Yahweh, with the assumption that 'the name of Jesus Christ' is functionally the same as 'the name of Yahweh'.

Interim conclusions: the essential nature of biblical prayer

On one level it is surprising how infrequently the phrase 'calling on the name of the LORD/Lord' is used in the Bible. But on the other it is clear that when it does occur, it carries significant theological weight. This supports the contention that Genesis 4:25–26 is not simply a historical note, but is a 'load-bearing' verse, which establishes the trajectory for at least a significant strand of the Bible's teaching on prayer. This has at least three far-reaching implications for constructing a biblical theology of prayer.

This is the primary biblical trajectory of prayer

It is rarely noted that the primary biblical trajectory of prayer is not praise, or lament, or intercession, or meditation on the word of Yahweh. Prayer begins in the Bible as a cry for God to do what he has promised – to deal with the reality of sin by delivering on his covenant promises. Even if one does not accept that the Protevangelium (Gen. 3:15) lies behind the cries to God of Genesis 4:26, the link between God's promises and prayer becomes clear in the Abraham narratives beginning in Genesis 12.

This is a helpful orientation for the rest of my discussion. It will, of course, be necessary to make some comment on the variety of material usually included under the general category of 'prayer', but we must take care not to collapse all the biblical material into a single nebulous mass. This study will focus on the main trajectory of the biblical material, which is *asking God to do what he has already committed himself to do*, and will attempt to show how other more peripheral categories (e.g. lament) take their meaning (and their boundaries) from this central, 'covenantal' strand.[18]

From the beginning, prayer and the gospel cannot be separated

Prayer is established (perhaps even defined as) calling on God to come through on his promises. To pray is to ask God to do for us what we cannot do for ourselves. It is to admit our weaknesses and appeal to his awesome strength. According to Genesis, people start to pray because they see both God's commitment to us and their own

---

[18] For a broader discussion of the nature of prayer see Keller 2014: 35–49. At a different level, for a discussion of the vocabulary of prayer in the OT see e.g. Verhoef 1997.

helplessness. They pray because they know God is for them, because he has said so, and that they are weak because he has said so. In other words *prayer starts with the gospel*. It always has and always will. Once we recognize this, it will ensure that we avoid the simple but far-reaching mistake of separating what God has joined – *prayer and the gospel.*[19]

Surprisingly, this connection is seldom noted, either in commentaries on Genesis or in discussions of prayer (whether at an academic or more popular level). A marvellous exception is the comment of John Calvin noted in the introduction: 'Just as faith is born from the gospel, so through it our hearts are trained to call upon God's name [Rom. 10:14–17].'[20] The starting point of all our discussion of prayer should be the initiative of God in the gospel.

A clear pointer to this is the fact that long before humanity began to call on the name of Yahweh, Yahweh himself had spoken to his fallen creatures. In the immediate aftermath of the fall we read this:

> And they heard the sound of the LORD God walking in the garden in the cool of the day, and the man and his wife hid themselves from the presence of the LORD God among the trees of the garden. *But the LORD God called to the man* and said to him, 'Where are you?' And he said, 'I heard the sound of you in the garden, and I was afraid, because I was naked, and I hid myself.' (Gen. 3:8–10)

After rejecting Yahweh, Yahweh still seeks his creatures. He *calls to them* long before they start to call out to him.[21]

Instead of easily, naturally, delighting in Yahweh and enjoying his presence, Adam and Eve hide. They avoid God. Instead of feeling joy, they are ashamed at the very sound of his footsteps. They are afraid, on edge. They pretend. They lie. They justify themselves. Even as they speak, a huge chasm opens between them and God, as the most severe

---

[19] At an anecdotal level, evidence of this separation is to be found in almost every small-group Bible study prayer time in Christendom.

[20] Calvin 1960, 2: 850–851. See also the comment of Patrick Miller (1994: 174) on discussing OT words of divine assurance in the context of prayer: 'It may seem anachronistic to say so, but it is nevertheless profoundly true that in these words we hear the "gospel".'

[21] See the discussion of Goldsworthy (2003: 109–111), who draws out the nature of the divine initiative beautifully. Similarly, Seitz (2001: 15): 'Prayer is not humanity's effort to reach God from below by crying out to him. Rather it is the consequence of his having made himself known, and our faithful response to that prior knowledge. True prayer, therefore, means discourse with the one Lord, and that cannot be taken for granted as covered under some generic deity.'

shock in history hits. Before our eyes a huge gulf opens between us and God. But what happens? God calls to Adam long before Adam calls on him. Prayer starts with the gospel and is made possible by the gospel.

Prayer is clearly designed for a fallen world

The third and final preliminary observation is, again, seldom noted. It is the fact that prayer is designed *for a fallen world*. If we are correct in asserting that the conversations in the garden are, strictly speaking, something other than prayer, then prayer is clearly part of life in a post-fall world.

It is almost self-evident that prayer is necessary only in a fallen world. Genesis 4:25–26 is built on the recognition (flowing out of Gen. 3) that despite the profound break in our relationship with Yahweh he continues to speak to his creatures, and makes it possible for us to respond to him. We can call on Yahweh, but only because he has called on us. We can cry out to him to come through on his promises only because he has already made his promises. In this sense *all biblical prayer is covenantal – all prayer is gospel driven.*

That should shape our expectations when we pray. On the one hand, God through the gospel has made it possible for us to speak to him. But on the other? In the Bible God draws close and invites us to 'call on his name'. This means that prayer in the Bible has a very different tone from all other ANE prayers. We can see and feel that in the ancient Sumero-Akkadian prayer 'A prayer to every god', written about the time of Moses:

> The lord in his anger of heart looked at me
> The god in the rage of his heart confronted me
> When the goddess was angry with me she made me
>   become ill
> The god whom I know or do not know has placed
>   suffering upon me
> Although I am looking constantly for help, no-one
>   takes me by the hand.
> When I weep, they do not come to my side.
> I utter laments but no-one hears me.[22]

This is far from the situation in the Bible. God calls us, and invites us to call on his name.

---

[22] See Pritchard 1969: 391–392.

It is important, however, to realize that the biblical-theological implications of this are significant. In particular it highlights the fact that prayer is an interim measure. Prayer is what we do now – and until God intervenes to straighten everything out. Prayer is God's gift to help us cope with life with him in the mess – a world where we ache and get distracted and struggle with sin, and fail repeatedly. Prayer is designed for a world in which we hurt people and get hurt, where we let God down and ignore him, even though we belong to him. Prayer is a temporary balm in a world where we so often feel cut off from him, where we feel alone and discouraged and frustrated. But prayer will not always be necessary.

The book, letter or vision of Revelation alludes to several prayers (e.g. Rev. 5:8).[23] However, these prayers are prayed in John's present. When, at the end of the book, John is shown the new heavens and the new earth, rather than doing nothing but praying, there is no suggestion that we will pray at all. All the apparatus of earth-bound religion is replaced by the Lamb himself, and it seems reasonable to assume that, as in the first 'garden temple', immediate conversation (along with celebration) takes away any need to 'call on the name of Yahweh'.[24]

If prayer in the Bible is gospel-shaped, covenantal prayer, as we call on the name of Yahweh to come through on his promises, then this is exactly what would be expected. However, we need to ask if this understanding of prayer is reflected by the text of the rest of the Pentateuch itself.

Prayer in the Pentateuch – a thesis tested

So far, one might be forgiven for thinking that rather a lot has been built on one slightly cryptic phrase (calling on the name of Yahweh) in Genesis 4. If, however, it becomes clear that this same understanding of prayer is reflected elsewhere in the Pentateuch, that significantly strengthens my argument.

---

[23] Beale (1998: 357) helpfully argues that the prayers of 5:8 and 8:3–4 are to be identified with 6:10: 'Therefore, the prayers mentioned here are not just praises but especially requests that God defend the honour of his reputation for justice by judging the persecutors of his people.' Apart from this, all dialogue directed at God in Revelation happens in his immediate presence and is usually linked with the term 'worship' – clearly a different beast (!) to general biblical understanding of 'prayer'.

[24] These ideas are developed at some length in chapter 9.

Prayer in Genesis

It is interesting that prayer does not play a hugely significant role in Genesis – many of the key incidents unfold without any reference to anything resembling prayer.[25] However, that does not mean that the narrative has nothing to contribute to a biblical theology of prayer.

In the midst of the furore created by his fathering a son with Hagar, Abraham prays for the first time. After God announces that Sarai (now Sarah) will conceive and bear his heir, the child of promise, Abraham falls on his face, laughing, and says, 'Oh that Ishmael might live before you!' (Gen. 17:18). The subject of his prayer is, of course, the fulfilment of Yahweh's promise – a point underlined by God himself in the very next verse: 'God said, "No, but Sarah your wife shall bear you a son, and you shall call his name Isaac. I will establish my covenant with him as an everlasting covenant for his offspring after him."' This connection between prayer and covenant (or, as I have expressed it more generally, between prayer and the gospel), dominates the prayers in the rest of the book.[26]

After God himself alludes to prayer as he appears to Abimelek in a dream (20:4–7),[27] the next person to pray is the unnamed but godly servant who is sent by Abraham to procure a wife for Isaac:

> And he made the camels kneel down outside the city by the well of water at the time of evening, the time when women go out to draw water. And he said, 'O Lord, God of my master Abraham, please grant me success today and show steadfast love to my master Abraham.' (24:11–12; see also vv. 26–27)

Given the wider context, the focus of these prayers is undeniably the fulfilment of the covenant promises – the God who gave Abraham

[25] E.g. there is no reference to prayer in the Noah narrative, nor in the opening scenes of the Abraham cycle.

[26] Many (e.g. Clements 1985: 20; Balentine 1993: 40; P. D. Miller 1994: 262–280) simply assume that the dialogue between God and Abraham in v. 18 is a prayer, although there is nothing in the context to suggest this. This is a divine–human encounter that is more like the envisaged discussions between Adam and God in Eden than anything resembling 'prayer'.

[27] The reference is to Abraham as a *prophet* praying for Abimelek so that he may be forgiven. This is clearly *intercessory* prayer. However, we must not miss the fact that the context of this prayer is the *continuation of the covenant* in the face of Abraham's repeated actions that jeopardize it (see also 12:8–20).

this son of promise is now called upon to provide a wife for him, thereby ensuring that the covenant family continues.[28]

Isaac's own subsequent prayer life, it is fair to say, is limited. In fact it is limited to asking God to work to ensure the continuance of the life of the covenant family: 'And Isaac prayed to the LORD for his wife, because she was barren. And the LORD granted his prayer, and Rebekah his wife conceived' (25:21). The verb here is *'tr* (entreat), and it is paired with its own niphal form in the second half of the verse ('and Yahweh *granted*'). Prayer is depicted quite straightforwardly as Isaac's requesting and God's fulfilling his request in line with his prior covenantal commitment.

It is important not to overstate this – there is clearly significant overlap between the *personal desires of Isaac* (and the other patriarchs) and the urgency of preserving and extending the line of promise. Their prayers do reflect deeply personal longings, and these are brought to Yahweh. However, this does not mitigate the fact that *the emphasized focus in the text is tied to the history of redemption and the survival of the covenant line.*

This understanding of prayer in Genesis finds its most compelling example in Jacob's prayer in chapter 32. This is the longest recorded prayer in the book, and Jacob's first.[29]

It is worth including this prayer in full:

And Jacob said, 'O God of my father Abraham and God of my father Isaac, O LORD who said to me, "Return to your country and to your kindred, that I may do you good," I am not worthy of the least of all the deeds of steadfast love and all the faithfulness that you have shown to your servant, for with only my staff I crossed this Jordan, and now I have become two camps. Please deliver me from the hand of my brother, from the hand of Esau, for I fear him, that he may come and attack me, the mothers with the children. But you said, "I will surely do you good, and make your offspring as the sand of the sea, which cannot be numbered for multitude."' (Gen. 32:9–12)

---

[28] Interestingly, no special 'prayer vocabulary' is used in the narrative (or its repetition as reported narrative). The servant simply 'says to God'.

[29] At the end of his vow in 28:22 Jacob does move from the third to the second person – however, it is not clear that this should be understood as a prayer. And in any case Jacob's theological comprehension at this point is hardly exemplary, so it would be wise not to read too much into this.

Once more, the preoccupation of the prayer is the survival of the covenant line. In many ways this is the high point of 'patriarchal spirituality'. It is hardly replete with extravagant praise, but is built on a sense of personal unworthiness, gratitude for past interventions and a plea for Yahweh to honour his covenant promises. These words of Jacob are the perfect expression of the emerging biblical theology of prayer that this chapter has sought to highlight.[30]

Prayer in Exodus

The opening chapters of Exodus are closely tied to the book of Genesis, providing a transition from the Joseph Cycle to the advent of Moses. This bridging section concludes with these words:

> During those many days the king of Egypt died, and the people of Israel groaned because of their slavery and cried out for help. Their cry for rescue from slavery came up to God. And God heard their groaning, and God remembered his covenant with Abraham, with Isaac, and with Jacob. God saw the people of Israel – and God knew. (Exod. 2:23–25)

The vocabulary differs from that of Genesis, but the thought is exactly the same.[31] To pray is to cry out to the God of Abraham, Isaac and Jacob for rescue.[32]

This same understanding is reflected consistently in the prayers of Moses, which are scattered throughout the Exodus narratives.[33] So, for example, in 5:22 Moses 'turns' to Yahweh:

> Then Moses turned to the LORD and said, 'O Lord, why have you done evil to this people? Why did you ever send me? For since I

---

[30] There are no other explicit prayers in the book of Genesis. The related category of 'blessing' does occur at e.g. 43:14, 48:15–16, 20, but 'blessing' is beyond the purview of this study. P. D. Miller (1994: 165) makes the interesting observation that there are no prayers in the Joseph Cycle. This may be because in this story the focus is on the preservation of the line of Judah and little else.

[31] The language is particularly intense here – with groans, sighs and cries (understandably).

[32] Interestingly, P. D. Miller (1994: 94–95) discusses this passage at some length, but does not seem to recognize its foundational nature.

[33] In keeping with the treatment of God's interaction with Adam and Eve in the garden of Eden, 'face to face interactions' with Yahweh (or perhaps, better, theophanic encounters) are not included in my discussion, on the basis that they are not, strictly speaking, prayers. However, particularly in ch. 32, it is not easy to distinguish between these two situations.

came to Pharaoh to speak in your name, he has done evil to this people, and you have not delivered your people at all.' (5:22–23)

His complaint is essentially that Yahweh has not kept his promises. This is confirmed by the specific response from God:

But the LORD said to Moses, 'Now you shall see what I will do to Pharaoh; for with a strong hand he will send them out, and with a strong hand he will drive them out of his land.'
God spoke to Moses and said to him, 'I am the LORD. I appeared to Abraham, to Isaac, and to Jacob, as God Almighty, but by my name the LORD I did not make myself known to them. I also established my covenant with them to give them the land of Canaan, the land in which they lived as sojourners. Moreover, I have heard the groaning of the people of Israel whom the Egyptians hold as slaves, and I have remembered my covenant. Say therefore to the people of Israel, "I am the LORD, and I will bring you out from under the burdens of the Egyptians, and I will deliver you from slavery to them, and I will redeem you with an outstretched arm and with great acts of judgement. I will take you to be my people, and I will be your God, and you shall know that I am the LORD your God, who has brought you out from under the burdens of the Egyptians. I will bring you into the land that I swore to give to Abraham, to Isaac, and to Jacob. I will give it to you for a possession. I am the LORD."' (Exod. 6:1–8)

There has, of course, been much discussion of the origins of this material, and the perceived problems created by 6:2 in reconstructing the history of Yahwism.[34] However, we must not miss the obvious point the writer is making about prayer – Moses' prayer is based on confidence in the commitment of Yahweh to his people, and God's answer does not disavow him of that notion. Rather, Yahweh answers by affirming his commitment to the covenant, and therefore underlines that he will, in fact, answer Moses' prayer.

The same could be said of the interactions in chapters 17 and 32:

So Moses cried to the LORD, 'What shall I do with this people? They are almost ready to stone me.' And the LORD said to Moses, 'Pass on before the people, taking with you some of the elders of

---

[34] See e.g. the discussion in Dozemann (2009: 163–168).

Israel, and take in your hand the staff with which you struck the Nile, and go. Behold, I will stand before you there on the rock at Horeb, and you shall strike the rock, and water shall come out of it, and the people will drink.' And Moses did so, in the sight of the elders of Israel. And he called the name of the place Massah and Meribah, because of the quarrelling of the people of Israel, and because they tested the LORD by saying, 'Is the LORD among us or not?' (Exod. 17:4–7)

But Moses implored the LORD his God and said, 'O LORD, why does your wrath burn hot against your people, whom you have brought out of the land of Egypt with great power and with a mighty hand? Why should the Egyptians say, "With evil intent did he bring them out, to kill them in the mountains and to consume them from the face of the earth"? Turn from your burning anger and relent from this disaster against your people. Remember Abraham, Isaac, and Israel, your servants, to whom you swore by your own self, and said to them, "I will multiply your offspring as the stars of heaven, and all this land that I have promised I will give to your offspring, and they shall inherit it for ever."' (Exod. 32:11–13)

In both cases what is at stake is the survival of the newly formed 'people of God'. In Exodus 17 the thought is that without the presence of Yahweh not only will the people fail in every project, but they cannot lay claim to being considered Yahweh's people at all. In chapter 32 the connection with the covenant with Abraham, Isaac and Jacob is more explicit. But in both cases Moses' prayer is focused on the continuation of the covenant, and the survival of hope in the promises of God.

The final 'prayer' in Exodus comes later in the same chapter. On the surface the sentiments expressed by Moses seem broadly similar, but there are profound differences. Rather than simply asking Yahweh to honour his commitments to Israel, Moses raises the possibility of *making atonement* for the people:

The next day Moses said to the people, 'You have sinned a great sin. And now I will go up to the LORD; perhaps I can make atonement for your sin.' So Moses returned to the LORD and said, 'Alas, this people has sinned a great sin. They have made for themselves gods of gold. But now, if you will forgive their sin – but if not, please blot me out of your book that you have written.' But the LORD said to Moses, 'Whoever has sinned against me, I will blot out of my book. But now go, lead the people to the place about which I have spoken to you; behold, my angel shall go before you. Nevertheless, in the day when I visit, I will visit their sin upon them.' (Exod. 32:30–34)[35]

In seeking to 'make atonement' (a piel cohortative form of *kpr*) Moses may reflect the common thinking of the ANE.[36] What is fascinating, however, is that Moses brings no offering (or religious activity) to cause this forgiveness, other than a plaintive request that he be blotted out in place of his people. It seems as if he is trapped somewhere between traditional ANE modes of thought and a Yahwistic (grace-based) approach.[37] The fact that Yahweh effectively ignores his request in verses 33–34 and simply asserts his divine right *and commitment to keeping his promises to those who have not abandoned him* draw these threads of covenant and atonement together, in a way that creates an intriguing link with the material that follows in Leviticus.

Prayer in Leviticus

One of the intriguing features of Leviticus, the sacral text par excellence in the Old Testament, is the fact that there is *not a single reference to prayer in the entire book*.[38] This is not often noticed, although both Israel Knohl and Jacob Milgrom have highlighted the issue.[39] Knohl contends that there was neither music nor prayer in the pre-Hezekian (*sic*) temple. Milgrom, however, dismisses his argument as 'an argument from silence', and insists that there are no grounds at all for conceiving of an Israelite temple ritual that was silent.

---

[35] In this case it may be that Moses said all this to Yahweh 'face to face', which would mean that, strictly speaking, it is not a prayer. However, there is little evidence that the writer is emphasizing this dynamic here in the narrative – the question is one of whether or not a mediator/intercessor can bring about atonement for sin.

[36] Mesopotamian thinking reflected a concern for sin and guilt; their prayers seek absolution/stay of punishment. See e.g. the Mesopotamian wisdom text (Walton 2006: 144) stating, 'reverence begets favour, sacrifice prolongs life, prayer atones for guilt'. General ANE knee-jerk reaction to misfortune was to assume one had done something wrong and to pray, offer restitution, etc. in hope of restoring the god's favour (ibid. 144–146); but it is hard to ascertain if this is atonement in its proper sense.

[37] The standard ANE response to wrongdoing is to try to appease God with something, but what he offers is a sort of desperate prayer for mercy (note pleas for mercy and compassion were common in Egyptian prayer; see ibid. 109–111).

[38] This point is seldom observed, let alone addressed, in the literature.

[39] Knohl 1988; Milgrom 1991: 18–19.

I strongly suspect that Milgrom is right to assert that there must have been both prayer and music in the temple. In particular Leviticus 16:21 at least implies that something close to prayer was involved in the Day of Atonement.[40] The weakness in his discussion is that while exposing the problems in Knohl's position, he gives no adequate explanation for the absence of prayer in the book. Given the all-pervasive nature of prayer in other similar ANE rituals, it is hard to believe that this is simply accidental, or the result of a focus on the mechanics of sacrifice.[41]

This is where the unfolding theology of prayer in the Pentateuch provides us with a credible (if not yet completely compelling) explanation of the 'silence' in Leviticus when it comes to prayer. In Exodus 32 Moses has already inadvertently highlighted the fact that Yahweh alone can provide atonement. Performing ritual actions (including prayer) cannot influence the God of Israel, nor can even the most godly individual act as a substitute. The logic of Leviticus takes us further along this trajectory. The need for atonement is abundantly clear. However, the shortfall in provision in the sacrificial system[42] leading to the necessity of the Day of Atonement as a proleptic celebration of God's intention to provide the ultimate sacrifice and the comprehensive symbolism of the Holiness Code underline the fact that God alone has the power to atone for the sins of Israel. It is also possible that the absence of prayer in Leviticus is built on the idea that Israel is a 'kingdom of priests' where access to Yahweh (calling on his name) is not simply limited to the priestly class.[43]

To summarize, given the material on prayer in Genesis and Exodus, it may well be that the absence of prayer in Leviticus functions both *to distinguish prayer in Israel from prayer in the ANE* (which typically consisted of pleading with the gods to be favourable) and *to establish that prayer does not lead to forgiveness*. This, of course, is completely

[40] Wenham (1979: 61) argues that prayer is also implied in the laying on of hands in Lev. 1:4.

[41] I am aware that this line of argument is vulnerable to Milgrom's criticism of being an argument from silence, but where the absence of material is so striking (and completely out of step with other contemporary material) it is perfectly reasonable to seek a credible explanation for the silence.

[42] This centres on the oft-noted virtual absence of any sacrifice for *deliberate* sin. This 'omission' is picked up by the chronicler in his use of the concept of *ma'al* (see e.g. Johnstone 1986).

[43] See Balentine 1993: 45; Greenberg 1983: 52. I am also grateful for discussions with David Peterson on this subject.

consistent with the thoroughly Levitical idea that only a perfect sacrificial death can possibly achieve atonement.

Prayer in Numbers

When reading through the Pentateuch canonically, the 'silence' in Leviticus becomes all the more noticeable when we reach Numbers, and the key section of Numbers 11 – 14 in particular.

The notion of Moses' praying for the people is introduced in 11:1–2:

> And the people complained in the hearing of the LORD about their misfortunes, and when the LORD heard it, his anger was kindled, and the fire of the LORD burned among them and consumed some outlying parts of the camp. Then the people cried out to Moses, and Moses prayed to the LORD, and the fire died down.

There is a clear (and deliberate) contrast between the people (who complain *to each other* 'in the hearing of Yahweh', and then cry out in an intensified complaint about Yahweh to Moses) and Moses himself, who is the only one who addresses God.[44] The implication seems to be that only Moses is thinking in covenantal terms, and therefore is the only one to whom it occurs to 'call on the name of Yahweh'.

However, the situation becomes more complex when, in the wake of the rabble's ingratitude (11:4–9), fire from God falls again, and Moses rails against him:

> Moses said to the LORD, 'Why have you dealt ill with your servant? And why have I not found favour in your sight, that you lay the burden of all this people on me? Did I conceive all this people? Did I give them birth, that you should say to me, *"Carry them in your bosom, as a nurse carries a suckling child," to the land that you swore to give their fathers?* Where am I to get meat to give to all this people? For they weep before me and say, "Give us meat, that we may eat." I am not able to carry all this people alone; the burden is too heavy for me. If you will treat me like this, kill me at once, if I find favour in your sight, that I may not see my wretchedness.' (Num. 11:11–15)

Moses' prayer is extremely forthright – so what is it that gives him the right (or at least the boldness) to express himself to the Lord of all in

---

[44] Incidentally, this is the first reference to the conventional verb 'to pray' in the Bible.

such blunt terms? The answer is found in verse 12 – Moses' complaint (or perhaps better, rant) is based on the implications of God's covenant commitment to his people. Once again, prayer is based on the prior fact of God's promise.

In chapter 12 the existence of the covenant people is once more under threat – this time because of the sinful attitude of Miriam and Aaron, who along with Moses carry the burden of leadership of the nation. Their resentment (which was a mixture of jealousy and naked racism) spills over into an implicit rejection of the word of God himself:

> 'With him I speak mouth to mouth, clearly, and not in riddles, and he beholds the form of the LORD. Why then were you not afraid to speak against my servant Moses?' And the anger of the LORD was kindled against them, and he departed.
>
> When the cloud removed from over the tent, behold, Miriam was leprous, like snow. (Num. 12:8–10)

In the ensuing dialogue Aaron pleads with Moses as the leader of Israel to intercede on behalf of their sister, which Moses does.[45] However, it is vital to see that this prayer for healing (the first in the Bible) cannot easily be extricated from its context – (1) it is a prayer in *direct response* to an intervention of Yahweh to punish Miriam in real time, (2) it is deeply embedded in a narrative in which the future of the covenant people of God is under threat, and (3) it is tied to the complaints of the people in the previous chapter, making the point that rebellion is endemic among the Hebrews under Moses. It then becomes clear that this is not a 'prayer for healing' in any straightforward sense – this prayer is part of a nexus of events in which God reasserts his leadership (through Moses) of the covenant people. Even this prayer cannot be separated from covenantal concerns.

This becomes even more obvious in the climax to this section in Numbers 14. The events at Kadesh Barnea call into question once more the viability of God's 'covenant project' given the propensity of the people to disobey. The words of Yahweh himself are ominous:

> And the LORD said to Moses, 'How long will this people despise me? And how long will they not believe in me, in spite of all the signs

---

[45] Moses' prayer is simple: 'O God, please heal her – please' (v. 13).

that I have done among them? I will strike them with the pestilence and disinherit them, and I will make of you a nation greater and mightier than they.' (Num. 14:11–12)

At this point Moses intervenes.

Once more, it is not completely clear that Moses is *praying*, rather than 'speaking with Yahweh face to face',[46] but either way his words serve to underline the theological point that interaction with Yahweh (including prayer) is predicated on his commitment to his people through his promises:

> But Moses said to the LORD, 'Then the Egyptians will hear of it, for you brought up this people in your might from among them, and they will tell the inhabitants of this land. They have heard that you, O LORD, are in the midst of this people. For you, O LORD, are seen face to face, and your cloud stands over them and you go before them, in a pillar of cloud by day and in a pillar of fire by night. Now if you kill this people as one man, then the nations who have heard your fame will say, "It is because the LORD was not able to bring this people into the land that he swore to give to them that he has killed them in the wilderness." And now, please let the power of the Lord be great as you have promised, saying, "The LORD is slow to anger and abounding in steadfast love, forgiving iniquity and transgression, but he will by no means clear the guilty, visiting the iniquity of the fathers on the children, to the third and the fourth generation." Please pardon the iniquity of this people, according to the greatness of your steadfast love, just as you have forgiven this people, from Egypt until now.' Then the LORD said, 'I have pardoned, according to your word.' (Num. 14:13–20)

Yahweh answers Moses' prayer not because of the character of the intercessor, nor his negotiating skill, but on the basis that appeal is made to his prior 'gospel' commitments.[47] This also undergirds Moses and Aaron's response to the rebellion of Korah in 16:22, and Moses' request that Yahweh appoint a godly successor in 27:16–17, when Moses is told of his impending death outside the land. Prayer

---

[46] See the discussion of Gen. 18 above.
[47] Contra Levine (1993: 280), who regards this as a confrontation between Moses and God. For a more helpful discussion of this passage see Olson 1996: 80–84.

is made and answered in Numbers purely on the basis of appeal to God's promises, and for the well-being of his people.

Prayer in Deuteronomy

The final piece in this covenantal puzzle is found in Deuteronomy. The only unique prayer in Deuteronomy is the prayer of Moses before his death, reported in 3:23–26:[48]

> And I pleaded with the LORD at that time, saying, 'O Lord GOD, you have only begun to show your servant your greatness and your mighty hand. For what god is there in heaven or on earth who can do such works and mighty acts as yours? Please let me go over and see the good land beyond the Jordan, that good hill country and Lebanon.' But the LORD was angry with me because of you and would not listen to me. And the LORD said to me, 'Enough from you; do not speak to me of this matter again.'

This is the first example of a prayer in the Bible that is explicitly rejected. Not only does Yahweh refuse to answer this prayer, but he is 'angered' by the request. Why is this? This is a vital question, as any attempt to outline a biblical theology of prayer must say something about the delicate and pastorally sensitive issue of 'unanswered prayer'. So why is the prayer of Moses, the great intercessor, portrayed in such a negative light, and why does it receive such a severe rebuke from Yahweh?

Yahweh's response here is completely predictable, because it is completely consistent with everything we have seen about prayer in the opening books of the Bible. Prayer is inherently *covenantal*, and is both driven by and based on the commitments Yahweh has made concerning the future of his covenant people, and his plans to reveal his glory to all nations. How does Moses' prayer fit with all this? The short answer is, 'It does not!' Despite beginning with an admirable statement of the greatness of God, it moves quickly on to a request that can only be described as 'selfish'. Moses' prayer may be completely understandable from a human point of view, but, for the first time in the Pentateuch we have a prayer that has no essential

---

[48] See Deut. 9:25–29 for the rehearsal of the events of Exod. 32. If anything, the focus on the nature of Israel as God's covenant people is intensified in the Deuteronomic version (see the phrases 'your people and your heritage').

connection with the progress of the plans of Yahweh. Moses, it seems, should have known better.[49]

The other statement in Deuteronomy that demands some attention (even though it is not a prayer itself) comes in the fascinating declaration of 4:5–8, which celebrates the uniqueness of Yahweh's dealings with Israel. In 4:7–8 Moses exclaims, 'For what great nation is there that has a god so near to it as the LORD our God is to us, whenever we call upon him? And what great nation is there, that has statutes and rules so righteous as all this law that I set before you today?' One of the twin privileges enjoyed by Israel is the proximity of Yahweh when they 'call on him', which clearly carries with it the implication that he hears and answers, acting on their behalf.[50] As Daniel Block vividly expresses it:

> When other people pray to their gods they remain both aloof and silent. Craftsmen may design them with big ears, but they remain silent. Ironically, although the Israelites' God was not represented by images they could set up in their homes or anywhere else, he was near, and although he had no ears, *he heard their cries whenever they called on him*.[51]

Yet again, prayer is understood in the context of Yahweh's covenant commitment to his people.[52]

Conclusion

In most previous studies of prayer in the Pentateuch discussion has been dominated either by a 'history of religions' approach to the text,

---

[49] Of course, there are times when what we long for and what may be good for the growth of the kingdom overlap – it is not always easy to discern what is best for the work of the gospel in the world. This passage should not lead us into the paralysis that comes from endless self-examination in a desire to pray with pure motives. But it is also equally clear that sometimes we simply pray for *what we want*, without any thought of or reference to the glory of God. Those prayers, it seems, are best left unprayed.

[50] The other benefit is, not surprisingly, possession of the Torah.

[51] Block 2012: 119 (emphasis mine).

[52] Seitz (2001: 17) makes an interesting point on the relationship of prayer to Deut. 30: 'It is prayer, Deuteronomy insists, which re-establishes the relationship (30:1–5). Here we touch upon the fundamental sacrificial reality, which lies just below the unitive character of sacrificial offerings, a broken and a contrite heart.' While it would be extremely helpful to the argument of this chapter if this were true, I can find nothing in Deut. 30 to suggest that the text describes the envisaged repentance and resultant return from exile as involving prayer.

or by discussions of the types of prayer presented. I would suggest that these approaches have missed something fundamental to the text as we now have it. Reading these five books canonically, it is startlingly obvious that a coherent biblical-theological approach to prayer emerges, which, as we will see, sets the trajectory for the rest of the Bible. Prayer in the Pentateuch is restricted to texts predicated on God's covenantal initiative. Speaking in terms of biblical theology, then, prayer is made possible only by 'the gospel'. All prayer is *gospel prayer*. It is calling on the name of Yahweh, who is the God of the covenant, the God of salvation. This has profound theological and practical implications. As I will now seek to demonstrate, this view of prayer is also borne out as we move through the rest of the Old Testament.

Chapter Two

Big prayers and the movements of history: prayer in the Former Prophets

Given the oft-noted continuity running from Genesis to 2 Kings, if the thesis proposed in chapter 1 is correct (that prayer is 'calling on the name of Yahweh'), then it seems reasonable to expect that the same ('Pentateuchal') view of prayer would be obvious from Joshua onwards.[1] This turns out to be exactly what we find.

Prayer in the book of Joshua

The first prayer in the book of Joshua comes in the wake of defeat at Ai in chapter 7:[2]

> Then Joshua tore his clothes and fell to the earth on his face before the ark of the LORD until the evening, he and the elders of Israel. And they put dust on their heads. And Joshua said, 'Alas, O Lord GOD, why have you brought this people over the Jordan at all, to give us into the hands of the Amorites, to destroy us? Would that we had been content to dwell beyond the Jordan! O Lord, what can I say, when Israel has turned their backs before their enemies! For the Canaanites and all the inhabitants of the land will hear of it and will surround us and cut off our name from the earth. And what will you do for your great name?' (Josh. 7:6–9)

---

[1] This clearly begs a significant number of questions about the authorship and composition of the Former Prophets. However, it matters little for the purposes of this study whether one views the activity of the 'publishers' in exile as simply bringing earlier essentially coherent material together, or, drawing on some earlier sources, producing a dramatically new work. For a very different perspective see e.g. Greenberg 1983.

[2] This is in line with my approach, which excludes theophanic appearances from this discussion.

The play on the linked fortunes of the 'name' of Israel and the 'name' of Yahweh in 7:9 is the key to this prayer, which immediately forges a strong link between the place of prayer in Joshua and the Pentateuch.[3] Joshua's protest is made on the basis that Yahweh appears to have forgotten his covenant promises, and has therefore put his good reputation in jeopardy. A vigorous (probably theophanic) response ensues (Josh. 7:10–14). In effect, Joshua's prayer is an example of the right principle applied to the wrong situation, but there can be little mistaking the fact that his understanding of the purpose of prayer coheres perfectly with all that we have seen so far.

Slightly unusually, the next allusion to prayer comes in the context of an implied rebuke to Joshua and the Israelites for *neglecting to pray*.[4] The root of their failure to see through the Gibeonites' elaborate and understandable subterfuge is ascribed to the fact that 'the men took some of their provisions, but did not ask counsel from the LORD' (Josh. 9:14). The course of salvation history it seems is potentially threatened by the failure of God's people to cry to him so that he might work out his agenda.[5]

The final passage in Joshua where prayer plays a part is the remarkable account of the battle against the Amorites in chapter 10. There is perhaps no miracle in the Old Testament that causes more puzzlement among commentators than this.[6] However, our primary interest is not in how God allowed the battle to continue to the great advantage of Israel, but rather the secondary issue that all these events unfolded in direct response to the prayers of Joshua:

At that time Joshua spoke to the LORD in the day when the LORD gave the Amorites over to the sons of Israel, and he said in the sight of Israel,

'Sun, stand still at Gibeon,
and moon, in the Valley of Aijalon.'

---

[3] Most discussions of this passage rightly focus on the similarity between Joshua's response and the complaint of the people in the wilderness, rather than on his prayer per se. However, see the discussion in Boling and Wright (1995: 224).

[4] We cannot be certain whether the neglected enquiry would have been a simple prayer or a more concrete divination process (see e.g. Woudstra 1981: 160). On balance, however, it seems most natural to take this as a reference to prayer.

[5] Ultimately, however, as with the incorporation of Rahab into the covenant people, the sovereignty of Yahweh is more than able to cope with the sinful foolishness and disobedience of Israel.

[6] See the helpful discussion of Pitkänen (2012: 224).

> And the sun stood still, and the moon stopped,
>   until the nation took vengeance on their enemies.

> Is this not written in the Book of Jashar? The sun stopped in the midst of heaven and did not hurry to set for about a whole day. There has been no day like it before or since, when the LORD heeded the voice of a man, for the LORD fought for Israel. (Josh. 10:12–14)

On this occasion Joshua simply speaks to Yahweh. There is no explanation of what he said, let alone of how Yahweh responded. But the outcome is clear – Joshua commands the sun and moon to stand still, and the battle continues until the victory is complete. The verdict in Joshua 7:14 is striking (esp. given the ambiguous encounter in 5:13–15). Joshua's prayer has been heard. Yahweh has heard their cries, intervened and fought for his people, just as he did in Egypt according to Joshua 24:7. His plan of salvation remains on track.

Prayer in the book of Judges

Given the darkness of the book of Judges (and the period of the judges in general), one would hardly expect it to be a rich source of material on prayer, and yet it proves to be probably the most important of the Former Prophets when it comes to formulating a biblical theology of prayer.[7]

The opening statement of the book sets the tone – calling on the name of Yahweh is set to be a key theme in this book:

> After the death of Joshua, the people of Israel enquired of the LORD, 'Who shall go up first for us against the Canaanites, to fight against them?' The LORD said, 'Judah shall go up; behold, I have given the land into his hand.' (Judg. 1:1–2)

The prayer of the people and the answer of Yahweh are intertwined in the outworking of God's covenant project, as his people continue the judicial campaign against the Canaanites. However, the connection between prayer and the safety/victory of Israel is not limited

---

[7] Contrast this with the fact that many books on prayer (even at the academic level) barely nod in the direction of Judges (see e.g. Clements 1985).

to the initial conquest. The repeated calling on Yahweh by Israel is one of the key features of this book:[8]

> But when the people of Israel cried out to the LORD, the LORD raised up a deliverer for the people of Israel, who saved them, Othniel the son of Kenaz, Caleb's younger brother. (Judg. 3:9)

> Then the people of Israel cried out to the LORD, and the LORD raised up for them a deliverer, Ehud, the son of Gera, the Benjaminite, a left-handed man. The people of Israel sent tribute by him to Eglon the king of Moab. (Judg. 3:15)

> Then the people of Israel cried out to the LORD for help, for he had 900 chariots of iron and he oppressed the people of Israel cruelly for twenty years. (Judg. 4:3)

> And Israel was brought very low because of Midian. And the people of Israel cried out for help to the LORD.
> When the people of Israel cried out to the LORD on account of the Midianites . . . (Judg. 6:6–7)

> And the people of Israel cried out to the LORD, saying, 'We have sinned against you, because we have forsaken our God and have served the Baals.' (Judg. 10:10)

In each case the cycle of rebellion and divine punishment leads eventually to repentance and 'crying out to Yahweh'. Interestingly, however, after Judges 10 the cycle grinds to a halt. Commenting on Judges 10:11–14, Barry Webb writes, 'Clearly the relationship between the two parties has reached a major point of crisis, with a complete breakdown of it looking like a real possibility,'[9] with Yahweh declaring in verses 13–14, 'Yet you have forsaken me and served other gods; therefore I will save you no more. Go and cry out to the gods whom you have chosen; let them save you in the time of your distress.'[10] Significantly, there are no further national cries for mercy, nor does

---

[8] See the helpful comments of Barry Webb (2012: 32–35).

[9] Ibid. 303.

[10] This anticipates a theme that will become extremely significant in the Latter Prophets: God's people cannot take it for granted that he will always listen to their prayers, irrespective of their behaviour.

Yahweh rescue his people in the same definitive way during the rest of the period of the judges.

It would be a mistake to assume that this emphasis on prayer is limited to national, corporate pleas of desperation. Prayer punctuates the entire narrative, with several of the most prominent judges praying on more than one occasion. What is most striking is the almost universal connection between the prayers of the judge and the desire for 'salvation'.[11]

So Deborah concludes the song of Judges 5 with this prayer:

> So may all your enemies perish, O LORD!
> But your friends be like the sun as he rises in his might.
>
> (Judg. 5:31)

Gideon, not renowned for his theological acumen, takes part in the remarkable interchange of Judges 6:36–40:

> Then Gideon said to God, 'If you will save Israel by my hand, as you have said, behold, I am laying a fleece of wool on the threshing floor. If there is dew on the fleece alone, and it is dry on all the ground, then I shall know that you will save Israel by my hand, as you have said.' And it was so. When he rose early next morning and squeezed the fleece, he wrung enough dew from the fleece to fill a bowl with water. Then Gideon said to God, 'Let not your anger burn against me; let me speak just once more. Please let me test just once more with the fleece. Please let it be dry on the fleece only, and on all the ground let there be dew.' And God did so that night; and it was dry on the fleece only, and on all the ground there was dew. (Judg. 6:36–40)

As Boling comments, 'At this point, the depiction of the Judges period begins to resemble the modern theatre of the absurd.'[12] Gideon asks for, and, even more surprisingly, receives, an utterly unnecessary commitment from Yahweh that, yes, he is committed to saving his people.

This principle is played out repeatedly in the rest of the book, as Yahweh graciously responds to some highly deficient prayers, offered by highly misguided supplicants.

---

[11] It is often hard to discern whether the judge conceives of this merely as deliverance from a military oppressor, or, as the reader inevitably does, also in terms of the fulfilment of the promises to Abraham, Isaac and Jacob.

[12] Boling 1975: 141.

Manoah, Samson's father, knows enough to ask for help, but little more. The help is graciously provided.[13] Samson himself, despite being the very antithesis of a model judge, does pray on two occasions. On each one his prayers show some awareness that prayer is a matter of calling on the name of Yahweh to deliver his people:

> And he was very thirsty, and he called upon the LORD and said, 'You have granted this great salvation by the hand of your servant, and shall I now die of thirst and fall into the hands of the uncircumcised?' (Judg. 15:18)

Similarly, at his death, while his prayer is hardly a model of piety,[14] his prayer is still heard, as Yahweh acts to ease the circumstances of his people:

> Then Samson called to the LORD and said, 'O Lord GOD, please remember me and please strengthen me only this once, O God, that I may be avenged on the Philistines for my two eyes.' And Samson grasped the two middle pillars on which the house rested, and he leaned his weight against them, his right hand on the one and his left hand on the other. And Samson said, 'Let me die with the Philistines.' Then he bowed with all his strength, and the house fell upon the lords and upon all the people who were in it. (Judg. 16:28–30)

Even though the remaining chapters of Judges are, arguably, the most depressing chapters of the Bible, it is striking that God in his grace has not abandoned his people, and when they cry to him he continues to listen (despite the warning of Judg. 10:13). When the civil war breaks out with Benjamin in chapter 20, we read these words:

> The people of Israel arose and went up to Bethel and enquired of God, 'Who shall go up first for us to fight against the people of Benjamin?' And the LORD said, 'Judah shall go up first.'
> Then the people of Israel rose in the morning and encamped against Gibeah. And the men of Israel went out to fight against Benjamin, and the men of Israel drew up the battle line against them

---

[13] Judg. 13:8–9.
[14] Butler (2006: 353) states bluntly that 'Samson's motive is not religious. He does not ask God to help him to fulfill a forgotten mission of deliverance. His motive is still selfish revenge.'

at Gibeah. The people of Benjamin came out of Gibeah and destroyed on that day 22,000 men of the Israelites. . . . And the people of Israel went up and wept before the LORD until the evening. And they enquired of the LORD, 'Shall we again draw near to fight against our brothers, the people of Benjamin?' And the LORD said, 'Go up against them.'

So the people of Israel came near against the people of Benjamin the second day. And Benjamin went against them out of Gibeah the second day, and destroyed 18,000 men of the people of Israel. All these were men who drew the sword. Then all the people of Israel, the whole army, went up and came to Bethel and wept. They sat there before the LORD and fasted that day until evening, and offered burnt offerings and peace offerings before the LORD. And the people of Israel enquired of the LORD (for the ark of the covenant of God was there in those days, and Phinehas the son of Eleazar, son of Aaron, ministered before it in those days), saying, 'Shall we go out once more to battle against our brothers, the people of Benjamin, or shall we cease?' And the LORD said, 'Go up, for tomorrow I will give them into your hand.' (Judg. 20:18–21, 23–28)

This strange cycle of events is not easy to fathom. With his inimitable clarity Dale Ralph Davis sums up the issue:

> If Yahweh was acting in judgment on Benjamin, why did Israel suffer those two laming defeats, especially when they had received direction from Yahweh both times? . . . There is another possibility: Israel's initial defeats may not point to the suffering of Yahweh's judgment but to the mystery of his ways.[15]

After the book of Judges it would not be possible to assume that prayer works automatically – already it has been made very clear that Yahweh answers prayer by grace alone, but also that in his sovereignty there may be times when he no longer listens or, worse, acts in judgment even in the face of the prayers of his people. None can take him for granted; and yet even as Judges comes to an end, he is still acting in response to his people's cries in order to keep his promises and pour out his covenant blessings on his undeserving (and divided) people:

---

[15] Davis 2000: 217.

> And the people came to Bethel and sat there till evening before God, and they lifted up their voices and wept bitterly. And they said, 'O LORD, the God of Israel, why has this happened in Israel, that today there should be one tribe lacking in Israel?' (Judg. 21:2–3)

Prayer in the books of Samuel

It is interesting that, relatively speaking, prayer has been a greatly neglected theme in the books of Samuel and Kings. This is doubly surprising given the fact that the books of Samuel open with the remarkable prayers of Hannah, the mother of the eponymous hero.

The very human drama of a dysfunctional household and the pain of childlessness has often led readers to miss the stunning impact of 1 Samuel 2. The writer is tantalizingly brief on the content of Hannah's vow-prayer in chapter 1, and the reason why her prayers are so angst-ridden. We are deliberately left to assume that this is simply an extreme case of a woman longing to start a family:

> And she vowed a vow and said, 'O LORD of hosts, if you will indeed look on the affliction of your servant and remember me and not forget your servant, but will give to your servant a son, then I will give him to the LORD all the days of his life, and no razor shall touch his head.'[16]
>
> As she continued praying before the LORD . . . (1 Sam. 1:11–12)

However, the fact that Eli, the leader of Israel, appears to lack any spiritual discernment when it comes to real piety alerts us to the fact that this 'everyday story' is anything but that. This becomes extremely obvious when we come to 1 Samuel 2:1–10.

The most remarkable feature of this prayer is the virtual lack of reference to Hannah's own situation.[17] It is not the typical prayer of a woman who has just conceived and given birth. So crucial is this to my argument that it is worth reproducing her prayer in full:

---

[16] V. 12 makes clear that this 'vow' was also a prayer: 'As she continued praying before the LORD . . .' See Woodhouse's (2008: 20–21) excellent discussion of this whole section.

[17] It is normal simply to ascribe this to the (surely clumsy?) insertion of later psalmic material (see e.g. McCarter 1980: 74–76; Alter 1999: 9), but this is not a satisfactory solution.

And Hannah prayed and said,

'My heart exults in the LORD;
   my horn is exalted in the LORD.
My mouth derides my enemies,
   because I rejoice in your salvation.
'There is none holy like the LORD:
   there is none besides you;
   there is no rock like our God.
Talk no more so very proudly,
   let not arrogance come from your mouth;
for the LORD is a God of knowledge,
   and by him actions are weighed.
The bows of the mighty are broken,
   but the feeble bind on strength.
Those who were full have hired themselves out for bread,
   but those who were hungry have ceased to hunger.
The barren has borne seven,
   but she who has many children is forlorn.
The LORD kills and brings to life;
   he brings down to Sheol and raises up.
The LORD makes poor and makes rich;
   he brings low and he exalts.
He raises up the poor from the dust;
   he lifts the needy from the ash heap
to make them sit with princes
   and inherit a seat of honour.
For the pillars of the earth are the LORD's,
   and on them he has set the world.
'He will guard the feet of his faithful ones,
   but the wicked shall be cut off in darkness,
   for not by might shall a man prevail.
The adversaries of the LORD shall be broken to pieces;
   against them he will thunder in heaven.
The LORD will judge the ends of the earth;
   he will give strength to his king
   and exalt the horn of his anointed.'

(1 Sam. 2:1–10)

This is one of the most remarkable prayers in the whole Bible. But what are its central concerns? The prayer is full of allusions to (or

53

anticipations of) other Old Testament passages. Hannah's prayer breathes in the world of Deuteronomy 32 and Psalm 2.[18] Intriguingly, the climax of the prayer is not the birth of Samuel but the coming of a messiah/king.

This text is often taken to be a piece of monarchical propaganda.[19] However, when one reads 1 Samuel 2 in the light of the unfolding picture of prayer in the Pentateuch, Joshua and Judges, the chapter looks very different. Here is another prayer in the spirit of Genesis 4 – for the God of Judges to send a rescuer, who is now identified explicitly as a messiah.

It is worth pointing out that this towering prayer, which, apart from the possible exception of the Song of Moses, is the longest and most theologically rich we have encountered so far, is prayed *by a woman who has no relationship to the central cult or the priesthood*. This is extremely unusual in the ancient world, and cannot be an accident in the masterly account of Israel's history in Samuel and Kings. Rather, it is a reminder that prayer is, in essence, *calling on the name of Yahweh to deliver on his covenant promises*.

This perspective finds substantial support in the very next chapter. In the well-known narrative of young Samuel's first encounter with Yahweh, alongside the repeated emphasis on 'hearing' (*šmʿ*) and the 'word' (*dbr*) of Yahweh is a pronounced play on 'calling' (*qrʾ*). Despite Eli's obvious failure to 'call on Yahweh' (and his initial failure to discern that Yahweh is speaking), Yahweh repeatedly *calls on* Samuel. The initiative Yahweh had taken in the garden with Adam after the fall was, it seems, not a one-off. The same balance of judgment and hope pronounced in Genesis 3 is present in 1 Samuel 2:27–36: God reveals to Samuel that the Elide dynasty is finished, but also reveals himself 'by the word of Yahweh' at Shiloh, as he establishes a new kind of leadership.[20]

Right at the beginning of Samuel–Kings, then, prayer that is essentially covenantal (precisely the kind of prayer described, and by implication prescribed in the Pentateuch) is once again front and centre.

---

[18] See the helpful discussion of Firth (2009: 59–63). Practically every second line of Hannah's prayer is echoed somewhere in Psalms. See also Job 1:21; 5:11; 36:7; 38:4–6.

[19] E.g. Gordon, 'a psalm composed in the pre-monarchical period would be unlikely to speak of Yahweh's anointed king'; although he does allow that if the prayer is genuinely Hannah's, verse 10b could be an addition 'to take account of the advent of the monarchy' (Gordon 1986: 23). Hertzberg (1964: 29) says it is clearly not Hannah's prayer. Davis (1999: 24, n.) gives a good overview of the discussion, and a defence.

[20] See e.g. Firth 2009: 80.

As we continue to read through the books of Samuel, the validity of this understanding of prayer is confirmed over and over. After the loss and recovery of the Ark in chapter 6, 1 Samuel 7 records a national repentance that, on the face of it at least, seems to be of almost Deuteronomic proportions (1 Sam. 7:4). This moment of 'covenant renewal' is rapidly followed by prayer – specifically, prayer for deliverance from the Philistines. Samuel prays (*pll*) and cries to Yahweh (*z 'q*), but although the vocabulary varies, the content of the request remains constant – Samuel is asking Yahweh to come through on his covenant promises and rescue his people once more ('Then Samuel said, "Gather all Israel at Mizpah, and I will pray to the LORD for you"').[21] This is the understanding of prayer in the historical books.

This explains the otherwise slightly puzzling response of Samuel to the request for a king in 1 Samuel 8:6–8:

> But the thing displeased Samuel when they said, 'Give us a king to judge us.' *And Samuel prayed to the LORD.* And the LORD said to Samuel, 'Obey the voice of the people in all that they say to you, for they have not rejected you, but they have rejected me from being king over them. According to all the deeds that they have done, from the day I brought them up out of Egypt even to this day, forsaking me and serving other gods, so they are also doing to you.'

It would be easy to overlook this little note in the midst of such a climactic moment in the history of Israel. *Why does Samuel pray?* The prophet is clearly aware of the Mosaic prohibition on such kings, so why not simply correct or confront the people, pointing them back to the words of Deuteronomy? It can only be because Samuel sees this request as a threat to the covenant itself, and so, quite naturally, cries to the God of the covenant to come to the rescue of his people.

When Samuel briefly returns to centre stage in 1 Samuel 12, it becomes even clearer (if that were possible) that prayer is inextricably linked to the covenant. After a long rehearsal of covenant history (1 Sam. 12:6–17), Samuel 'called upon the LORD, and the LORD sent thunder and rain that day, and all the people greatly feared the LORD and Samuel' (12:18). This micro-covenant curse leads the people to

---

[21] The phrasing here is a little unusual – this is a striking offer of intercession. Presumably, this is a consequence of the spiritual declension of the period of the judges.

beg Samuel to pray for them (6:19), culminating in the striking words of 12:23–25:

> Moreover, as for me, far be it from me that I should sin against the LORD by ceasing to pray for you, and I will instruct you in the good and the right way. Only fear the LORD and serve him faithfully with all your heart. For consider what great things he has done for you. But if you still do wickedly, you shall be swept away, both you and your king.

What is Samuel committing himself to pray? It can be only one thing – Samuel is praying *covenantally*. The prophet is praying that God will equip his covenant people to live in a way that fits with the covenant. He is praying that Yahweh will come through on his promises. This begs an important question: In what sense will Samuel be 'sinning against Yahweh' by failing to pray for them? There is nothing in the text to suggest that Samuel has been given a special ministry of intercession on behalf of the people.[22] A better explanation is simply to say that it is a fundamental responsibility of God's covenant people to 'call on the name of Yahweh', crying out to God to keep his promises to his people, including that most basic of covenantal promises to be with his people, strengthening and equipping them to keep in step with him.

In marked contrast to Samuel, Saul is not depicted as either grasping or practising 'biblical' prayer. The only reference to anything close to prayer in the Saul narratives comes in 1 Samuel 14 in the wake of Saul's rash vow. For Israel's first king 'prayer' is a means of extracting the requisite guidance or information from Yahweh.[23] Saul enquires (the verb shares the same root as the name 'Saul') of God in verse 36, and then complains when the answer is not forthcoming. While the language of enquiring of God is not pejorative,[24] in the context the introduction of the Urim and Thummim, Saul's preoccupation with his own immediate concerns (rather than those of the nation per se) added to the fact that the prayer leads to the exposure of his sin and stupidity all suggest that his understanding of prayer is highly deficient.

---

[22] Although that could possibly be an implication of 1 Sam. 7:5.

[23] Incidentally, this is borne out by Saul's approach to the medium of Endor in 1 Sam. 28, which is described in essentially the same terms as his approach to Yahweh in that chapter. The result of Saul's prayer there is even less effective (28:7).

[24] The language of enquiry can be used of various other gods as well as Yahweh (see e.g. the disastrous events of 2 Kgs 1).

When Yahweh finally reveals his 'verdict' on Saul's reign in 15:10–11, it leads Samuel to cry to Yahweh all night in anger. The text does not spell out whether Samuel is angry with Saul or with Yahweh (on balance, it seems more likely that he is angry with Saul[25]), but either way his response to this divinely allowed covenantal crisis is to cry out to Yahweh all night. Although many commentators simply say that the content of his prayer is unknown,[26] there is no need for such uncertainty. The narrative of 1 Samuel so far has made it clear that Samuel's key concern in all this (despite his own personal issues[27]) is the future progress of Yahweh's covenant, which is now in jeopardy thanks to the foolish actions of the ungodly 'people's choice'. However, as 1 Samuel 16 makes plain, Yahweh himself will not stand by and allow his people to lose their way.

The remaining references to prayer in 1 Samuel and those in the early part of 2 Samuel are a little more puzzling. Formally, at least, David's approaches to Yahweh in 23:1–5, 30:7–10 (in which David puts on the 'ephod' before enquiring of Yahweh), 2 Samuel 2:1–2 and even 5:19 seem to have more in common with Saul's methods than Samuel's. David routinely enquires of Yahweh and Yahweh gives him victory (usually over the Philistines). However, two things need to be borne in mind: (1) the fact that the narrator is at pains to stress the fact that David enquires of *Yahweh* (rather than simply Elohim) immediately sets his prayers apart from those of Saul; (2) during David's 'wilderness period', the narrative interest is focused on the preservation of David as Israel's 'messiah', and his eventual return to Jerusalem in triumph. Again, in contrast to Saul, David's interest is not simply in self-preservation, but in serving Yahweh (see explicitly in 1 Sam. 30:6) and in living obediently (within the covenant), albeit in a unique and abnormal situation. David's prayers here, despite first appearances, fit neatly with the emphasis on covenant that is so obvious earlier in 1 Samuel.[28] Each victory over the Philistines is a reminder that Yahweh will overcome his enemies, and will install *his* king over his people.

This theme is picked up in one of the most important prayers not just in the Former Prophets but in the entire Bible – the prayer of

---

[25] See Gunn 1980: 146.

[26] E.g. Firth 2009: 174.

[27] This is implied in 1 Sam. 8:1–5.

[28] This is confirmed by the climax of the narrative in 2 Sam. 2:1–7, where the blessings exchanged with the men of Jabesh Gilead and the bald statement of 2:4 make it clear where this whole section has been leading.

David in response to Yahweh's dynastic promise in 2 Samuel 7:18–29. This prayer merits slightly more detailed consideration.

In 2 Samuel 7:18 David goes in and sits before Yahweh. This is a highly unusual posture for prayer, which presumably underscores the fact that David, Yahweh's messiah-king is speaking to his Lord. This has already been made clear by the preponderance of first-person statements made by Yahweh in the previous verses. It is obvious that once more it is Yahweh who is taking all the initiative (in marked contrast to the normal ANE pattern[29]). The course of the rest of David's prayer is determined by the connection between the promise just made to him (concerning his 'house') and the grand sweep of Yahweh's great covenant project. The language of verses 22–24 is typically Deuteronomic and leads to the heart of David's petition in verse 25.[30] And what does David ask of Yahweh? Simply that he do what he has already promised through his word: 'And now, O LORD God, confirm for ever the word that you have spoken concerning your servant and concerning his house, and do as you have spoken.' This takes us right to the heart of biblical prayer. Prayer is, in essence, calling on Yahweh to do what he has said. This is confirmed once more in the conclusion of David's prayer in verses 28–29:

> And now, O Lord GOD, you are God, and your words are true, and you have promised this good thing to your servant. Now therefore may it please you to bless the house of your servant, so that it may continue for ever before you. For you, O Lord GOD, have spoken, and with your blessing shall the house of your servant be blessed for ever.

It is worth pointing out, however, that Yahweh is silent on David's (probably instinctive) commitment to build a 'house' (temple) for Yahweh. According to 7:13, this does not seem to be part of the plan, and jars slightly with the rest of David's prayer, which is so determined to root all that has happened in the firm ground of Yahweh's sovereignty.

Of the remaining possible references to prayer in 2 Samuel, *bqš* occurs twice: in the first occurrence David 'sought God' (2 Sam. 12:16), and in the other he 'sought the face of the LORD' (2 Sam. 21:1);

---

[29] See Davis 1999: 74–75 for a helpful list of ancient human initiatives designed to elicit divine favour.
[30] See Deut. 4:7, 34; 9:26; 10:21; 33:29; also 26:18.

whereas in the final reference to prayer David simply speaks to Yahweh, confessing his pride. In each case it is important to realize that the prayers have dynastic (or perhaps, better, covenantal overtones.) David prays for his sick infant son, and for the nation in the face of famine, and for his own 'house' in the wake of his own arrogant presumption. Even in these brief references to prayer it seems that the connection with covenant cannot be broken.

Prayer in the books of Kings

In the books of Kings there are fewer passing references to prayer, but a similar amount of space is devoted to long prayers at key points in the narrative (notably those prayed by Solomon and Hezekiah). In addition throughout the Elijah and Elisha narratives the significance of prayer is repeatedly highlighted. This shape will guide our discussion.

The prayers of Solomon

There is a sense in which Solomon's 'prayer' in 1 Kings 3 should be excluded from our discussion, in that it is not a prayer at all. The interaction between Solomon and Yahweh in 1 Kings 3:1–15 takes place in a dream. However, ensuing events make clear that this 'dream sequence' has 'real-world' consequences, as Solomon's request is answered. Although normal prayer language is missing from the narrative, it seems reasonable to include it in our discussion, not least because of parallels with other prayers (e.g. 2 Sam. 7).

The wording of Solomon's request is often interpreted primarily as the gift of a personal attribute. Solomon himself, however, is quick to link his petition both to the legacy of his father, David, and to the fulfilment of the promises made to Abraham, their forefather:

> And Solomon said, 'You have shown great and steadfast love to your servant David my father, because he walked before you in faithfulness, in righteousness, and in uprightness of heart towards you. And you have kept for him this great and steadfast love and have given him a son to sit on his throne this day. And now, O LORD my God, you have made your servant king in place of David my father, although I am but a little child. I do not know how to go out or come in. And your servant is in the midst of your people whom you have chosen, a great people, too many to be numbered or counted for multitude. Give your servant therefore an understanding mind to govern your people, that I may discern between

good and evil, for who is able to govern this your great people?'
(1 Kgs 3:6–9)

This prayer is some considerable distance from a personal request for
the ability to make good decisions. This is a request for divine help in
discharging the role of messiah.[31] Yahweh is delighted with this suggestion precisely because Solomon is the messiah – the wisdom
supplied is to enable Solomon to lead Yahweh's people well and
promote covenant faithfulness. The necessity of such wisdom is
evidenced both in 1 Kings 2 (where in both v. 6 and v. 9 David charges
Solomon to act 'wisely' by killing Joab and Shimei, to clean up some
of the political fallout created by David himself) and in 1 Kings
3:16–28 (where the national declension is seen in the fact that brothels
are hardly worthy of remark, never mind censure[32]). This covenantal
perspective is confirmed by 1 Kings 3:11–15, where Yahweh himself
confirms that this prayer is answered so that Solomon may be a king
without equal, *and that he himself may walk in covenant faithfulness*,
even managing to handle unparalleled wealth.

In passing, it is worth noting that this goes a little way to easing the
oft-observed tension between the fact that Solomon is the wisest man
on the planet and his personal life, which shows evidence of some
dubious choices (see e.g. 1 Kgs 7:8; 11:1–8). Solomon's wisdom is given
by Yahweh to his anointed king to lead his people in covenant faithfulness.[33] It hinges on the degree to which he listens to Yahweh. All this is
obvious from the moment he dreams to the end of his reign. And it
is obvious in the central pillar of the account of his reign in 1 Kings 8.

In many ways this is the high point of the Old Testament. Too many
sheep to be counted are sacrificed before the party gets started, and
then later a mere 142,000 are added. This is a Feast of Tabernacles
unlike any other, a breathtaking moment in the history of God's
people, as the long-awaited temple is commissioned. But there is
something deeply surprising about Solomon's prayer of dedication
– it *barely mentions the temple itself*. This is not a prayer about sacrifice,
ritual or priesthood, or even atonement. It is about *covenant*.[34]

---

[31] See e.g. House 1995: 110–111.

[32] This confusion could only have arisen where the women were living together
without any husbands present – in other words, in a brothel, which is an index of the
moral declension in Israel.

[33] See also the explicitly covenantal language of 1 Kgs 4:29–34. God's equipping of
Solomon leads to an interim fulfilment of the promises to Abraham.

[34] Peter Leithart (Leithart 2006: 68–69) has an excellent discussion of the Deutero-
nomic/Mosaic links in 1 Kgs 8.

That fact is everywhere in 1 Kings 8. The prominence of the *Ark of the Covenant* in the opening section sets the tone for all that follows. The emphasis is on God's people *assembling*, just as they did on Mount Sinai when they became a nation proper. The word 'Israel' is used thirty-five times. There are constant references to God's *keeping the promises he made to David* (8:15, 20, 24–25, 66) and the covenant promises *made at Sinai* (8:21, 53, 56), and the promises made to Abraham (8:40, 48), and the characterization of God as a *covenant-keeping God* in 8:23.

This emphasis on the covenant is crucial in understanding the deep paradox at the heart of Solomon's prayer. The paradox is spelled out in 8:27–30:

> But will God indeed dwell on the earth? Behold, heaven and the highest heaven cannot contain you; how much less this house that I have built! Yet have regard to the prayer of your servant and to his plea, O Lord my God, listening to the cry and to the prayer that your servant prays before you this day, that your eyes may be open night and day towards this house, the place of which you have said, 'My name shall be there', that you may listen to the prayer that your servant offers towards this place. And listen to the plea of your servant and of your people Israel, when they pray towards this place. And listen in heaven your dwelling place, and when you hear, forgive.

This is a very strange prayer to pray at a temple dedication. But this tension between the transcendence and immanence of God is right at the heart of Deuteronomic covenant theology,[35] and makes clear that the temple is not an end in itself, but the servant of a much bigger agenda.[36]

This striking emphasis on covenant (rather than temple or sacrifice per se) continues in verse 31, where Solomon picks up a list of covenant curses from Deuteronomy 28 and Leviticus 26. In one way this is deeply pessimistic, yet there is also the possibility of forgiveness. But once again, drawing on Deuteronomy, Solomon links this forgiveness not to temple rituals, but to covenantal repentance:

---

[35] See e.g. Deut. 4, and in particular the work of I. Wilson (1995) and McConville (1992; 1993a).

[36] 'It is prayer rather than sacrifice which is envisaged as the medium of communication between God's people and their Lord, and also as their means of seeking his forgiveness' (M. E. W. Thompson 1996: 191).

yet if they turn their heart in the land to which they have been carried captive, and repent and plead with you in the land of their captors, saying, 'We have sinned and have acted perversely and wickedly', if they repent with all their mind and with all their heart in the land of their enemies, who carried them captive, and pray to you towards their land, which you gave to their fathers, the city that you have chosen, and the house that I have built for your name, then hear in heaven your dwelling place their prayer and their plea, and maintain their cause and forgive your people who have sinned against you, and all their transgressions that they have committed against you, and grant them compassion in the sight of those who carried them captive, that they may have compassion on them (for they are your people, and your heritage, which you brought out of Egypt, from the midst of the iron furnace). (1 Kgs 8:47–51)

If one needed any further evidence that this most powerful of biblical prayers is essentially covenantal, the repeated appeals to actions and promises through Moses (8:52–54), and the startling provision for foreigners (with the attendant expectation that Yahweh will hear their prayers too; 8:41–43, 60), presumably fulfilling the promise made to Abraham, puts the matter beyond all reasonable doubt.[37] When Solomon prays, he prays for Yahweh to come through on his covenant promises.

The prayers of Elijah and Elisha

The largest cluster of references to prayer in Kings comes in the Elijah–Elisha narratives. Elijah prays for the resuscitation of a dead boy (17:20–24), for vindication in his contest with the prophets of Baal on Mount Carmel (18:36–37) and for God to end his life (19:4). In each case the prayer is connected in a significant way to the promises of Yahweh.

When the son of the widow of Zarephath is raised, not only is this another example of blessing accruing to people outside Israel (Zarephath is in the heart of Jezebel country) and a demonstration of the supremacy of Yahweh, the God of the covenant, over Baal and Anat,[38] but the miracle also acts as a vindication of the divine word as delivered by the prophet (1 Kgs 17:24: 'And the woman said to Elijah, "Now I know that you are a man of God, and that the word

---

[37] McConville 1992: 42.
[38] See House 1995: 215; Sweeney 2007: 14.

of the LORD in your mouth is truth"'). In the context of 1 Kings (and, as we have just seen, particularly in the light of 1 Kgs 8) it is impossible to speak about the word of Yahweh without also invoking the *presence of Yahweh*, the covenant God who says, 'I will be your God and you will be my people.' This is a covenantal miracle.

When praying mid-confrontation on Mount Carmel, Elijah makes explicit reference to the covenant with Abraham, Isaac and Jacob:

> O LORD, God of Abraham, Isaac, and Israel, let it be known this day that you are God in Israel, and that I am your servant, and that I have done all these things at your word. Answer me, O LORD, answer me, that this people may know that you, O LORD, are God, and that you have turned their hearts back. (1 Kgs 18:36–37)

Elijah's prayer is at root a prayer for God to act to vindicate himself and keep his commitments.

Even Elijah's prayer of desperation in 1 Kings 19:4 cannot be adequately understood without reference to a covenantal context. If I am right in proposing that the verb in 19:3 should be read with the MT as 'saw' (rather than 'was afraid'),[39] it is almost certain that Elijah's motivation is not one of fear or personal collapse, but of frustration at his own failure, following on from the epic failures of generation after generation of his forebears. Despite the events of Carmel, nothing has changed. Like those who have gone before, he too has failed to call God's people back to covenant obedience. That same note is echoed in verses 10 and 14, where, when he is taken back to Horeb, that covenant place par excellence, Elijah says twice that God's people 'have forsaken your covenant'. Yet again we see that the understanding of prayer in the Old Testament is calling on God to do what he has already committed to do in his covenant promises.

Like his mentor, Elisha also prays for a dead son (2 Kgs 4:32–37). Although the language is much less explicitly covenantal in the Elisha incident, the close parallels with the Elijah encounter make it clear that the writer of Kings wants us to understand that Yahweh is still acting to bring life out of death, and to uphold his commitments to his people. In 2 Kings 6:15–19 the links with covenantal thought are much clearer – Elisha prays, and then God acts to preserve his people – opening the eyes of the servant to the 'real' situation, and closing the eyes of the Syrian army to ensure their defeat, and allowing them

---

[39] The MT reads, 'he saw'; e.g. Davis 2007: 257–258; Provan 1995: 144.

to be led safely into the heart of the Israelite garrison! Prayer, it seems, cannot be easily reduced to anything less than asking God to do what he has promised.

The prayers of Hezekiah

The final piece of the puzzle in constructing the Former Prophets' theology of prayer is found in two narratives concerning King Hezekiah of Judah in 2 Kings 19 and 20. In the first, Hezekiah responds well to a threat from Assyria; in the second, he responds badly to his own impending death. The contrast between these two prayers provides yet more evidence that in the Old Testament prayer is asking Yahweh to come through on his promises to the nation.

In 2 Kings 19 Hezekiah's reaction to the arrogance of the Rabshakeh (who asserts, among other things, that Yahweh cannot be trusted to come through on his promises, 19:10) is highly commendable.[40] He goes to the temple, spreads out the letter before Yahweh and prays. His prayer is based on the fact that Yahweh is both the God of Israel and the God of all nations. His concern is for Yahweh's honour, which he understands is bound up with the fate of his covenant people. In that, his prayer in 19:14–19 fits the pattern that has been established very well. As we might expect, Yahweh answers this prayer dramatically (19:35), and *explicitly on the basis of his covenant with David*: 'For I will defend this city to save it, for my own sake and for the sake of my servant David' (19:34).

However, Hezekiah's prayer in 2 Kings 20 stands in stark contrast. Even though Yahweh continues to operate on a covenantal basis, it seems that Hezekiah's concerns fail to rise above self pity:[41]

> Hezekiah turned his face to the wall and prayed to the LORD, saying, 'Now, O LORD, please remember how I have walked before you in faithfulness and with a whole heart, and have done what is good in your sight.' And Hezekiah wept bitterly. (2 Kgs 20:2–3)

What is interesting is that even in his despair *Hezekiah still prays on the basis of the covenant* (whether or not he was justified in praying such a prayer). What is even more interesting is the basis on which Yahweh responds – once more, it is the covenant with David:

[40] See the discussion of Wray Beal (2014: 464–465).
[41] Commentators are divided on whether or not this passage is an implied criticism of Hezekiah. With Hobbs (1986: 290) I think that the contrast with the previous chapter makes it highly likely that it is.

Turn back, and say to Hezekiah the leader of my people, Thus says the Lord, the God of David your father: I have heard your prayer; I have seen your tears. Behold, I will heal you. On the third day you shall go up to the house of the Lord, and I will add fifteen years to your life. I will deliver you and this city out of the hand of the king of Assyria, and I will defend this city for my own sake and for my servant David's sake. (2 Kgs 20:5–6)

Such is Yahweh's commitment to his covenant (and his covenant king) that he is even willing to make shadows go backwards (2 Kgs 20:10; the writer to Kings does not explain whether God distorts the space-time continuum in order to do this, or simply makes the shadow shorten) in order to convince him of his commitment.

For our purposes neither the utterly self-preoccupied reaction of Hezekiah to Isaiah's prophecy nor his foolishness in inviting Merodach-Baladan into his treasury changes the fact that when he prays, Hezekiah calls on the name of Yahweh to deliver on his covenant commitments. There are 'good' prayers and 'bad' prayers, worthy prayers and unworthy prayers – but God answers both in line with his commitments to his king and kingdom.[42]

Conclusion

While it would be overstating it to say that prayer is one of the major themes of Joshua to 2 Kings, it is fair to say that there is a consistent strand of teaching on prayer in these books. From Joshua through Judges and all through the books of Samuel and Kings there is an insistence that one of the great needs of the people of Yahweh is to call on his name; that is, to ask him to do what he has said he will do and to keep his covenant promises.

This is generally how prayer is understood, described and practised in this part of the Old Testament. The theology of prayer, if one can call it that, laid down in the Pentateuch is developed and applied consistently through these books with a remarkable degree of unity. Prayer is calling on the name of Yahweh, our covenant God.

---

[42] I am indebted to Don Carson for helping to sharpen my thinking on these passages.

Chapter Three

Praying in the light of the future: prayer in the Latter Prophets

Prayer probably is not the first subject that comes to mind when we think of the writing prophets in the Bible. Rather surprisingly, however, a significant amount of their material has a bearing on my discussion.

Obviously, to step into the world of the 'Latter Prophets' is to enter a minefield of critical and historical issues, which I cannot hope to begin to address here.[1] My approach will essentially be synchronic, treating each of the Major Prophets as a whole, and then discussing the material on prayer in the Book of the Twelve in a broadly similar fashion.

Long prayers and large books

Isaiah

Surprisingly, the first mention of prayer in the book of Isaiah is a statement from Yahweh himself through his prophet, warning the people that their petitions are completely ineffective:

> When you spread out your hands,
>   I will hide my eyes from you;
> even though you make many prayers,
>   I will not listen;
>   your hands are full of blood.
>   (Isa. 1:15)[2]

This silence dominates large tracts of the book.

---

[1] Particularly when it comes to Isaiah, and the nature and composition of the 'Book of the Twelve'.

[2] A similar comment is made of the prayers of Moab in 16:12. See also Isa. 59:1–3.

The theophany (or theophanic vision) in Isaiah 6 does contain conversation with Yahweh – however, it is hard to say whether or not this should be construed as prayer. If so, Isaiah's visceral cry for mercy fits broadly into the pattern of 'calling on the name of Yahweh' that we have seen repeatedly up to this point. However, we have to wait until chapter 12 before we encounter the first substantial communication with God in the book.

Isaiah 12 comes at the climax of the first 'movement' of the book, by which time Yahweh has made it clear that he will intervene by sending Immanuel, the 'shoot from the stump of Jesse', to bring in his victory and summon the nations to bow before him (see 11:1–16). Chapter 12 then provides the capstone of this section. The interesting feature of the section is that, rather than 'calling on the name of Yahweh', praise is offered at some point in the future *after* Yahweh has acted to rescue his people. So is it, strictly speaking, a *prayer*? I am not sure it is.

It seems that the Old Testament maintains a distinction between *prayer*, which is what we do in crying to God for deliverance, and *praise*, which is what we do after God has delivered us. Of course, this distinction can be overplayed – conversations with God which are, on any understanding, *prayers* often freely mingle prayer and praise, as the one praying moves easily from past deliverance to appeal for future deliverance. But nonetheless there is significant value in maintaining the distinction in principle at least, particularly as we seek to clarify if in fact there is a consistent understanding of prayer in the Old Testament.

This distinction becomes obvious in the section of the book usually referred to as the 'Isaiah Apocalypse'. As both Isaiah himself and those who will experience the events he describes reflect on them, their statements focus on the fact that Yahweh has acted according to his commitments, which in this case are experienced as 'curse' rather than 'blessing'. This is entirely in keeping with the prophet's warning in Isaiah 1:15 that God had stopped listening to the prayers of his people. So in 25:1–2 we read:

> O LORD, you are my God;
>   I will exalt you; I will praise your name,
> for you have done wonderful things,
>   plans formed of old, faithful and sure.
> For you have made the city a heap,
>   the fortified city a ruin;

the foreigners' palace is a city no more;
it will never be rebuilt.

This could be understood as 'anti-prayer' – what to say to God when the time for asking is past. But it is clear that the *content* of this prophetic praise is governed by precisely the same concern as the prayers we have seen – the promises and plans of God.

This perspective is mirrored in the envisaged response in the land of Judah to God's action, as anticipated by Isaiah in chapter 26. The chapter begins with what is designated a 'song'; but as the song progresses, there is a movement from simply reacting to the judgment of God to waiting for him to save. One could say that the song becomes a prayer. It is worth unpacking this in some detail.

After celebrating the establishment of Zion post-judgment as a stronghold, and enjoining their brothers and sisters to trust Yahweh (26:1–7), the focus of the song shifts to petition. At this point it is difficult to see any formal difference between the song and prayer, particularly as the focus of the petitions is the 'name of Yahweh':

In the path of your judgements,
O LORD, we wait for you;
your name and remembrance
are the desire of our soul.
My soul yearns for you in the night;
my spirit within me earnestly seeks you.
For when your judgements are in the earth,
the inhabitants of the world learn righteousness.
If favour is shown to the wicked,
he does not learn righteousness;
in the land of uprightness he deals corruptly
and does not see the majesty of the LORD.
O LORD, your hand is lifted up,
but they do not see it.
Let them see your zeal for your people, and be ashamed.
Let the fire for your adversaries consume them.
O LORD, you will ordain peace for us,
for you have indeed done for us all our works.
O LORD our God,
other lords besides you have ruled over us,
but your name alone we bring to remembrance.

(Isa. 26:8–13)

The expressed desire (or prayer) of the song is that God's enemies will be confronted with his power and greatness, that his plans for his people will come to fruition, and that his name will therefore be honoured. The fact that God has already acted in judgment (in the prophetic perspective of Isaiah) is evidence that this will come to pass:

> They are dead, they will not live;
>> they are shades, they will not arise;
> to that end you have visited them with destruction
>> and wiped out all remembrance of them.
> But you have increased the nation, O LORD,
>> you have increased the nation; you are glorified;
>> you have enlarged all the borders of the land.
>
> (Isa. 26:14–15)

Even the counter-example of the prayers not heard (again, in keeping with 1:15), the prayers of God's recalcitrant people, shows that the perspective underlying these verses is that prayer is essentially calling on the name of Yahweh to deliver on his promises.

> O LORD, in distress they sought you;
>> they poured out a whispered prayer
>> when your discipline was upon them.
> Like a pregnant woman
>> who writhes and cries out in her pangs
>> when she is near to giving birth,
> so were we because of you, O LORD;
>> we were pregnant, we writhed,
>> but we have given birth to wind.
> We have accomplished no deliverance in the earth,
>> and the inhabitants of the world have not fallen.
>
> (Isa. 26:16–18)

It is only after judgment that Yahweh will hear the cries of his people once more, and intervene decisively to bring both life and justice (26:19–21). It becomes increasingly clear that even in the radically different perspective of Isaiah, a world in which judgment is a fast-approaching reality and calling on the name of Yahweh will bring no relief in the short-term at least, *prayer* continues to be

understood as intrinsically linked to God's working out his covenantal purposes.[3]

The pivotal historical section of the book in chapters 36–39 includes
two prayers offered by Hezekiah (37:16–20; 38:2–3). Aside from the
rhetorical function of these chapters in Isaiah,[4] Hezekiah's prayers bring
together two prominent ideas in any discussion of the biblical theology
of prayer. His *first* prayer focuses on the fate of the nation, and therefore
on Yahweh's commitment to honour his promises made to Abraham,
David, and so on. His *second* prayer is focused entirely on Hezekiah's
own fate (a fact confirmed by his appalling reaction in 39:8). This
Davidide has a singularly unhealthy view of messianic suffering, which
stands in marked contrast to the approach of Psalms to this subject.[5]

The virtual absence of any reference to prayer continues through
Isaiah all the way to chapter 55. Here, however, we find the prophet
exhorting God's people to turn to the Lord in repentance and obedience,
seeking his pardon. This call to return should lead to prayer:[6]

> Seek the LORD while he may be found;
>   call upon him while he is near;
> let the wicked forsake his way,
>   and the unrighteous man his thoughts;
> let him return to the LORD, that he may have
>   compassion on him,
>   and to our God, for he will abundantly pardon.
>   (Isa. 55:6–7)

As the section continues, it becomes apparent that to follow this
injunction and call on God is to embrace the fact that he is sovereign,
and to ask him to advance his agenda in our world (see further Isa.
55:8–11). And the outworking of this? It is nothing less than the
outpouring of the eschatological blessing of Yahweh. In other words,
to 'call on the name of Yahweh' is seen, yet again, to be inseparable
from asking God to do what he has promised:

---

[3] This is also reflected in the words of Isa. 31:1–2. Again, while not a prayer, it
reflects this theological understanding.

[4] Motyer (1999: 247–272) has a particularly helpful treatment of these chapters.

[5] See my comments in chapter 5.

[6] Blenkinsopp (2002: 371) says that 'the exhortation to seek God . . . in the later
period is generalized in the sense of a positive and open religious attitude expressed in
prayer and penitential practice'.

Motyer (1999: 389) says that to call on Yahweh is at one and the same time to
acknowledge him in worship and to appeal to him in need (as in Ps. 50:15).

For you shall go out in joy
   and be led forth in peace;
the mountains and the hills before you
   shall break forth into singing,
     and all the trees of the field shall clap their hands.
Instead of the thorn shall come up the cypress;
   instead of the brier shall come up the myrtle;
and it shall make a name for the LORD,
   an everlasting sign that shall not be cut off.
                     (Isa. 55:12–13)

This view is echoed at several points in the closing section of the book. In marked contrast to the command to stay silent, the watchmen are now encouraged to keep reminding *Yahweh himself* of his covenant obligations:

On your walls, O Jerusalem,
   I have set watchmen;
all the day and all the night
   they shall never be silent.
You who put the LORD in remembrance,
   take no rest,
and give him no rest
   until he establishes Jerusalem
   and makes it a praise in the earth.
                 (Isa. 62:6–7)[7]

Isaiah 63:15 – 64:12 is the longest prayer in the book, and rather like Deuteronomy 30 it envisages God's people calling on Yahweh after the judgment of exile. Finally, in 64:7–8 the silence is broken and someone *does* call on the name of Yahweh, pleading with him to turn back the clock to the days when the promises to Abraham, Isaac and Jacob were being fulfilled. This striking prayer is worth including in full:

Look down from heaven and see,
   from your holy and beautiful habitation.
Where are your zeal and your might?
   The stirring of your inner parts and your compassion

---

[7] These verses are most naturally taken to refer to prayer. See Childs 2001: 512; Motyer 1999: 432.

are held back from me.
For you are our Father,
> though Abraham does not know us,
> and Israel does not acknowledge us;
you, O LORD, are our Father,
> our Redeemer from of old is your name.
O LORD, why do you make us wander from your ways
> and harden our heart, so that we fear you not?
Return for the sake of your servants,
> the tribes of your heritage.
Your holy people held possession for a little while;
> our adversaries have trampled down your sanctuary.
We have become like those over whom you have never ruled,
> like those who are not called by your name.

(Isa. 63:15–19)

Oh that you would rend the heavens and come down,
> that the mountains might quake at your presence –
as when fire kindles brushwood
> and the fire causes water to boil –
to make your name known to your adversaries,
> and that the nations might tremble at your presence!
When you did awesome things that we did not look for,
> you came down, the mountains quaked at your presence.
From of old no one has heard
> or perceived by the ear,
no eye has seen a God besides you,
> who acts for those who wait for him.
You meet him who joyfully works righteousness,
> those who remember you in your ways.
Behold, you were angry, and we sinned;
> in our sins we have been a long time, and shall we be saved?
We have all become like one who is unclean,
> and all our righteous deeds are like a polluted garment.
We all fade like a leaf,
> and our iniquities, like the wind, take us away.
There is no one who calls upon your name,
> who rouses himself to take hold of you;
for you have hidden your face from us,
> and have made us melt in the hand of our iniquities.
But now, O LORD, you are our Father;

> we are the clay, and you are our potter;
>> we are all the work of your hand.
> Be not so terribly angry, O LORD,
>> and remember not iniquity for ever.
>> Behold, please look, we are all your people.
> Your holy cities have become a wilderness;
>> Zion has become a wilderness,
>> Jerusalem a desolation.
> Our holy and beautiful house,
>> where our fathers praised you,
> has been burned by fire,
>> and all our pleasant places have become ruins.
> Will you restrain yourself at these things, O LORD?
>> Will you keep silent, and afflict us so terribly?
>>> (Isa. 64:1–12)

This plaintive appeal essentially comes down to one thing – it is a plea to God to remember his covenant beyond judgment. Yahweh is urged to remember mercy in the midst of wrath. We must not overlook the fact that this is something he has already promised to do, which puts Isaiah's teaching on prayer squarely in the centre of the flow of the teaching of the Old Testament as a whole. The prophet's last word demonstrates how radically the situation will change in that day:

> Before they call I will answer;
>> while they are yet speaking I will hear.
>>> (Isa. 65:24)

Jeremiah

In the early chapters of Jeremiah Yahweh himself raises a similar issue to that highlighted in Isaiah – the prayers of God's people will not be answered in the short term, because they are offered by people who, rather than repenting, are hell-bent on spiritual adultery:

> Have you not just now called to me,
>> 'My father, you are the friend of my youth –
>> will he be angry for ever,
> will he be indignant to the end?'
> Behold, you have spoken,
>> but you have done all the evil that you could.
>>> (Jer. 3:4–5)

The change of pronoun (from 'you' in 3:4 to 'he' in 3:5) is indicative of the distance in relationship between Yahweh and his people. Their prayers will not be heard, because the covenant relationship has already been impaired by persistent disobedience and the absence of repentance. That notwithstanding, however, it demonstrates that in Jeremiah prayer is construed yet again as calling on the name of Yahweh to honour his promises.

This is confirmed by Yahweh's own statement in 3:19–20. The ideal scenario is depicted in the following terms:

> I said,
>> How I would set you among my sons,
> and give you a pleasant land,
>> a heritage most beautiful of all nations.
> And I thought you would call me, My Father,
>> and would not turn from following me.
> Surely, as a treacherous wife leaves her husband,
>> so have you been treacherous to me, O house of Israel,
> declares the LORD.
>
> (Jer. 3:19–20)

As Jeremiah's message of judgment unfolds, it becomes increasingly obvious that his people are beyond 'calling on the name of Yahweh', which in turn provides the foundation for the chilling command of 7:16: 'As for you, do not pray for this people, or lift up a cry or prayer for them, and do not intercede with me, for I will not hear you.' The die is cast – there is no point in praying for God to pour out his blessings, because the curses of the covenant are already being rolled out:

> Again the LORD said to me, 'A conspiracy exists among the men of Judah and the inhabitants of Jerusalem. They have turned back to the iniquities of their forefathers, who refused to hear my words. They have gone after other gods to serve them. The house of Israel and the house of Judah have broken my covenant that I made with their fathers. Therefore, thus says the LORD, Behold, I am bringing disaster upon them that they cannot escape. Though they cry to me, I will not listen to them. Then the cities of Judah and the inhabitants of Jerusalem will go and cry to the gods to whom they make offerings, but they cannot save them in the time of their trouble.' (Jer. 11:9–12)

At this point, however, the book of Jeremiah takes a dramatically different turn. Rather than looking forward to a day when true prayer is offered (on the other side of the exile), Jeremiah enters into a plaintive and impassioned discussion with Yahweh himself. In doing so Jeremiah provides us with one of the richest veins of material on prayer in the entire canon.

The so-called confessions of Jeremiah (although they are not, strictly speaking, 'confessional' in any sense of the word) are carefully ordered to provide a powerful indictment of Judah's rejection of the word of Yahweh.[8] Formally, they fall broadly into the category of 'laments', although even then there is significant variation.[9] For our purposes these 'confessions' (11:18–23; 12:1–6; 15:10–14, 15–21; 17:14–18; 18:18–23; 20:7–13, 14–18) provide an insight into the tensions at the very heart of biblical prayer.

Gordon McConville, in his excellent work on Jeremiah *Judgment and Promise*, makes the telling comment that 'The figure of Jeremiah, especially in the Confessions . . . is extremely complex. At once he represents the people, he represents YHWH, and he remains himself.'[10] This brings significant complexity to the prayers in these chapters. So McConville continues:

> In 14:9–22, for example, he speaks for the people. In doing so, he cannot but evoke their failure to take the prayer to themselves in any genuine way. His words, therefore, are a kind of criticism of the nation, sealing their fate. At the same time, they are words which he, Jeremiah, does sincerely take on his own lips. By virtue of his representative role, therefore, the prayer becomes, after all, a genuine prayer of the people. Their participation in the prayer, however, with the hope of salvation to which it gives rise, is secured only through the prophet.

These prayers, then, are simultaneously representative, exemplary and accusatory.

Despite this complexity, however, in the context of this study the point made by these prayers is both clear and simple: the major issue in the life of God's people is the fulfilment (or non-fulfilment) of God's promises, and this is the proper subject of the prayers of both

---

[8] See Allen's (2012: 431) helpful discussion.
[9] E.g. Baumgartner's (1987) classic treatment.
[10] McConville 1993b: 72.

his prophet and his people. Even a cursory glance through the confessions makes this obvious.

In the first of the confessions Jeremiah's primary concern is with the people's opposition to him, which flows from their rejection of the word of Yahweh, and therefore to Yahweh himself (Jer. 11:18–20).

This concern spills over into the second in the series in 12:1–6. Even though those who oppose him take the name of God on their lips (12:2), their hearts are far from Yahweh. The treachery of the people of God is front and centre, as Jeremiah begins to come to terms with the fact that judgment is inevitable:

> Righteous are you, O LORD,
> when I complain to you;
> yet I would plead my case before you.
> Why does the way of the wicked prosper?
> Why do all who are treacherous thrive?
> You plant them, and they take root;
> they grow and produce fruit;
> you are near in their mouth
> and far from their heart.
> But you, O LORD, know me;
> you see me, and test my heart towards you.
> Pull them out like sheep for the slaughter,
> and set them apart for the day of slaughter.
> How long will the land mourn
> and the grass of every field wither?
> For the evil of those who dwell in it
> the beasts and the birds are swept away,
> because they said, 'He will not see our latter end.'
> 'If you have raced with men on foot, and they have
>   wearied you,
> how will you compete with horses?
> And if in a safe land you are so trusting,
> what will you do in the thicket of the Jordan?
> For even your brothers and the house of your father,
> even they have dealt treacherously with you;
> they are in full cry after you;
> do not believe them,
> though they speak friendly words to you.'
>
>   (Jer. 12:1–12)

The first in the second pair of confessions (15:10–14) makes it plain that Jeremiah's inner turmoil is the result of his concern to see the promises of God fulfilled – he longs to see blessing in the land, but only experiences curse:

> Woe is me, my mother, that you bore me, a man of strife and contention to the whole land! I have not lent, nor have I borrowed, yet all of them curse me. . . .

> 'I will make you serve your enemies in a land that you do not know, for in my anger a fire is kindled that shall burn for ever.'
> (Jer. 15:10, 14)

The accompanying prayer that follows it is equally passionate, as the prophet rehearses how his acceptance of the word of Yahweh both isolated him from his peers and drew him into the experience of Yahweh himself:

> O Lord, you know;
>   remember me and visit me,
>   and take vengeance for me on my persecutors.
> In your forbearance take me not away;
>   know that for your sake I bear reproach.
> Your words were found, and I ate them,
>   and your words became to me a joy
>   and the delight of my heart,
> for I am called by your name,
>   O Lord, God of hosts.
> I did not sit in the company of revellers,
>   nor did I rejoice;
> I sat alone, because your hand was upon me,
>   for you had filled me with indignation.
> Why is my pain unceasing,
>   my wound incurable,
>   refusing to be healed?
> Will you be to me like a deceitful brook,
>   like waters that fail?
> (Jer. 15:15–18)

Jeremiah's pain is palpable as he tastes the apparent 'anguish of Yahweh'. This pain, expressed in prayer, flows from the realization that the words that brought him joy (which can only be the 'gospel words' of the covenant promises of Yahweh) have been rejected by the rest of his people, and therefore lead to judgment and curse.[11] As a result of Jeremiah's faithfulness he becomes an interim answer to his own prayers and longings, experiencing the salvation of Yahweh, so decisively rejected by his people:

> Therefore thus says the LORD:
> 'If you return, I will restore you,
>   and you shall stand before me.
> If you utter what is precious, and not what is worthless,
>   you shall be as my mouth.
> They shall turn to you,
>   but you shall not turn to them.
> And I will make you to this people
>   a fortified wall of bronze;
> they will fight against you,
>   but they shall not prevail over you,
> for I am with you
>   to save you and deliver you,
> declares the LORD.
> I will deliver you out of the hand of the wicked,
>   and redeem you from the grasp of the ruthless.'
> (Jer. 15:19–21)

As the series of confessions continues, Jeremiah calls on Yahweh to rescue him, looking for him to deliver on his word, whether in salvation or judgment:

> Heal me, O LORD, and I shall be healed;
>   save me, and I shall be saved,
>   for you are my praise.
> Behold, they say to me,
>   'Where is the word of the LORD?
>   Let it come!'
> I have not run away from being your shepherd,
>   nor have I desired the day of sickness.

---

[11] The relationship between Jeremiah's suffering, his outcry and the promises of Yahweh take us to the very heart of biblical prayer. The idea that prayer flows from the gospel does not *remove* such deeply personal cries from the category of prayer – it simply relocates them to a 'gospel-shaped' context.

You know what came out of my lips;
  it was before your face.
Be not a terror to me;
  you are my refuge in the day of disaster.
Let those be put to shame who persecute me,
  but let me not be put to shame;
let them be dismayed,
  but let me not be dismayed;
bring upon them the day of disaster;
  destroy them with double destruction!
                                    (Jer. 17:14–18)

This is one of the distinctives of prayer in Jeremiah (and the prayers of Jeremiah). The double-edged nature of the word of God (see e.g. Isa. 6:8–10), which has been played out in the prophetic books, now becomes a controlling feature of the prayers of the prophet, as is displayed by the increasingly angst-ridden outpourings of 18:18–23. The mounting tension in Jeremiah's prayers reaches fever pitch in chapter 20. In highly emotive language the prophet initially rails against Yahweh for manipulating and using him, before reasserting his confidence in Yahweh's ability to act both in judgment and ultimately in salvation, thus fulfilling his own prior word, where he promised first curse, and then blessing:

O LORD, you have deceived me,
  and I was deceived;
you are stronger than I,
  and you have prevailed.
I have become a laughing-stock all the day;
  everyone mocks me.
For whenever I speak, I cry out,
  I shout, 'Violence and destruction!'
For the word of the LORD has become for me
  a reproach and derision all day long.
If I say, 'I will not mention him,
  or speak any more in his name',
there is in my heart as it were a burning fire
  shut up in my bones,
and I am weary with holding it in,
  and I cannot.
For I hear many whispering.
  Terror is on every side!

'Denounce him! Let us denounce him!'
　　say all my close friends,
　　watching for my fall.
'Perhaps he will be deceived;
　　then we can overcome him
　　and take our revenge on him.'
But the LORD is with me as a dread warrior;
　　therefore my persecutors will stumble;
　　they will not overcome me.
They will be greatly shamed,
　　for they will not succeed.
Their eternal dishonour
　　will never be forgotten.
O LORD of hosts, who tests the righteous,
　　who sees the heart and the mind,
let me see your vengeance upon them,
　　for to you have I committed my cause.
Sing to the LORD;
　　praise the LORD!
For he has delivered the life of the needy
　　from the hand of evildoers.

（Jer. 20:7–13）

At this point the unexpected downward turn of the final confession has caused commentators all manner of problems. Jeremiah has been accused of everything from mental illness to simple contradiction.[12] However, placing the darkness of 20:14–18 at the climax of the series has a perfectly comprehensible rhetorical effect – it makes sure that we as readers appreciate that in the short term there will be neither relief nor hope. Jeremiah's people will face the curses of the covenant, and Jeremiah, their prophet, will suffer with them. As the prophet speaks, he 'incarnates' the reality of judgment:

Cursed be the day
on which I was born!

[12] Brueggemann (1998: 185) suggests, 'perhaps he is an unstable personality. No doubt his contemporaries found him so.' He goes on to admit, however, that the 'poem gives us no warrant for psychological analysis'. Harrison (1973: 116) describes Jeremiah as a person of 'sensitive disposition' who was 'embarrassed' by the fact that his prophetic words remained unfulfilled for so long and 'offended' by the ridicule of the people. J. A. Thompson (1980: 458) also says Jeremiah had a sensitive nature.

The day when my mother bore me,
   let it not be blessed!
Cursed be the man who brought the news to my father,
'A son is born to you',
   making him very glad.
Let that man be like the cities
   that the LORD overthrew without pity;
let him hear a cry in the morning
   and an alarm at noon,
because he did not kill me in the womb;
   so my mother would have been my grave,
   and her womb for ever great.
Why did I come out from the womb
   to see toil and sorrow,
   and spend my days in shame?

                     (Jer. 20:14–18)

The prayers of Jeremiah reveal a deep personal struggle in the life and experience of the prophet which mirror that in the life of the people of Judah. Undergirding his prayers are the dawning realization that in the short term calling on Yahweh can lead only to the confirmation of his purposes in judgment. The hope of answered prayer in the form of renewed blessing lies on the other side of the ultimate curse of exile. And in the meantime? The lone voice of the prayer of the prophet exposes both the pain in the heart of Yahweh and sounds a truly prophetic note which will only reach a crescendo in the salvation that lies beyond judgment – a perspective encapsulated in the prayer of 14:19–22, which although not formally designated one of the confessions nonetheless takes us to the heart of the message of the book:

Have you utterly rejected Judah?
   Does your soul loathe Zion?
Why have you struck us down
   so that there is no healing for us?
We looked for peace, but no good came;
   for a time of healing, but behold, terror.
We acknowledge our wickedness, O LORD,
   and the iniquity of our fathers,
   for we have sinned against you.
Do not spurn us, for your name's sake;

do not dishonour your glorious throne;
remember and do not break your covenant with us.
Are there any among the false gods of the nations
    that can bring rain?
Or can the heavens give showers?
Are you not he, O LORD our God?
    We set our hope on you,
    for you do all these things.

(Jer. 14:19–22)

Although the focus on prayer diminishes as the book continues, it does not disappear completely. Jeremiah's purchase of a field in chapter 32 both embodies the message of the confessions and brings it back to centre stage:

After I had given the deed of purchase to Baruch the son of Neriah, I prayed to the LORD, saying: 'Ah, Lord GOD! It is you who have made the heavens and the earth by your great power and by your outstretched arm! Nothing is too hard for you. You show steadfast love to thousands, but you repay the guilt of fathers to their children after them, O great and mighty God, whose name is the LORD of hosts, great in counsel and mighty in deed, whose eyes are open to all the ways of the children of man, rewarding each one according to his ways and according to the fruit of his deeds. You have shown signs and wonders in the land of Egypt, and to this day in Israel and among all mankind, and have made a name for yourself, as at this day. You brought your people Israel out of the land of Egypt with signs and wonders, with a strong hand and outstretched arm, and with great terror. And you gave them this land, which you swore to their fathers to give them, a land flowing with milk and honey. And they entered and took possession of it. But they did not obey your voice or walk in your law. They did nothing of all you commanded them to do. Therefore you have made all this disaster come upon them. Behold, the siege mounds have come up to the city to take it, and because of sword and famine and pestilence the city is given into the hands of the Chaldeans who are fighting against it. What you spoke has come to pass, and behold, you see it. Yet you, O Lord GOD, have said to me, "Buy the field for money and get witnesses" – though the city is given into the hands of the Chaldeans.'
(Jer. 32:16–25)

What is interesting about this prayer is the lack of any direct request. Instead, Jeremiah apparently processes the logic behind the divine command in conversation with Yahweh, slowly coming to the realization that the instruction to buy the field contains an implicit commitment to honour the promises to Abraham in the long term. Prayer, it seems, is intricately linked with the outworking of God's covenant commitments in the mind of the prophet – a connection underlined one more time in the final prose section of the book.

In Jeremiah 42 the remnant finally approach the prophet with a request to hear the word of Yahweh:

> Then all the commanders of the forces, and Johanan the son of Kareah and Jezaniah the son of Hoshaiah, and all the people from the least to the greatest, came near and said to Jeremiah the prophet, 'Let our plea for mercy come before you, and pray to the LORD your God for us, for all this remnant – because we are left with but a few, as your eyes see us – that the LORD your God may show us the way we should go, and the thing that we should do.' Jeremiah the prophet said to them, 'I have heard you. Behold, I will pray to the LORD your God according to your request, and whatever the LORD answers you I will tell you. I will keep nothing back from you.' Then they said to Jeremiah, 'May the LORD be a true and faithful witness against us if we do not act according to all the word with which the LORD your God sends you to us. Whether it is good or bad, we will obey the voice of the LORD our God to whom we are sending you, that it may be well with us when we obey the voice of the LORD our God.' (Jer. 42:1–6)

This time, unusually, both the prophet and the people associate prayer with seeking guidance from Yahweh. However, this is not simply a prescription for replacing the Urim and Thummim with a particular kind of prayer. This prayer for guidance comes at a unique moment of salvation history – God's judgment is at hand, and it is 'make your mind up time' for his people. Should they stay or go? God's answer comes back unequivocally – they should go to Babylon. But they refuse, and make for Egypt instead, and Jeremiah, the prophet who lives and breathes the word of God, goes with the people even in their disobedience.

There is, it turns out, a surprising amount of space in the book of Jeremiah devoted to the prayers of God's most intense spokesman.

As in Isaiah the prayers of the people are silenced by divine command, for the best they can muster are hypocritical ramblings. The prophet Jeremiah, however, prays on. He prays about Yahweh's determination to bring down his curse on his people. He prays about the blessing still promised beyond the curse. He prays about his purchase of land. He prays about the destination of Yahweh's people. His prayers revolve around and are dominated by the sovereign purposes of God.

Jeremiah revisited? The prayers of Lamentations

Assuming for a moment that Jeremiah was in some way connected with the book that we know as Lamentations, it makes sense to consider this material now, rather than as part of the short discussion of the Writings in the following chapter.[13]

As the title suggests, the book is made up of a series of 'laments'. However, of special interest to us are the sections of the book that consist of direct address to Yahweh (prayers). These sections are spread liberally throughout the text. So, for example, we read:

> Look, O LORD, for I am in distress;
>> my stomach churns;
> my heart is wrung within me,
>> because I have been very rebellious.
> In the street the sword bereaves;
>> in the house it is like death.
> They heard my groaning,
>> yet there is no one to comfort me.
> All my enemies have heard of my trouble;
>> they are glad that you have done it.
> You have brought the day you announced;
>> now let them be as I am.
> Let all their evildoing come before you,
>> and deal with them
> as you have dealt with me
>> because of all my transgressions;
> for my groans are many,
>> and my heart is faint.
>
> (Lam. 1:20–22)

---

[13] For the arguments concerning Jeremianic authorship or influence on Lamentations see e.g. Parry 2010: 3–5.

The writer, in a Jeremiah-like way as the representative of God's people, both faces the past rebellion, which has brought down the judgment of Yahweh, and cries to God for justice (more specifically for just punishment of those who have crushed Judah, namely the Babylonians).

This kind of 'calling on the name of Yahweh' continues in chapter 2, where the brutal experience of conquest gives rise to plaintive cries:

> Look, O LORD, and see!
>> With whom have you dealt thus?
> Should women eat the fruit of their womb,
>> the children of their tender care?
> Should priest and prophet be killed
>> in the sanctuary of the Lord?
> In the dust of the streets
>> lie the young and the old;
> my young women and my young men
>> have fallen by the sword;
> you have killed them in the day of your anger,
>> slaughtering without pity.
> You summoned as if to a festival day
>> my terrors on every side,
> and on the day of the anger of the LORD
>> no one escaped or survived;
> those whom I held and raised
>> my enemy destroyed.
>> (Lam. 2:20–22)

There is no suggestion that this fate is ill deserved, or even that Yahweh should have intervened. The sense is more that of unremitting anguish as the people of God try to come to terms with the fact that he appears to have turned against them:

> Let us test and examine our ways,
>> and return to the LORD!
> Let us lift up our hearts and hands
>> to God in heaven:
> 'We have transgressed and rebelled,
>> and you have not forgiven.
> 'You have wrapped yourself with anger and pursued us,
>> killing without pity;

> you have wrapped yourself with a cloud
> > so that no prayer can pass through.
> You have made us filth and rubbish
> > among the peoples.
> 'All our enemies
> > open their mouths against us;
> panic and pitfall have come upon us,
> > devastation and destruction;
> my eyes flow with rivers of tears
> > because of the destruction of the daughter
> > > of my people.'
>
> (Lam. 3:40–48)

However, the direct addresses to God take on a different hue as Lamentations moves on. In due course the visceral reaction to the horrors of the exile is replaced by a healthy self-examination, a renewed call for justice and eventually even an appeal to God to save his people on the other side of exile:

> I called on your name, O LORD,
> > from the depths of the pit;
> you heard my plea, 'Do not close
> > your ear to my cry for help!'
> You came near when I called on you;
> > you said, 'Do not fear!'
> You have taken up my cause, O Lord;
> > you have redeemed my life.
> You have seen the wrong done to me, O LORD;
> > judge my cause.
> You have seen all their vengeance,
> > all their plots against me.
> You have heard their taunts, O LORD,
> > all their plots against me.
> The lips and thoughts of my assailants
> > are against me all the day long.
> Behold their sitting and their rising;
> > I am the object of their taunts.
> You will repay them, O LORD,
> > according to the work of their hands.
> You will give them dullness of heart;
> > your curse will be on them.

You will pursue them in anger and destroy them
  from under your heavens, O LORD.
                                    (Lam. 3:55–66)

The final chapter of Lamentations draws all these elements together in a way that is highly reminiscent of Jeremiah 14. The prayer is realistic about the situation facing Yahweh's people – they are under judgment. They do, however, call on the name of Yahweh himself to reverse their fortunes. To move beyond curse to blessing, and once more to fulfil his ancient promises:

Remember, O LORD, what has befallen us;
  look, and see our disgrace!
Our inheritance has been turned over to strangers,
  our homes to foreigners.
We have become orphans, fatherless;
  our mothers are like widows.
We must pay for the water we drink;
  the wood we get must be bought.
Our pursuers are at our necks;
  we are weary; we are given no rest.
We have given the hand to Egypt, and to Assyria,
  to get bread enough.
Our fathers sinned, and are no more;
  and we bear their iniquities.
Slaves rule over us;
  there is none to deliver us from their hand.
We get our bread at the peril of our lives,
  because of the sword in the wilderness.
Our skin is hot as an oven
  with the burning heat of famine.
Women are raped in Zion,
  young women in the towns of Judah.
Princes are hung up by their hands;
  no respect is shown to the elders.
Young men are compelled to grind at the mill,
  and boys stagger under loads of wood.
The old men have left the city gate,
  the young men their music.
The joy of our hearts has ceased;
  our dancing has been turned to mourning.

The crown has fallen from our head;
    woe to us, for we have sinned!
For this our heart has become sick,
    for these things our eyes have grown dim,
for Mount Zion which lies desolate;
    jackals prowl over it.
But you, O LORD, reign for ever;
    your throne endures to all generations.
Why do you forget us for ever,
    why do you forsake us for so many days?
Restore us to yourself, O LORD, that we may be restored!
    Renew our days as of old –
unless you have utterly rejected us,
    and you remain exceedingly angry with us.

                                         (Lam. 5:1–22)

Because the sovereign Lord remains in control, and because somehow his plans remain intact, his people can still call on him with hope. Ultimately, this is the message of both Jeremiah and Lamentations.

Ezekiel

In marked contrast to the extended examples of prayer in Jeremiah, prayer barely raises its head in Ezekiel in any form. There may be a very simple reason for this. The prophecy of Ezekiel is designed in large measure to reassure the exiles that the story of Judah is not over – in other words the book is written to give the exiles *a reason to pray* rather than to encourage them to pray per se. The prayers of the exiles should flow out of reading the prophecy of Ezekiel, rather than be codified in the book.

That said, it is still remarkable that the four prayers of Ezekiel himself in this book all deal with key issues in salvation history:

Then I said, 'Ah, Lord GOD! Behold, I have never defiled myself. From my youth up till now I have never eaten what died of itself or was torn by beasts, nor has tainted meat come into my mouth.' (Ezek. 4:14)

And while they were striking, and I was left alone, I fell upon my face, and cried, 'Ah, Lord GOD! Will you destroy all the remnant of Israel in the outpouring of your wrath on Jerusalem?' (Ezek. 9:8)

> And it came to pass, while I was prophesying, that Pelatiah the son of Benaiah died. Then I fell down on my face and cried out with a loud voice and said, 'Ah, Lord GOD! Will you make a full end of the remnant of Israel?' (Ezek. 11:13)

> Then I said, 'Ah, Lord GOD! They are saying of me, "Is he not a maker of parables?"' (Ezek. 20:49)

It should be pointed out, of course, that each of these prayers is spontaneous. There is little evidence of the careful crafting and arrangement of the prayers of Jeremiah, for instance. However, it is also clear that each of these prayers expresses and engages the angst experienced by the Judahites in exile.

The first prayer (Ezek. 4:14) is the priestly Ezekiel's protest at being asked to defile himself in the course of his prophetic ministry, through which God will provoke his people into both facing the reality of exile and starting to deal with it in a godly way. This was obviously a highly charged issue, as it raised issues of covenant, purity and election.

The second brief prayer, in 9:8, is also occasioned by an outrageous pronouncement from Yahweh. This time it seems that God is willing to allow his people to be obliterated, without even a tiny rump of survivors remaining to keep the quickly fading hopes of his chosen people alive.

The third, in 11:13, is similar, although this time occasioned by the rather startling and permanent impact made by Ezekiel's preaching among the exiles.

The final prayer, in 20:49, is prompted when Ezekiel's words meet a similar response to those of his prophetic predecessors, and no one appears to want to listen to the word of Yahweh, even when clearly proclaimed. In each case, then, the prayers of the prophet are prompted by a shattering announcement or event, which gives rise to fears that, as far as the people of God are concerned, this may be the end of the road.

It is part of the function of Ezekiel to bring the good news to God's people that this is not the case. In fact, rather than closing down the opportunity to pray (as both Jeremiah and Isaiah do), it is Ezekiel's role to recommission prayer:

> Thus says the Lord GOD: This also I will let the house of Israel ask me to do for them: to increase their people like a flock. Like the flock for sacrifices, like the flock at Jerusalem during her appointed

feasts, so shall the waste cities be filled with flocks of people. Then they will know that I am the LORD. (Ezek. 36:37–38)

This rapid overview of the place of prayer in the Major Prophets has added another level to the argument that prayer in the Old Testament is essentially calling on Yahweh to come through on his promises. Isaiah and Jeremiah develop this concept in nuanced and complex ways, seeking to enable God's people to understand the place of curse as well as blessing, and judgment as well as salvation, while encouraging them to continue to call on the name of Yahweh, clinging to hope in a difficult world. Ezekiel moves the discussion a step further, as he reopens the divine conversation after the traumatic events of the exile, encouraging God's people once more to call on the name of Yahweh.

Short prayers and short(ish) books

Since the publication of Paul House's game-changing work *The Unity of the Twelve* in 1990, synchronic readings of the Minor Prophets as a whole have proliferated. And while the scholarly jury is still out on the extent of the redactional unity of this 'collection', it is safe to say that significant thematic connections between these books have been established.[14] For the sake of this study we will assume both a substantial connection between these smaller prophetic books and the veracity of House's original observation, that there is a movement from warning through judgment to hope in the collection.[15]

Given the perspectives on prayer in the books of Isaiah, Jeremiah and Ezekiel, in which the possibility of prayer is initially closed down, recalibrated and then opened up again, one might expect to find a similar 'prophetic' pattern in the Book of the Twelve. This turns out to be the case.

The end of prayer?

In the three larger pre-exilic minor prophets (Hosea, Amos and Micah) the pattern is very similar to that of their larger contemporaries.

In Hosea prayer is virtually absent, apart from the desperate,

---

[14] See e.g. House's own recent survey paper given to the Institute of Biblical Research Conference 2014, '*The Unity of the Twelve* Twenty-Five Years Later: Synchronic Readings of the Book of the Twelve' (unpublished).

[15] There has been significant discussion, criticism and modification of House's original thesis, but his underlying observations remain essentially sound. For further discussion of this see Cumerford 2015.

self-justifying cry of 8:2, which in context is clearly a prayer to which Yahweh will not listen:

> Set the trumpet to your lips!
>   One like a vulture is over the house of the LORD,
> because they have transgressed my covenant
>   and rebelled against my law.
> To me they cry,
>   'My God, we – Israel – know you.'
> Israel has spurned the good;
>   the enemy shall pursue him.
>
> (Hos. 8:1–3)

This is entirely consistent with the situation in the run-up to the exile in both Isaiah and Jeremiah. God's people occasionally 'cry to him' in self-serving panic, but they neither know nor serve him, and their cry falls on deaf ears.

The prophet Hosea experiences a parallel to Yahweh's own rejection by his people in his personal life, but Amos, like Jeremiah, works this through explicitly in the context of direct conversation with God. As in Hosea there is virtual silence when it comes to prayer in Amos, with the striking exception of Amos 7:2–9. The prophet encounters Yahweh in a similar context to Moses in Genesis 18 – however, rather than interceding for twin pagan cities, Amos is crying out for the people of Yahweh. We break into Amos' vision as he baulks at the impending judgment of Israel:

I said,

> 'O Lord GOD, please forgive!
> How can Jacob stand?
> He is so small!'
> The LORD relented concerning this:
> 'It shall not be,' said the LORD.

This is what the Lord GOD showed me: behold, the Lord GOD was calling for a judgement by fire, and it devoured the great deep and was eating up the land. Then I said,

> 'O Lord GOD, please cease!
> How can Jacob stand?

He is so small!'
The LORD relented concerning this:
'This also shall not be,' said the Lord GOD.

This is what he showed me: behold, the Lord was standing beside a wall built with a plumb line, with a plumb line in his hand. And the LORD said to me, 'Amos, what do you see?' And I said, 'A plumb line.' Then the Lord said,

> 'Behold, I am setting a plumb line
>   in the midst of my people Israel;
>   I will never again pass by them;
> the high places of Isaac shall be made desolate,
>   and the sanctuaries of Israel shall be laid waste,
>   and I will rise against the house of Jeroboam
>   with the sword.'

(Amos 7:2–9)

In the same way that Jeremiah would several centuries later, Amos faces the emotional trauma of coming to terms with the reality of judgment.

Interestingly, Micah's experience (and presentation) is different again. There is no reference to calling on Yahweh or prayer of any kind in the book of Micah until the last stanza. However, here Micah anticipates a day when the silence will be broken once more, when people (initially in the guise of the prophet) will call out to Yahweh again, and experience healing and forgiveness as a fulfilment of the patriarchal promises:

> Who is a God like you, pardoning iniquity
>   and passing over transgression
>   for the remnant of his inheritance?
> He does not retain his anger for ever,
>   because he delights in steadfast love.
> He will again have compassion on us;
>   he will tread our iniquities underfoot.
> You will cast all our sins
>   into the depths of the sea.
> You will show faithfulness to Jacob
>   and steadfast love to Abraham,
> as you have sworn to our fathers
>   from the days of old.

(Mic. 7:18–20)

That leaves me to comment only on the shorter book of Joel. It is notoriously difficult to fix the provenance of Joel,[16] but for the purposes of this study I will simply state that in my opinion it is almost certainly pre-exilic, and leave it at that. As we will see, in terms of our understanding of prayer, not much hinges on this.

Two prayers are included in Joel's prophecy – the first is a prayer of the prophet himself in the wake of the destruction that provokes the prophecy (1:19–20), and the second is a prayer prescribed for the priests to pray (2:17). In both cases the subject of the prayer is the apparent gap between the current experience of the people of God and the historical understanding of the promises of God:

> To you, O LORD, I call.
> For fire has devoured
>   the pastures of the wilderness,
> and flame has burned
>   all the trees of the field.
> Even the beasts of the field pant for you
>   because the water brooks are dried up,
> and fire has devoured
>   the pastures of the wilderness.
>   (Joel 1:19–20)

> Between the vestibule and the altar
>   let the priests, the ministers of the LORD, weep
> and say, 'Spare your people, O LORD,
>   and make not your heritage a reproach,
>   a byword among the nations.
> Why should they say among the peoples,
>   "Where is their God?"'
>   (Joel 2:17)

Why does the prophet pray like this? Why are the priests to pray like this? Because prayer is essentially calling on the name of Yahweh to keep his promises, and the reality of their experience is that Yahweh has reneged on that. He is neither hearing nor answering their prayers. As the book progresses, however, it appears that Joel shares the pre-exilic prophetic perspective that the time for praying is over – the only

---

[16] See e.g. the comments of Garrett (2012: 449) or Dillard (1992: 239).

thing that God's people can do is return to the Lord in the hope that he may relent (e.g. 2:12).

And yet even here, where the note of judgment sounds long and clear, there is also the accompanying insistence that beyond judgment lies a new day, when once again people will call upon the name of Yahweh and be saved:

> And I will show wonders in the heavens and on the earth, blood and fire and columns of smoke. The sun shall be turned to darkness, and the moon to blood, before the great and awesome day of the LORD comes. And it shall come to pass that everyone who calls on the name of the LORD shall be saved. For in Mount Zion and in Jerusalem there shall be those who escape, as the LORD has said, and among the survivors shall be those whom the LORD calls. (Joel 2:30–32)

I should acknowledge at this point that three of the Twelve make little or no mention of prayer. Two of the books, of course, address the enemies of God's people. Both Obadiah's announcement of judgment against Edom and Nahum's polemic against the Assyrians brook no reply. There is nothing for these nations to say to Yahweh (although, see the discussion of Jonah below). They have acted against the people of Yahweh in deliberate and decisive ways. Now they must pay the price. But the question is, does this have any bearing on our discussion of prayer in the life of the people of Yahweh?

If House et al. are justified in seeing some coherence in the ordering and 'message' of the Book of the Twelve, then it may well be that the inclusion of these books at the heart of the collection is, in part, a reflection of the situation Judah themselves have experienced through the exile – having no answer and nothing to say – in the face of both the command and the judgment of Yahweh. They have, in essence, been reduced to the status of the 'nations'.

Haggai is a slightly different case. It may simply be that the brevity and subject matter of the book mean that Haggai has nothing to contribute to our discussion. On the other hand, it could be another example of the desperate need for the people of Yahweh to find their voices, and call again to Yahweh – a theme that, perhaps unexpectedly, grows ever stronger as we progress through the Twelve.

The rebirth of prayer

None of the 'Minor Prophets' has attracted so much attention both from the church and the academy over the years as the book of Jonah.

However, Jonah's contribution to the Bible's teaching on prayer has often been overlooked. In addition, in the flow of the Book of the Twelve, it is Jonah's quirky and open-ended narrative that most compellingly presents readers with the possibility of the 'rebirth of prayer'.

For our purposes the most significant feature of the text is the repetition of calling on the name of Yahweh. This is obvious on a cursory glance at both chapters 1 and 3:

> Then the mariners were afraid, and each *cried out to his god*. And they hurled the cargo that was in the ship into the sea to lighten it for them. But Jonah had gone down into the inner part of the ship and had lain down and was fast asleep. So the captain came and said to him, 'What do you mean, you sleeper? Arise, *call out to your god*! Perhaps the god will give a thought to us, that we may not perish.' . . .
>
> Therefore they *called out to the* LORD, *'O* LORD, *let us not perish for this man's life, and lay not on us innocent blood, for you, O Lord, have done as it pleased you.'* (Jon. 1:5–6, 14)

> Then the word of the LORD came to Jonah the second time, saying, 'Arise, go to Nineveh, that great city, and *call out against it* the message that I tell you.' So Jonah arose and went to Nineveh, according to the word of the LORD. Now Nineveh was an exceedingly great city, three days' journey in breadth. Jonah began to go into the city, going a day's journey. *And he called out*, 'Yet forty days, and Nineveh shall be overthrown!' And the people of Nineveh believed God. *They called for a fast* and put on sackcloth, from the greatest of them to the least of them. The word reached the king of Nineveh, and he arose from his throne, removed his robe, covered himself with sackcloth, and sat in ashes. And he issued a proclamation and published through Nineveh, 'By the decree of the king and his nobles: Let neither man nor beast, herd nor flock, taste anything. Let them not feed or drink water, but let man and beast be covered with sackcloth, and *let them call out mightily to God*. Let everyone turn from his evil way and from the violence that is in his hands. Who knows? God may turn and relent and turn from his fierce anger, so that we may not perish.' When God saw what they did, how they turned from their evil way, God relented of the disaster that he had said he would do to them, and he did not do it. (Jon. 3:1–10)

The pagan sailors initially call out to their god(s); but on discovering that Jonah's God is responsible for the storm, they quickly readdress their pleas to Yahweh. Their prayer shows a remarkable degree of theological sensitivity. Unlike Jonah's countrymen,[17] the sailors are convinced of Yahweh's power, sovereignty and ability to save.

Similarly, when Jonah (probably enthusiastically) in obedience to the command of Yahweh in 3:4 'calls out' judgment on the Ninevites, these Assyrians unexpectedly respond – they 'called for a fast' and then 'call out mightily' to Jonah's God![18] God is using an assortment of pagans to teach his prophet – and his people – to pray again. Yahweh is inviting his people to call on his name.

A parallel feature of the text – and one that drives us decisively to read the text in this direction – is the way in which Jonah addresses Yahweh:

Then Jonah *prayed to the Lord* his God from the belly of the fish, saying,

> '*I called out to the Lord*, out of my distress,
>   and he answered me;
> out of the belly of Sheol I cried,
>   and you heard my voice.'

(Jon. 2:1)

But it displeased Jonah exceedingly, and he was angry. *And he prayed to the Lord* and said, 'O Lord, is not this what I said when I was yet in my country? That is why I made haste to flee to Tarshish; for I knew that you are a gracious God and merciful, slow to anger and abounding in steadfast love, and relenting from disaster. Therefore now, O Lord, please take my life from me, for it is better for me to die than to live.' (Jon. 4:1–3)

Unlike the pagan sailors and Assyrians, Jonah *prays* (*pll*). However, I would suggest that in chapter 2 Jonah's technically and theologically

---

[17] Assuming that the prophet Jonah is the same Jonah mentioned in 2 Kgs 14:25. If this is the case, irrespective of whether one shares my convictions concerning the historicity of the events depicted in the book, the point holds – in the narrative world of Jonah God's people as a whole signally fail to call on the name of Yahweh.

[18] There is some variation in the vocabulary here. In ch. 1 the sailors *z'q*, but in ch. 3 the Ninevites *qr'* – as these terms fall within the same semantic range, the best explanation of the variation is simply for literary effect.

correct address to God simply exposes the fact that he has stopped praying. In chapter 4 theological appropriateness is left far behind, as Jonah exposes the issues in his own heart as well as those in the heart of his people.

It is worth examining Jonah's prayer in some detail, as the import of his prayer is often missed. It is often read at face value that Jonah comes to his senses in the belly of the fish. I would argue strongly that the reverse is the case, and that, in fact, the orthodox prayer he utters rather reveals the depths of his issues![19]

> I called out to the LORD, out of my distress,
>   and he answered me;
> out of the belly of Sheol I cried,
>   and you heard my voice.
>
> (Jon. 2:2)

One of the puzzles of the text is that up to this point there has been no hint that Jonah has had any intention of 'calling out to Yahweh' – in fact, in the preceding narrative he has *refused* to do just that. This could, of course, simply mean that the prophet has been brought to his senses and is now crying out to God with all sincerity; but the slightly odd tense of this prayer,[20] and, more compellingly, the jarring note that Jonah's claim sounds should at least raise questions for the reader. This tension becomes increasingly apparent as Jonah 'prays' on:

> For you cast me into the deep,
>   into the heart of the seas,
>   and the flood surrounded me;
> all your waves and your billows
>   passed over me.
> Then I said, 'I am driven away
>   from your sight;

---

[19] A similar line is taken by Jenson (2008: 58), who points out that 'if Jonah were fully realigned to God's will, then we would expect a confession of sin. The absence of any such element can be interpreted to indicate that there is disjunction between his actions (ie orthodox prayer) and will. It is this contradiction that sets up the attempt by God to persuade him in ch 4.'

[20] It is theoretically possible to construe Jonah's words as referring to what he is doing (give justification), or that this 'psalm' was written after the event and simply inserted, despite being written from a different perspective, but it is more likely that he is using a simple past tense, thus raising the possibility that he is piously trumpeting something he has not done.

> yet I shall again look
> upon your holy temple.'
> (Jon. 2:3–4)

At this point poetic licence seems to turn into something resembling post-apocalyptic dystopian teenage fiction. While it may be theologically accurate to claim that Yahweh cast him into the deep, it is at best only part of the story. To assert that 'I am driven away from your sight', however, leaves the reality of the situation far behind. There is no acknowledgment that Jonah is fleeing Yahweh in disobedience, nor does he allude at any level to his refusal to engage with 'his' God on the ship. Instead, we have what seems to be a highly melodramatic account of his (admittedly traumatic!) experience (2:5–6), and a slightly enigmatic reference to the 'temple'. I would suggest that any adequate explanation of this prayer needs to deal satisfactorily with this surprising feature of the text (which recurs in 2:7).

Perhaps the most likely reason for Jonah's citing the Jerusalem temple at this point is to reinforce the fact that his strongly nationalistic view of Yahweh has not changed. Despite the irony of his departure from Joppa in an attempt *to escape the God of the temple*, Jonah twice expresses the fact that for him there is an inextricable link between Yahweh and Jerusalem, his capital city. This is confirmed immediately by the 'anti-idolatry' statement of 2:8, and the self-congratulatory (and legalistic) note of verse 9:

> When my life was fainting away,
>   I remembered the LORD,
> and my prayer came to you,
>   into your holy temple.
> Those who pay regard to vain idols
>   forsake their hope of steadfast love.
> But I with the voice of thanksgiving
>   will sacrifice to you;
> what I have vowed I will pay.
>   Salvation belongs to the LORD!
> (Jon. 2:7–9)

Jonah's sloganeering notwithstanding, there are significant problems with this part of the prayer when read in the context of the book itself. For example, only a few verses earlier *it is those who pay regard to vain idols who showed spiritual discernment, genuine piety, fear of Yahweh and end up praying real prayers.* Jonah, however, who knows 'how' to pray, whose 'temple theology' is completely orthodox and who has a clear grasp on the fact that 'Salvation belongs to Yahweh', is the one who seems to have significant problems in calling on the name of Yahweh in a way that is authentic – based on repentance and flowing from faith. Christopher Seitz comments that 'Prayer therefore is to address God by name. And to name God's name is to deal with God as he truly is, without remainder – yet always under the obligation of having invoked the one holy and jealous God.'[21] Jonah seems to be some way from realizing this.

That is confirmed both by the language and the import of the closing chapter of the book. We have already seen the odd juxtaposition of 4:1–2:

> But it displeased Jonah exceedingly, and he was angry. And he prayed to the LORD and said, 'O LORD, is not this what I said when I was yet in my country? That is why I made haste to flee to Tarshish; for I knew that you are a gracious God and merciful, slow to anger and abounding in steadfast love, and relenting from disaster.'

The prophet who has been shown mercy himself seems somewhat reluctant to welcome mercy being shown anywhere else. The fact of his anger shows that once more (as in ch. 2), even though he is addressing God, Jonah is still some way from 'calling on the name of Yahweh'. He even cites Yahweh's classic covenantal pronouncement *against him*, before, in an astonishing piece of illogic, asking the gracious and merciful God who relents from disaster to take his life!

Jonah, then, is the prophet who cannot, and will not, pray. In that he is the perfect representative of his people. It also explains why the book ends the way it does. Yahweh's invitation to Jonah to rejoin the conversation with him, perhaps even to begin to pray again, to call on his name for the first time in the book, is left suspended in the air. It is reasonable to suggest that at least a part of the purpose of this remarkable book is to invite God's people to begin to call on him again.

Not surprisingly, this invitation is echoed in several places in the Book of the Twelve, not least in the book of Habakkuk.

Habakkuk is often understood as a kind of theodicy, albeit one dealing with the issue of *unanswered prayer.* This finds prima facie justification right at the start of the book:

[21] Seitz 2001: 13.

> O LORD, how long shall I cry for help,
>   and you will not hear?
> Or cry to you 'Violence!'
>   and you will not save?

(Hab. 1:2)

However, given what we have already seen of the prophetic emphasis on the silencing of the prayers of God's people (both by their failure to call on the name of Yahweh, and by Yahweh's own insistence that he will no longer listen until he has poured out the curses of the covenant), there may well be a significantly more fruitful line of approach.

The question Habakkuk asks is not an abstract one, detached from all historical considerations. It is an issue that arises at a particular point in salvation history.[22] Rather than asking 'Why does God not answer us?', Habakkuk addresses the question 'Why is God not answering us *now*?' The answer the book provides reiterates something we have seen over and over again – there is no benefit in calling on the name of Yahweh until judgment has passed. For now, at least, the die is cast.

This emerges very early on in the text. Society is breaking down. Habakkuk continues to 'call on the name of Yahweh', asking him to act in line with his prior covenantal commitments, but to no avail. His opening prayer (usually called a 'complaint') rehearses the awfulness of the situation in Judah:

> Why do you make me see iniquity,
>   and why do you idly look at wrong?
> Destruction and violence are before me;
>   strife and contention arise.
> So the law is paralysed,
>   and justice never goes forth.
> For the wicked surround the righteous;
>   so justice goes forth perverted.

(Hab. 1:3–4)

The situation is a significant declension from that envisaged by the prophet in the light of God's promises. And Yahweh's response? His

---

[22] It is likely that Habakkuk was a contemporary of Nahum, Zephaniah and Jeremiah, prophesying in Jerusalem in the seventh century BC (see e.g. Bruckner 2003: 300).

explanation in 1:5–11 is simple – Habakkuk's prayers are not being heard and society continues to break down because God is on the point of acting in judgment through the Chaldeans (Babylonians). Habakkuk continues to press for answers (1:12 – 2:1), this time on the question of how it could be just of Yahweh to use such brutal instruments, a charge Yahweh quickly refutes with an assurance of ultimate judgment on the future oppressors as well as the oppressed. That brings us to the heart and climax of the book, the prayer (*těpillâ*) of Habbakkuk. It is this prayer that confirms the understanding set out above.

The opening statement of Habakkuk's prayer identifies the key issue at stake:

> O LORD, I have heard the report of you,
> and your work, O LORD, do I fear.
> In the midst of the years revive it;
> in the midst of the years make it known;
> *in wrath remember mercy.*
>
> (Hab. 3:2)

Habakkuk has grasped the fact that, as far as God is concerned, 'service has been temporarily suspended'. There is no point in praying for mercy now, for this is the day of wrath. So, in chapter 3, the terms of his prayers have changed – now he simply asks Yahweh to 'remember mercy'. Habakkuk asks effectively that Yahweh will one day begin to listen to the prayers of his people once more.

Drawing on imagery from elsewhere in the Old Testament,[23] Habakkuk describes in vivid terms the actions of Yahweh in judgment and salvation. The difference is that he now understands the wider context. Even in judgment he can perceive salvific purposes (a principle made clear as far back as the exodus):

> You went out for the salvation of your people,
> for the salvation of your anointed.
> You crushed the head of the house of the wicked,
> laying him bare from thigh to neck. . . .
> You trampled the sea with your horses,
> the surging of mighty waters.
>
> (Hab. 3:13, 15)

---

[23] Bruce 1993: 890–891.

The point is not so much that Habakkuk is now convinced that Yahweh answers prayer after all, but rather than he understands the flow of salvation history in a new way. He grasps the fact that this may not be the time for Yahweh to answer the prayers of his people, but that day will come again – first, he will judge the oppressors, and then act to fulfil all his eschatological promises:

> I hear, and my body trembles;
>> my lips quiver at the sound;
> rottenness enters into my bones;
>> my legs tremble beneath me.
> Yet I will quietly wait for the day of trouble
>> to come upon people who invade us.
> Though the fig tree should not blossom,
>> nor fruit be on the vines,
> the produce of the olive fail
>> and the fields yield no food,
> the flock be cut off from the fold
>> and there be no herd in the stalls,
> yet I will rejoice in the LORD;
>> I will take joy in the God of my salvation.
> GOD, the Lord, is my strength;
>> he makes my feet like the deer's;
>> he makes me tread on my high places.
>
> (Hab. 3:16–19)

As with the book of Jonah the message of Habakkuk is inextricably linked to the idea that God's people have stopped calling on Yahweh's name, and Yahweh has stopped answering if and when they do call. More than that, however, both books envisage a day when Yahweh's people will cry out to him again, and he is delighted to respond to their calls.

This same idea is found embedded in the message of Zephaniah. The double problem in Josiah's day, according to the prophet, is that God's people do not seek him and Yahweh has silenced them:

> 'those who have turned back from following the LORD,
>> who do not seek the LORD or enquire of him.'
> Be silent before the Lord GOD!
>> For the day of the LORD is near . . .
>
> (Zeph. 1:6–7)

This situation is then resolved in 3:9, when Yahweh himself gives the undertaking that

> For at that time I will change the speech of the peoples
>> to a pure speech,
> that all of them may call upon the name of the LORD
>> and serve him with one accord.
>
> (Zeph. 3:9)

While prayer is not one of the main themes of the complex and powerful prophecy of Zechariah, the same ideas on prayer continue to be played out. God's people are no longer calling on the name of Yahweh, and Yahweh is no longer listening to his people. However, a day is envisaged when the people will pray, and Yahweh will be delighted to answer:

They made their hearts diamond-hard lest they should hear the law and the words that the LORD of hosts had sent by his Spirit through the former prophets. Therefore great anger came from the LORD of hosts. 'As I called, and they would not hear, so they called, and I would not hear,' says the LORD of hosts, 'and I scattered them with a whirlwind among all the nations that they had not known. Thus the land they left was desolate, so that no one went to and fro, and the pleasant land was made desolate.' (Zech. 7:12–14)

Thus says the LORD of hosts: Peoples shall yet come, even the inhabitants of many cities. The inhabitants of one city shall go to another, saying, 'Let us go at once to entreat the favour of the LORD and to seek the LORD of hosts; I myself am going.' Many peoples and strong nations shall come to seek the LORD of hosts in Jerusalem and to entreat the favour of the LORD. Thus says the LORD of hosts: In those days ten men from the nations of every tongue shall take hold of the robe of a Jew, saying, 'Let us go with you, for we have heard that God is with you.' (Zech. 8:20–23)

> I will strengthen the house of Judah,
>> and I will save the house of Joseph.
> I will bring them back because I have compassion on them,
>> and they shall be as though I had not rejected them,
>> for I am the LORD their God and I will answer them.
>
> (Zech. 10:6)

And I will put this third into the fire,
   and refine them as one refines silver,
   and test them as gold is tested.
They will call upon my name,
   and I will answer them.
I will say, 'They are my people';
   and they will say, 'The LORD is my God.'
                  (Zech. 13:9)[24]

The cumulative effects of these texts is substantial. The idea of the rebirth of prayer – of a restored connection between Yahweh and his people embodied in the people calling on the name of Yahweh, and Yahweh responding by pouring out the promised blessing of the covenant, is visible at many key points, especially in the second half of the Book of the Twelve. The only remaining question is, 'Does this emphasis continue all the way through to the end of the Minor Prophets?'

The concern of Malachi is not so much with prayer, as with the contradiction that is the life of God's people (and the priesthood in particular). The words with which Yahweh takes issue in the book are not so much those addressed directly to him (although these are not free from problems; see e.g. 2:13) as the declarations made to other people. However, at the root of many of the problems of this diffident generation is a lack of awe of the name of Yahweh (2:5). It is when people who fear Yahweh get together (and presumably begin to talk to him)[25] that their concerns are heard, and the fulfilment of his eschatological promises begins:

Then those who feared the LORD spoke with one another. The LORD paid attention and heard them, and a book of remembrance was written before him of those who feared the LORD and esteemed his name. 'They shall be mine, says the LORD of hosts, in the day when I make up my treasured possession, and I will spare them as a man spares his son who serves him. Then once more you shall see the distinction between the righteous and the wicked, between one who serves God and one who does not serve him.' (Mal. 3:16–18)

---

[24] See the excellent commentary of Petterson (2015), but esp. pages 234, 278 on the fact that on this day their prayers will again be heard.
[25] Ibid. 379–380.

Conclusion

In this chapter we have covered a huge amount of prophetic ground. Despite covering a wide range of genres and diverse historical situations, both the Major Prophets and the Book of the Twelve share a common view of the place of prayer in and around the time of the exile. The privilege of 'calling on the name of Yahweh' is temporarily withdrawn as the curses of the covenant are poured out on the recalcitrant people of God, and they are taken out of the land promised to them into exile in Babylon. Coming to terms with this earth-shattering turn of events is not easy (as is evinced by Jeremiah and Lamentations, as well as Habakkuk and even Jonah). But the prophets speak with one voice – this is not a permanent situation.

Beyond the day of judgment lies a day of hope, a day when once more the people of Yahweh will call on his name, and he will answer them. This is a day when 'everyone who calls on the name of Yahweh will be saved' (Joel 2:32), and

> Before they call I will answer;
> while they are yet speaking I will hear.
> (Isa. 65:24)

Chapter Four

Praying for a new covenant: prayer in the Writings

Having established a continuity in the theology of prayer displayed in the Law and the Prophets (both the Former and Latter Prophets), we now turn to examine the way in which prayer is presented and practised in the Writings.[1]

The wisdom of prayer

Aside from the special case of Psalms, to which we will return, it would be highly misleading to suggest that prayer plays a major role in the Wisdom Literature.[2] However, that is not to say that this part of the Bible has nothing to say on the subject. Proverbs, for example, is insistent that there is a link between an obedient life and Yahweh's answering prayer:

> The sacrifice of the wicked is an abomination to the LORD,
> but the prayer of the upright is acceptable to him.
> (Prov. 15:8)

> The LORD is far from the wicked,
> but he hears the prayer of the righteous.
> (Prov. 15:29)

> If one turns away his ear from hearing the law,
> even his prayer is an abomination.
> (Prov. 28:9)

While phrased somewhat differently, this is similar to the perspective that undergirds the prophetic insistence in the years leading up to the

---

[1] For practical reasons I have already discussed the material in Lamentations, and will devote chapter 5 to a short discussion of Psalms.
[2] The only possible exception to this is the book of Job, but even here, as we will see, prayer is hardly central.

destruction of Israel and the exile of Judah that Yahweh will not listen to the prayers of his people any longer, because they are rebelling against him.

Neither the pre-evangelistic address of Ecclesiastes,[3] nor the Song of Songs[4] contains any reference to prayer.[5] However, the book of Job makes up for this apparent lack of interest in the subject.

The main concern of Job has been characterized in a variety of different ways. For some it is the ultimate theodicy; for others it is a more focused discussion of the concept of innocent suffering; for others still it is essentially a prophetic book developing the concept of the righteous sufferer, anticipating the life and work of the Lord Jesus.[6] But however the purpose of the book is construed, a significant amount of time and space along the way are devoted to the prayers of Job. This cannot be by accident.

While much of the dialogue in Job is directed at Job himself or one of his four friends, at points the narrative blends seamlessly into prayer, and Job starts to take his complaints directly to Yahweh. So for example in chapter 7 he moves smoothly from challenging Bildad to challenging Yahweh himself:

> Remember that my life is a breath;
>   my eye will never again see good.
> The eye of him who sees me will behold me no more;
>   while your eyes are on me, I shall be gone.
> As the cloud fades and vanishes,
>   so he who goes down to Sheol does not come up;
> he returns no more to his house,
>   nor does his place know him anymore.
> Therefore I will not restrain my mouth;
>   I will speak in the anguish of my spirit;
>   I will complain in the bitterness of my soul.
> Am I the sea, or a sea monster,
>   that you set a guard over me?
> When I say, 'My bed will comfort me,
>   my couch will ease my complaint',

---

[3] See Fredericks on this in Fredericks and Estes 2010.

[4] I take the book to be a Solomonic reflection on the elusive nature of real love.

[5] Although Eccl. 5:2, 'Be not rash with your mouth, nor let your heart be hasty to utter a word before God, for God is in heaven and you are on earth. Therefore let your words be few,' while not primarily addressing prayer, does have some application here.

[6] See Christopher Ash's brilliant exposition *Job: The Wisdom of the Cross* (2014).

then you scare me with dreams
and terrify me with visions,
so that I would choose strangling
and death rather than my bones.
I loathe my life; I would not live for ever.
Leave me alone, for my days are a breath.
What is man, that you make so much of him,
and that you set your heart on him,
visit him every morning
and test him every moment?
How long will you not look away from me,
nor leave me alone till I swallow my spittle?
If I sin, what do I do to you, you watcher of mankind?
Why have you made me your mark?
Why have I become a burden to you?
Why do you not pardon my transgression
and take away my iniquity?
For now I shall lie in the earth;
you will seek me, but I shall not be.

(Job 7:7–21)

This outpouring is gut-wrenchingly emotional,[7] but we must not miss the theological underpinnings of expressing such sentiments to Yahweh. Job's conviction is that (as in Ps. 8) humanity is created for relationship with God, which entails being blessed by God. The intensity of his prayer flows from the fact that in the life and experience of God's servant there is now scant evidence of this 'covenantal' blessing.[8]

The tenor of the anticipated prayer from 10:2 is similarly angst ridden. Even though Job is aware of Yahweh's creative action (10:3, 8–9, 11) and salvific action (10:12), there is a huge disjunction between his theological convictions and his experience:[9]

Do not condemn me;
let me know why you contend against me.

---

[7] Balentine (2006: 141) comments, 'With his second speech, Job continues his free fall into suffering that seems to have no end.'

[8] Even though there is little explicit covenantal language in Job, the whole book lives and breathes in an atmosphere of Israelite covenantal piety.

[9] There is some discussion over the object of these complaints. With Ash (2014: 148–149) contra Balentine (2006: 198) and Clines (1989: 288), I see Job's words as primarily addressed to God rather than to his friends.

Does it seem good to you to oppress,
   to despise the work of your hands
   and favour the designs of the wicked?
Have you eyes of flesh?
   Do you see as man sees?
Are your days as the days of man,
   or your years as a man's years,
that you seek out my iniquity
   and search for my sin,
although you know that I am not guilty,
   and there is none to deliver out of your hand?
Your hands fashioned and made me,
   and now you have destroyed me altogether.
Remember that you have made me like clay;
   and will you return me to the dust?
Did you not pour me out like milk
   and curdle me like cheese?
You clothed me with skin and flesh,
   and knit me together with bones and sinews.
You have granted me life and steadfast love,
   and your care has preserved my spirit.
Yet these things you hid in your heart;
   I know that this was your purpose.
If I sin, you watch me
   and do not acquit me of my iniquity.
If I am guilty, woe to me!
   If I am in the right, I cannot lift up my head,
for I am filled with disgrace
   and look on my affliction.
And were my head lifted up, you would hunt me like a lion
   and again work wonders against me.
You renew your witnesses against me
   and increase your vexation towards me;
   you bring fresh troops against me.
'Why did you bring me out from the womb?
   Would that I had died before any eye had seen me
and were as though I had not been,
   carried from the womb to the grave.
Are not my days few?
   Then cease, and leave me alone, that I may find a
     little cheer

> before I go – and I shall not return –
>> to the land of darkness and deep shadow,
> the land of gloom like thick darkness,
>> like deep shadow without any order,
>> where light is as thick darkness.'
>>>>> (Job 10:2–22)

In reproducing these long outpourings of prayer it becomes clear that at a biblical-theological level these prayers of Job are remarkably similar to the many and various prayers we have seen up to this point. Whatever the precise nuance and intricacies of his debates with his friends, when it comes to his *prayers* Job is essentially *calling on the name of Yahweh to do what the Almighty has promised.* Job's expectations seem entirely reasonable. Is Yahweh not committed to blessing him? Then why is he experiencing darkness and death and *curse*? He understandably says:

>> I, who called to God and he answered me,
>> a just and blameless man, am a laughing-stock.
>>>>> (Job 12:4)

It seems that one of the questions at the heart of Job is a familiar one (particularly from the prophetic books). If Yahweh stops listening to the prayers of the disobedient (as he says he has done with his people), does that mean that one can extrapolate from individual suffering to the 'spiritual state' of that individual? Or, to put it bluntly, has Yahweh stopped listening to Job because of his sin? At one level it seems a reasonable assumption to make (certainly Job's friends think so). But at another this simple equation breaks down. What is true at the 'national level', even in the theocratic world of the Old Testament, cannot readily be transferred to the realm of personal spirituality, and in particular to the enigma of unanswered prayer.

In the long section from 13:18 to 14:22 Job's reply to Zophar spills over into direct address to God, and once again his dominant concern is the extent to which Yahweh seems already to have condemned and abandoned him. The silence is apparently driving him crazy. The extracts below make this abundantly clear:

>> Only grant me two things,
>>> then I will not hide myself from your face:

withdraw your hand far from me,
    and let not dread of you terrify me.
Then call, and I will answer;
    or let me speak, and you reply to me.
How many are my iniquities and my sins?
    Make me know my transgression and my sin.
Why do you hide your face
    and count me as your enemy?
Will you frighten a driven leaf
    and pursue dry chaff?
For you write bitter things against me
    and make me inherit the iniquities of my youth.
                          (Job 13:20–26)

And do you open your eyes on such a one
    and bring me into judgement with you?
Who can bring a clean thing out of an unclean?
    There is not one.
Since his days are determined,
    and the number of his months is with you,
    and you have appointed his limits that he
        cannot pass,
look away from him and leave him alone . . .
                          (Job 14:3–6)

Oh that you would hide me in Sheol,
    that you would conceal me until your wrath be past,
    that you would appoint me a set time, and remember me!
If a man dies, shall he live again?
    All the days of my service I would wait,
    till my renewal should come.
You would call, and I would answer you;
    you would long for the work of your hands.
For then you would number my steps;
    you would not keep watch over my sin;
my transgression would be sealed up in a bag,
    and you would cover over my iniquity.
                          (Job 14:13–17)

According to his friends (and Eliphaz in particular), Job's outpourings are making things worse, rather than better:

> But you are doing away with the fear of God
> and hindering meditation before God.
> (Job 15:4)

The only orthodox way to deal with the silence of Yahweh is to think, repent and wait for him to 'open his ears' again to his people. Job, however, has no time for that approach:

> Since you have closed their hearts to understanding,
> therefore you will not let them triumph.
> (Job 17:4)[10]

Job's remarkable certainty that prayer is both possible and of great advantage to him continues to emerge periodically through the rest of the book. In his description of the wicked he maintains that *there is benefit* in someone like him praying to Yahweh:

> [The wicked] say to God, 'Depart from us!
> We do not desire the knowledge of your ways.
> What is the Almighty, that we should serve him?
> And what profit do we get if we pray to him?'
> (Job 21:14–15)[11]

In the face of Eliphaz' insistence that if only he will repent, then 'you will delight yourself in the Almighty / and lift up your face to God. / You will make your prayer to him, and he will hear you . . .' (22:26–27), Job maintains his convictions, even if the pain of his situation weighs heavily on him – see chapter 23, especially verses 16–17:

> God has made my heart faint;
>   the Almighty has terrified me; yet I am not silenced
>   because of the darkness,
>   nor because thick darkness covers my face.

The issue for Job can be summarized in his own words from chapter 30:

---

[10] Longman (2012: 241) captures Job's sentiments well: 'Job believes, at least for the moment, that God has closed the mocking friends' minds so that they too will be defeated and bring glory to the situation.'

[11] See also Job 27:9–10.

> God has cast me into the mire,
>> and I have become like dust and ashes.
> I cry to you for help and you do not answer me;
>> I stand, and you only look at me.
> You have turned cruel to me;
>> with the might of your hand you persecute me.
> You lift me up on the wind; you make me ride on it,
>> and you toss me about in the roar of the storm.
> For I know that you will bring me to death
>> and to the house appointed for all living.
>
>> (Job 30:19–23)

When the bold Elihu shows up, he, of course, has a straightforward solution to Job's problem (33:23–26), but his harsh and simplistic words meet with no response.

As is often the case through these chapters, Elihu does speak better than he knows. Ultimately, the tension between the rebellion of God's people and God's determination to bless will be resolved by a mediator who comes from the outside – who will not only pay a ransom, but will be a ransom, who will both declare righteousness and bring righteousness, who will make it possible for our prayers to be heard, even though we are deeply unworthy. But the fulfilment of this vision will have to wait. In the meantime, however, *Yahweh speaks*.

The immediate resolution of the tension comes from the mouth of Yahweh himself. The sovereign God speaks 'out of the whirlwind' (38:1) and silences all debate. It seems that when it comes to individual suffering, and the questions of when and how God answers prayer in the life of any of his people, the answers are to be found only in the brute fact of his sovereignty. Job gradually (see 40:3–5) submits to his God in the face of a torrent of evidence that he (along with his friends) has been approaching this question from the wrong angle entirely:

Then Job answered the LORD and said:

> 'I know that you can do all things,
>> and that no purpose of yours can be thwarted.
> "Who is this that hides counsel without knowledge?"
> Therefore I have uttered what I did not understand,
>> things too wonderful for me, which I did not know.
> "Hear, and I will speak;
>> I will question you, and you make it known to me."

114

I had heard of you by the hearing of the ear,
    but now my eye sees you;
therefore I despise myself,
    and repent in dust and ashes.'

(Job 42:1–6)

Now that Job has a deepened appreciation of God's sovereignty and a new level of submission to his will, the way to call on Yahweh – and have his cries heard – is reopened. This is underlined by the delicious irony of 42:8. Alongside the theological significance of Job's mediatorial role,[12] the one to whom apparently God could and would not listen is now heard not only on his own terms, but on behalf of others:

Now therefore take seven bulls and seven rams and go to my servant Job and offer up a burnt offering for yourselves. And my servant Job shall pray for you, for I will accept his prayer not to deal with you according to your folly. For you have not spoken of me what is right, as my servant Job has. (Job 42:8)

The book of Job has much more to say about prayer than is often observed. This is no abstract meditation on the nature of good and evil, or even on the reality of innocent suffering. Job's focus is significantly more specific than that. At the very least, a minor theme of the book deals with the issue of prayer. Does Yahweh hear our prayers and act? On what basis? What is the place of the godliness of the individual? In that, the wisdom literature provides a deeply personal companion to the commentary on 'national spirituality' provided by both the Former and Latter Prophets. There is, however, an easily observed coherence between the theological frameworks in which prayer is discussed. For nations (i.e. Israel and Judah) the picture is clear – 'calling on the name of Yahweh' is a privilege extended by grace alone, and can justly be withheld by Yahweh in the face of the disobedience of his people. But when it comes to individuals? Yes, as Proverbs makes clear, there is a similar theological principle at work – one cannot separate godliness from prayer. But for godly individuals in this broken world, as Job both discovers and explains, nothing is quite so simple, and our ultimate refuge can be only

---

[12] See Ash 2014: 431 on the glorious reversal of Job's interceding for his three friends.

in the fact that we cry out to a sovereign God, who will eventually hear our cries.

Praying through the exile

In the words of the first Bible song I can remember learning:

> Daniel was a man of prayer,
> Daily prayed he three times,
> Even when they had him cast
> In the den of lions.

The problem is that for much of the book of Daniel his prayers (or anyone else's for that matter) are barely to be seen.[13]

It is true that when confronted with the initial challenge of interpreting Nebuchadnezzar's dream, Daniel urges his three friends Hananiah, Mishael and Azariah (better known by their Babylonian sobriquets Shadrach, Meshach and Abednego) to 'seek mercy' from God:

> Then Daniel went to his house and made the matter known to Hananiah, Mishael, and Azariah, his companions, and told them to seek mercy from the God of heaven concerning this mystery, so that Daniel and his companions might not be destroyed with the rest of the wise men of Babylon. (Dan. 2:17–18)

No doubt their own fates and the potential drastic impact on the people of God in exile (losing their four key voices within the government) concentrated their minds.[14] While it is not made explicit in the text, the prayer was answered and the day saved.

It is a little surprising that in the following chapters there is no further mention of prayer. Daniel's friends come through the furnace unscathed, Nebuchadnezzar falls and rises apparently without any explicit reference to prayer per se, and Daniel the senior citizen is dragged out of retirement by the obnoxious Belshazzar to perform

---

[13] I am not convinced of the arguments put forward for a late date for the book of Daniel. However, even if one takes a different view of the provenance of the book, the narrative world of the book is obviously the exile.

[14] Daniel Block, during a visit to Queensland Theological College, made the intriguing and plausible suggestion that Judah's procurement of a prime part of the city of Babylon in which to settle (near the Chebar canal; see Ezek. 1) was in all likelihood due to the intervention of Daniel.

his party piece somewhat perfunctorily without 'calling on the name of Yahweh'.[15] It is only in chapter 6 that Daniel does anything that even begins to warrant his reputation.

In clear defiance of the edict of Darius Daniel, who by now is an old man, does what he has always done:

> When Daniel knew that the document had been signed, he went to his house where he had windows in his upper chamber open towards Jerusalem. He got down on his knees three times a day and prayed and gave thanks before his God, as he had done previously. (Dan. 6:10)[16]

For our purposes the most interesting feature of this prayer is the fact that he prayed 'towards Jerusalem'. This could, of course, simply be an indicator of his religious allegiance (in much the same way as Muslims take great care to ensure they pray 'towards Mecca'). However, on balance, I think there is a more satisfactory explanation (which fits neatly with the subsequent prayers in the book of Daniel). The writer is more interested in Daniel's salvation-historical commitment than his geographical orientation. The implication may well be that Daniel's prayers have little to do with lions and his own longevity but everything to do with the covenantal promises of Yahweh. To pray towards Jerusalem is best understood as 'calling on the name of Yahweh' from exile.

This finds oblique support from the fact that the conclusion of this story (as was the case repeatedly in the Nebuchadnezzar narratives) is the reassertion of the sovereignty of Yahweh, with this affirmation coming from the lips of a pagan ruler, and being backed up by the quiet note underlining the fact that Yahweh ensured that he had his 'man' in place at the heart of successive regimes all the way through to the end of the exile. The point of Daniel 1 – 6 is not the prayerfulness of Daniel, but rather the sovereignty of Yahweh, the one whom they could call and depend on both to protect his servants in exile and keep his promises.

The obvious place to test this thesis (and this reading of Daniel) is in the extended prayer of Daniel 9. This oft-quoted 'model prayer'

---

[15] Although, to be fair to Nebuchadnezzar he does give credit to the Most High (4:1–2, 34).

[16] The 'three times a day' has given rise to much comment. Was this simply Daniel's usual practice? Is it an oblique reference to Ps. 55:17? It is hard to say with any confidence.

is of enormous significance in trying to ascertain the importance and nature of prayer in the exilic and post-exilic periods. That is why it is important to look at it in some detail. 'I prayed to the LORD my God and made confession, saying, "O Lord, the great and awesome God, who keeps covenant and steadfast love with those who love him and keep his commandments . . ."' (Dan. 9:4).

The first thing to note is the striking conjunction of prayer and confession in the introduction to this prayer. This instantly roots the prayer in salvation history, for it is not a *personal prayer of confession*. Daniel is speaking on behalf of the entire exilic community (if not the entire people of God). This is a new departure in prayer for the people of Yahweh.[17] One could perhaps even argue that this is a turning point for the people of God. Daniel's prayer continues:

we have sinned and done wrong and acted wickedly and rebelled, turning aside from your commandments and rules. We have not listened to your servants the prophets, who spoke in your name to our kings, our princes, and our fathers, and to all the people of the land. To you, O Lord, belongs righteousness, but to us open shame, as at this day, to the men of Judah, to the inhabitants of Jerusalem, and to all Israel, those who are near and those who are far away, in all the lands to which you have driven them, because of the treachery that they have committed against you. (Dan. 9:5–7)[18]

The scope of Daniel's prayer is striking. His concern is not simply for Judah, but for all the people of God, including Israel, shattered by the Assyrians over 150 years earlier. Daniel's covenantal concerns are broad and deep, and this shapes his petitions. The origin of his theological mindset is avowedly Deuteronomy:

To us, O LORD, belongs open shame, to our kings, to our princes, and to our fathers, because we have sinned against you. To the Lord our God belong mercy and forgiveness, for we have rebelled against him and have not obeyed the voice of the LORD our God by walking in his laws, which he set before us by his servants the

---

[17] I mean this in the context of the 'narrative flow' of the history of Yahweh's people. There are obviously elements of confession embedded in the laments of Psalms (as well as Lamentations), but there is precious little confession in the recorded prayers either of leaders of God's people or of individual Israelites.

[18] See the excellent summary of biblical allusions to this prayer in Collins (1993: 350–351).

prophets. All Israel has transgressed your law and turned aside, refusing to obey your voice. And the curse and oath that are written in the Law of Moses the servant of God have been poured out upon us, because we have sinned against him. He has confirmed his words, which he spoke against us and against our rulers who ruled us, by bringing upon us a great calamity. For under the whole heaven there has not been done anything like what has been done against Jerusalem. As it is written in the Law of Moses, all this calamity has come upon us; yet we have not entreated the favour of the LORD our God, turning from our iniquities and gaining insight by your truth. Therefore the LORD has kept ready the calamity and has brought it upon us, for the LORD our God is righteous in all the works that he has done, and we have not obeyed his voice. And now, O Lord our God, who brought your people out of the land of Egypt with a mighty hand, and have made a name for yourself, as at this day, we have sinned, we have done wickedly. (Dan. 9:8–15)

Daniel's understanding of both the predicament of God's people and the only possibility for restoration is steeped in the earlier traditions of the Old Testament. He draws heavily on the language of Deuteronomy and the prophets, as he calls on the name of Yahweh to bring blessing out of curse.[19] This also adds support to the suggestion made above that Daniel's act of deliberately praying 'towards Jerusalem' should be understood biblical-theologically, where Jerusalem functions as a symbol of God's historic covenant purposes. This is evident from the conclusion of the prayer in 9:16–19:

O Lord, according to all your righteous acts, let your anger and your wrath turn away from your city Jerusalem, your holy hill, because for our sins, and for the iniquities of our fathers, Jerusalem and your people have become a byword among all who are around us. Now therefore, O our God, listen to the prayer of your servant and to his pleas for mercy, and for your own sake, O Lord, make your face to shine upon your sanctuary, which is desolate. O my God, incline your ear and hear. Open your eyes and see our desolations, and the city that is called by your name. For we do not present our pleas before you because of our righteousness, but because of your great mercy. O Lord, hear; O Lord, forgive. O

---

[19] See the helpful comments of Longman (1999: 225) on this passage.

Lord, pay attention and act. Delay not, for your own sake, O my God, because your city and your people are called by your name. (Dan. 9:16–19)

In the narrative flow of the Old Testament this prayer marks a new departure. The silence is well and truly over – God's stubborn people are repentant, and are again crying out to Yahweh to keep his promises. The moment anticipated in Deuteronomy 30 has come, and the way of return is now opening up. The dearth of prayer in the nation has now been superseded by vibrant confession and a revival of genuine piety.[20]

Praying for a new covenant (prayer in Ezra–Nehemiah and Chronicles)

Once the return from exile gets underway, there is a growing emphasis on the place of prayer in the unfolding purposes of God (now that they are 'back on track'). Arguably, the high point of both Ezra and Nehemiah is the extended Daniel-like prayer.

The scene is set for the prayer of Ezra at the end of chapter 8, where Ezra seeks God's help in undertaking a key part of the resettling of the land of promise:

Then I proclaimed a fast there, at the river Ahava, that we might humble ourselves before our God, to seek from him a safe journey for ourselves, our children, and all our goods. For I was ashamed to ask the king for a band of soldiers and horsemen to protect us against the enemy on our way, since we had told the king, 'The hand of our God is for good on all who seek him, and the power of his wrath is against all who forsake him.' So we fasted and implored our God for this, and he listened to our entreaty. (Ezra 8:21–23)

After the exile, prayer continues primarily to be understood as calling on Yahweh, *particularly at moments when the future of the covenant hangs in the balance*. This understanding is also reflected in chapter 9 in Ezra's reaction to the crisis precipitated by intermarriage.

[20] The obvious absence of such piety in the book of Esther implies that this 'movement' (if one can call it such) was limited to those who returned to Judah at the end of the exile.

The first part of Ezra's prayer is formally very similar to Daniel 9:[21]

> And at the evening sacrifice I rose from my fasting, with my garment and my cloak torn, and fell upon my knees and spread out my hands to the LORD my God, saying: 'O my God, I am ashamed and blush to lift my face to you, my God, for our iniquities have risen higher than our heads, and our guilt has mounted up to the heavens. From the days of our fathers to this day we have been in great guilt. And for our iniquities we, our kings, and our priests have been given into the hand of the kings of the lands, to the sword, to captivity, to plundering, and to utter shame, as it is today. But now for a brief moment favour has been shown by the LORD our God, to leave us a remnant and to give us a secure hold within his holy place, that our God may brighten our eyes and grant us a little reviving in our slavery. For we are slaves. Yet our God has not forsaken us in our slavery, but has extended to us his steadfast love before the kings of Persia, to grant us some reviving to set up the house of our God, to repair its ruins, and to give us protection in Judea and Jerusalem.' (Ezra 9:5–9)

When he starts to address the specific problem, it is clear that the burden of Ezra's prayer is that the fate of the nation now hangs in the balance. After Yahweh's beginning to bless his people again, keeping his promise to bring them (or at least a remnant) back into the land, the people have repeated the sins of the pre-exilic generation:

> And now, O our God, what shall we say after this? For we have forsaken your commandments, which you commanded by your servants the prophets, saying, 'The land that you are entering, to take possession of it, is a land impure with the impurity of the peoples of the lands, with their abominations that have filled it from end to end with their uncleanness. Therefore do not give your daughters to their sons, neither take their daughters for your sons, and never seek their peace or prosperity, that you may be strong and eat the good of the land and leave it for an inheritance to your children for ever.' And after all that has come upon us for our evil deeds and for our great guilt, seeing that you, our God, have punished us less than our iniquities deserved and have given us such a remnant as this, shall we break your commandments again

---

[21] See e.g. Williamson 1985: 128.

and intermarry with the peoples who practise these abominations? Would you not be angry with us until you consumed us, so that there should be no remnant, nor any to escape? O LORD, the God of Israel, you are just, for we are left a remnant that has escaped, as it is today. Behold, we are before you in our guilt, for none can stand before you because of this. (Ezra 9:10–15)[22]

This prayer, then, issues in a general act of repentance for 'breaking faith' and a covenant renewal.[23]

For the key leaders of the post-exilic community prayer is seen to be a central part of the covenant work of God. At key moments of opportunity and threat for the people of Yahweh the nation prays. This understanding is played out in some detail throughout the book of Nehemiah.

The first prayer in the book comes in the opening scene, as Nehemiah, still in exile, gets news of the state of Jerusalem (and, by extension, God's covenant project). When he does so, he prays:

As soon as I heard these words I sat down and wept and mourned for days, and I continued fasting and praying before the God of heaven. And I said, 'O LORD God of heaven, the great and awesome God who keeps covenant and steadfast love with those who love him and keep his commandments, let your ear be attentive and your eyes open, to hear the prayer of your servant that I now pray before you day and night for the people of Israel your servants, confessing the sins of the people of Israel, which we have sinned against you. Even I and my father's house have sinned. We have acted very corruptly against you and have not kept the commandments, the statutes, and the rules that you commanded your servant Moses. Remember the word that you commanded your servant Moses, saying, "If you are unfaithful, I will scatter you among the peoples, but if you return to me and keep my commandments and do them, though your outcasts are in the uttermost parts of heaven, from there I will gather them and bring them to the place that I have chosen, to make my name dwell there." They are your servants and your people, whom you have redeemed by your great power and by your strong hand. O Lord, let your ear be attentive

---

[22] Much of the phraseology is used widely in the OT, but see particularly Deut. 7:1–3; 11:8; 23:6; 2 Kgs 21:16; Isa. 1:19.
[23] See the discussion in Baltzer's classic work *The Covenant Formulary* (1971: 47–48).

to the prayer of your servant, and to the prayer of your servants who delight to fear your name, and give success to your servant today, and grant him mercy in the sight of this man.'

The common elements with the prayers of Daniel and Ezra are obvious: strong expressions of trust in Yahweh, the covenant God; convincing confession on behalf of the nation; reference to the law of Moses (and Deuteronomy in particular); an appeal to Yahweh for success in a venture that will materially affect the progress of the people of God. The link between prayer and advance in the fortunes of the people of God is clear, and becomes clearer still in 2:3–4:

I said to the king, 'Let the king live for ever! Why should not my face be sad, when the city, the place of my fathers' graves, lies in ruins, and its gates have been destroyed by fire?' Then the king said to me, 'What are you requesting?' So I prayed to the God of heaven.

When Nehemiah arrives in Jerusalem he is in no doubt that if the work of Yahweh in Jerusalem is to progress, it will be in large measure down to the prayers of the people, who will call on Yahweh to keep his promises. This is reflected in the 'prayerful pragmatism' of 4:9 ('And we prayed to our God and set a guard as a protection against them day and night.') It is also the background to the series of highly personal 'Remember me' prayers Nehemiah prays in the remainder of the book. He prays like this five times:

Remember for my good, O my God, all that I have done for this people. (Neh. 5:19)

Remember me, O my God, concerning this, and do not wipe out my good deeds which I have done for the house of my God and for his service. (Neh. 13:14)

Remember this also in my favour, O my God, and spare me according to the greatness of your steadfast love. (Neh. 13:22)

Remember them, O my God, because they have desecrated the priesthood and the covenant of the priesthood and the Levites. (Neh. 13:29)

Remember me, O my God, for good. (Neh. 13:31)

On the face of it these prayers of Nehemiah are slightly problematic. They have a strange whiff of 'works righteousness', which would separate them both from the view of prayer that we have seen so far in the book of Nehemiah, but also the perspective of the rest of the Old Testament. So what are we to make of these atypical prayers? Not surprisingly, the key to reading these prayers is in giving proper weight to the context. These are no ordinary prayers.

In the same way that the prayers in the early part of the book are intricately linked to key developments in the restorative work of God after the exile, so too these prayers of Nehemiah are not to be taken as the slightly disgruntled outbursts of a frustrated governor. The text makes very clear that Nehemiah's motivation for returning to Jerusalem, as well as the vision that undergirds his building projects, is profoundly *covenantal*. It would be a mistake to sunder these later 'Remember me' prayers from this covenantal agenda. This finds support in the prayer of 13:29, where the same 'remember' language is used to mourn the departure of the priests and Levites from covenantal norms.

So what is Nehemiah praying for when he asks Yahweh to 'remember him'? He is asking Yahweh to use his apparently fruitless efforts to advance the work of God in the world. He is calling out to Yahweh to come through on his promises, in a context where it seems like all his (Nehemiah's) efforts have been in vain. The colourful events of chapter 13, where Nehemiah's frustration boils over at several points, lead this servant of Yahweh to reach a point where he knows that there is nothing more he can do. His administrative and motivational gifts notwithstanding, things are starting to go backwards rapidly. What can he do? All that is left for him is to 'call on the name of Yahweh'. This is what he does, in simple words that represent faith in virtual defeat: 'Remember me, O my God, for good.'

It may be, of course, that Nehemiah's four cries to God to remember *him* in a chapter replete with rebellion, while understandable, are a worrying sign that he is falling into a dangerous attitude of self-righteousness. Or it may be that, theologically speaking, Nehemiah's words show he has reached the point where he realizes there is little left to do but call on God to deliver the new covenant arrangements hinted at in Deuteronomy 30 and explicitly promised in both Jeremiah and Ezekiel. It is impossible to be certain about this, but the more optimistic view does find some support in the long prayer prayed by the Levites in Nehemiah 9.

The first part of the prayer may helpfully be summarized as follows:

9:6   Opening theological affirmations
9:7–8   Rehearsal of promises to Abraham
9:9–12   Rehearsal of the events of the Exodus
9:13–21 Rehearsal of the events at Sinai and in the wilderness
9:22–25 Rehearsal of fulfilment of promise in occupying the land
9:26–31 Potted history of Joshua to 2 Kings

It is worth quoting the final part of the prayer in full:

Now, therefore, our God, the great, the mighty, and the awesome God, who keeps covenant and steadfast love, let not all the hardship seem little to you that has come upon us, upon our kings, our princes, our priests, our prophets, our fathers, and all your people, since the time of the kings of Assyria until this day. Yet you have been righteous in all that has come upon us, for you have dealt faithfully and we have acted wickedly. Our kings, our princes, our priests, and our fathers have not kept your law or paid attention to your commandments and your warnings that you gave them. Even in their own kingdom, and amid your great goodness that you gave them, and in the large and rich land that you set before them, they did not serve you or turn from their wicked works. Behold, we are slaves this day; in the land that you gave to our fathers to enjoy its fruit and its good gifts, behold, we are slaves. And its rich yield goes to the kings whom you have set over us because of our sins. They rule over our bodies and over our livestock as they please, and we are in great distress.

Because of all this we make a firm covenant in writing; on the sealed document are the names of our princes, our Levites, and our priests. (Neh. 9:32–38)

This prayer is strangely depressing. The wording of verse 36, for example, at least in the mind of these Levites and the author of Nehemiah, suggests that the people of God *are still in exile*. The fact that the prayer ends on a slightly lame note, with the recommitment in another covenant does not promise a bright new national future (esp. in the light of the historical summary in the first part of the prayer). The prayer leaves one with a nagging question: Is this it? Is there not something else that can be done? In that sense this prayer coheres with Nehemiah's elemental cry at the end of chapter 13. Surely the only thing that can remedy this situation is a radical intervention of God himself, as anticipated all those years earlier by Moses in Deuteronomy 30. Surely what is needed is the national transformation that can come only from a new covenant.

If this analysis is correct, it would go some way to explaining the massive significance of prayer in the books of Chronicles: What is the future for Israel? What hope is there for God's people? All that is left to do is to *call on the name of Yahweh.*

It would be an overstatement to say that prayer is everywhere in 1 and 2 Chronicles, but the fact that kings pray ten times more in Chronicles than in 1 and 2 Kings shows that there was a substantial shift in the attitudes and emphases of Israel's historians in the post-exilic period.[24]

Even in the long introductory genealogies the chronicler flags his intention to call God's people to prayer. The prayer of Jabez and the lesser-known prayer of the Reubenites, Gadites and Manassites are included at the heart of 1 Chronicles 1 – 9:

> Jabez called upon the God of Israel, saying, 'Oh that you would bless me and enlarge my border, and that your hand might be with me, and that you would keep me from harm so that it might not bring me pain!' And God granted what he asked. (1 Chr. 4:10)

> And when they prevailed over them, the Hagrites and all who were with them were given into their hands, for they cried out to God in the battle, and he granted their urgent plea because they trusted in him. (1 Chr. 5:20)

Rather than providing models of prayer, these 'cameo' prayers function as reminders that Yahweh is a promise-keeping God, who is still committed to blessing his people according to the commitments given to Abraham, Isaac and Jacob. In order to encourage God's people to throw themselves on him, these prayers are embedded in the middle of the long section designed to expound the heart of the Israelite problem.[25]

---

[24] M. E. W. Thompson 1996: 151. Thompson's discussion of the place of prayer in Chronicles is extremely insightful.

[25] Johnstone (1986) has identified the function of this genealogy as exposing the unfaithfulness of Israel. These prayers, however, reassure the people of Yahweh that he is still able and willing to act in line with his promises when his people cry to him.

Similarly, after David's long psalm of praise in 1 Chronicles 16 a short prayer is appended for all of God's people to proclaim:

Say also:

> 'Save us, O God of our salvation,
>> and gather and deliver us from among the nations,
> that we may give thanks to your holy name,
>> and glory in your praise.
> Blessed be the LORD, the God of Israel,
>> from everlasting to everlasting!'
>
>> (1 Chr. 16:35–36)

One could argue that this prayer is a template for all the other prayers that follow in Chronicles, drawing together neatly as it does a cry for salvation and an affirmation of Yahweh's unchanging nature. However, it is when Chronicles begins its account of the kings of Israel and Judah that its emphasis on the place of prayer becomes readily apparent.

Two long prayers of King David are recorded, one that is included in Samuel–Kings and one that is not.[26] First, David prays in response to the dynastic promise God makes him (1 Chr. 17:16–27), and then, more generally, he prays in the assembly of Israel (1 Chr. 29:10–19).

In addition to the now familiar elements of affirmation of the divine character and reference to the exodus tradition and the word through Moses, the elements that are particularly prominent in this prayer are marked in italic:

> Then King David went in and sat before the LORD and said, 'Who am I, O LORD God, and what is my house, that you have brought me thus far? And this was a small thing in your eyes, O God. You have also spoken of your servant's house *for a great while to come*, and have shown me *future generations*, O LORD God! And what more can David say to you for honouring your servant? For you know your servant. For your servant's sake, O LORD, and according to your own heart, you have done all this greatness, in *making known all these great things*. There is none like you, O LORD, and there is no God besides you, according to all that we have heard

---

[26] See 2 Sam. 7:18–29. Williamson (1977) discusses at some length the slightly differing versions of these prayers.

with our ears. And who is like your people Israel, the one nation on earth whom God went to redeem to be his people, making for yourself a name for great and awesome things, in driving out nations before your people whom you redeemed from Egypt? And you made your people Israel to be your people for ever, and you, O Lord, became their God. And now, O Lord, let the word that you have spoken concerning your servant and *concerning his house be established for ever*, and do as you have spoken, and *your name will be established and magnified for ever*, saying, "The Lord of hosts, the God of Israel, is Israel's God", and the house of your servant David *will be established before you*. For you, my God, have revealed to your servant that you will build a house for him. Therefore your servant has found courage to pray before you. And now, O Lord, you are God, and you have *promised this good thing* to your servant. Now you have been pleased to bless the house of your servant, *that it may continue for ever before you*, for it is you, O Lord, who have blessed, and it is blessed for ever. (1 Chr. 17:16–27)[27]

In the context of Chronicles, where the Davidic hope is being deliberately rehabilitated and rekindled, the emphasis on the eternal nature of the house of David is striking.[28]

The other long Davidic prayer is not dissimilar, although this time the emphasis falls not on the eternal nature of the Davidic covenant but on the fulfilment of the promise to the patriarchs through Solomon, David's son and heir. This time, however, it is clear that the answer to the prayer (the fulfilment of the promise) is dependent on the grace of God in enabling the petitioners to follow God wholeheartedly:

Therefore David blessed the Lord in the presence of all the assembly. And David said: 'Blessed are you, O Lord, the God of Israel our father, for ever and ever. Yours, O Lord, is the greatness and the power and the glory and the victory and the majesty, for all that is in the heavens and in the earth is yours. Yours is the kingdom, O Lord, and you are exalted as head above all. *Both riches and honour come from you, and you rule over all. In your hand*

---

[27] The chronicler has emphasized the eternal nature of the Davidic dynasty in 1 Chr. 17:16.
[28] Williamson 1977: 142.

128

are power and might, and in your hand it is to make great and to give strength to all. And now we thank you, our God, and praise your glorious name.

'But who am I, and what is my people, *that we should be able thus to offer willingly? For all things come from you, and of your own have we given you.* For we are strangers before you and sojourners, as all our fathers were. Our days on the earth are like a shadow, and there is no abiding. O LORD our God, all this abundance that we have provided for building you a house for your holy *name comes from your hand and is all your own.* I know, my God, that you test the heart and have pleasure in uprightness. In the uprightness of my heart I have freely offered all these things, and now I have seen your people, who are present here, offering freely and joyously to you. O LORD, the God of Abraham, Isaac, and Israel, our fathers, *keep for ever such purposes and thoughts in the hearts of your people, and direct their hearts towards you. Grant to Solomon my son a whole heart* that he may keep your commandments, your testimonies, and your statutes, performing all, and that he may build the palace for which I have made provision.' (1 Chr. 29:10–19)

As the chronicler consciously seeks to provide models for prayer for the post-exilic generation, this prayer is particularly powerful. Long experience has already made it clear that no generation of Israelites has the wherewithal to keep the covenant. Again, as Moses himself anticipated, both the desire and the ability to keep covenant would have to come from Yahweh alone. This prayer captures that beautifully, and in doing so offers powerful testimony that hope for the post-exilic generation can be found only in throwing themselves on God and calling on his name, asking him in mercy to fulfil his promises.

The only other prayer of David included in Chronicles underlines the necessity of divine grace in meeting the obligations God lays on his people. The prayer comes in the context of David's disobedience surrounding the ill-fated national census in 1 Chronicles 21:

And David lifted his eyes and saw the angel of the LORD standing between earth and heaven, and in his hand a drawn sword stretched out over Jerusalem. Then David and the elders, clothed in sackcloth, fell upon their faces. And David said to God, 'Was it not I who gave command to number the people? It is I who have sinned and done great evil. But these sheep, what have they done? Please let your hand, O LORD my God, be against me and against

my father's house. But do not let the plague be on your people.'
(1 Chr. 21:16–17)[29]

Unlike the previous Davidic prayers in Chronicles, this is presented
less as a model and more as a warning. In the same way that Moses
was excluded from the land as a result of his own disobedience David
is revealed to be a flawed messiah. But in this moment of major
national disappointment both the reaction of the king and the ensuing
response of Yahweh imply that the day is not lost entirely. Hope
remains both for the house of David and for Yahweh's people who
cry to him for mercy.

After the passing of David, the remaining narratives are peppered
with reminders that when Yahweh's people, and in the case of 2 Chronicles, generally, Yahweh's king, call on his name, Yahweh is delighted
to answer and to keep his promises both to David and to Abraham.
The pattern for these prayers is set by Solomon in 2 Chronicles 1:

> And Solomon said to God, 'You have shown great and steadfast
> love to David my father, and have made me king in his place. O
> LORD God, let your word to David my father be now fulfilled, for
> you have made me king over a people as numerous as the dust of
> the earth. Give me now wisdom and knowledge to go out and come
> in before this people, for who can govern this people of yours,
> which is so great?' (2 Chr. 1:8–10)

The wording of this prayer draws together both Davidic and
Abrahamic elements in a way typical of Chronicles.[30] As many of the
biblical-theological strands of the Old Testament converge, the nature
of the full-orbed commitment of Yahweh to do whatever it takes to
bring his people home becomes ever clearer.

Once again, it is established beyond any reasonable doubt that the
chronicler conceives of prayer as fundamentally being a matter of
calling on the name of Yahweh – asking God to do what he has
promised. The 'gospel shape of prayer' is, yet again, plain for all to see.
This emphasis runs all the way through to the end of Chronicles.

While most of the prayers in 2 Chronicles are unique to the book,
some, like the prayer of dedication of Solomon in 2 Chronicles 6, do
occur in Kings in another form. However, the chronicler's version of

---

[29] Compare the shorter version of this prayer in 2 Sam. 24:10.
[30] This idea is present in 1 Kgs 3:8, but is deliberately highlighted in Chronicles.

the 1 Kings 8 prayer confirms that my interpretation is running in the right direction. The overwhelming focus of this prayer is not the temple, but Yahweh's willingness to hear the prayers of his people:

> Although the dedicatory prayer of Solomon is taken almost verbatim from the parallel passage (1 Kgs. 8) the Chronicler has given the prayer a centrality and importance it does not have in the earlier history. The importance the Chronicler attaches to the prayer can be seen in several ways. (1) The prayer and the divine response to it are at the centre of a large chiastic narrative embracing the entire account of Solomon's reign . . . (2) The prayer at the dedication is longer than the actual account of the building itself (2 Chr. 3) unlike the parallel in 1 Kings 6 . . . (3) . . . For the Chronicler, the theology of immediate retribution grows out of Solomon's own prayer. The author has grounded the leitmotif of the remainder of his history in this prayer, giving the prayer a centrality not found in Kings.[31]

It is striking just how many direct references there are to prayer within this prayer itself:

> Yet have regard to the *prayer of your servant and to his plea*, O LORD my God, *listening to the cry and to the prayer that your servant prays before you*, that your eyes may be open day and night towards this house, the place where you have promised to set your name, *that you may listen to the prayer that your servant offers towards this place*. And *listen to the pleas of your servant and of your people Israel, when they pray towards this place. And listen from heaven your dwelling place, and when you hear, forgive.*
>
> If a man sins against his neighbour and is made to take an oath and comes and swears his oath before your altar in this house, then *hear from heaven and act and judge your servants* . . .
>
> If your people Israel are defeated before the enemy because they have sinned against you, *and they turn again and acknowledge your name and pray and plead with you in this house*, then *hear from heaven* and forgive the sin of your people Israel and bring them again to the land, which you gave to them and to their fathers.
>
> When heaven is shut up and there is no rain because they have sinned against you, *if they pray towards this place and acknowledge*

---

[31] Dillard 1987: 52.

your name and turn from their sin, when you afflict them, *then hear in heaven and forgive the sin of your servants*, your people Israel, when you teach them the good way in which they should walk, and grant rain upon your land, which you have given to your people as an inheritance.

If there is famine in the land, if there is pestilence or blight or mildew or locust or caterpillar, if their enemies besiege them in the land at their gates, whatever plague, whatever sickness there is, *whatever prayer, whatever plea is made by any man or by all your people Israel, each knowing his own affliction and his own sorrow and stretching out his hands towards this house, then hear from heaven your dwelling place and forgive* and render to each whose heart you know, according to all his ways, for you, you only, know the hearts of the children of mankind, that they may fear you and walk in your ways all the days that they live in the land that you gave to our fathers.

Likewise, when a foreigner, who is not of your people Israel, comes from a far country for the sake of your great name and your mighty hand and your outstretched arm, when he comes and prays towards this house, *hear from heaven your dwelling place and do according to all for which the foreigner calls to you, in order that all the peoples of the earth may know your name and fear you, as do your people Israel, and that they may know that this house that I have built is called by your name.*

If your people go out to battle against their enemies, by whatever way you shall send them, and they pray to you towards this city that you have chosen and the house that I have built for your name, *then hear from heaven their prayer and their plea, and maintain their cause.*

If they sin against you – for there is no one who does not sin – and you are angry with them and give them to an enemy, so that they are carried away captive to a land far or near, yet if they turn their heart in the land to which they have been carried captive, and repent and *plead with you* in the land of their captivity, *saying, 'We have sinned and have acted perversely and wickedly'*, if they repent with all their mind and with all their heart in the land of their captivity to which they were carried captive, and *pray towards their land*, which you gave to their fathers, the city that you have chosen and the house that I have built for your name, *then hear from heaven your dwelling place their prayer and their pleas, and maintain their cause and forgive your people who have sinned against you. Now, O my God, let your eyes be open and your ears attentive to the prayer of this place.* (2 Chr. 6:19–40)

Whatever else is happening in this long and rich prayer, it is clearly an encouragement to Yahweh's people that, whatever has gone on through the exilic period, Yahweh is once more listening to his people and answering their prayers. The chronicler desperately wants people to call on the name of Yahweh. This is confirmed by the way in which prayer is front and centre in the rest of the narrative of Chronicles.

When Yahweh's people are attacked and forced to go into battle, and ask for his help, Yahweh is sure to answer, as he did for Abijah in 2 Chronicles 13 and Asa in 2 Chronicles 14:

And when Judah looked, behold, the battle was in front of and behind them. And they cried to the LORD, and the priests blew the trumpets. Then the men of Judah raised the battle shout. And when the men of Judah shouted, God defeated Jeroboam and all Israel before Abijah and Judah. (2 Chr. 13:14–15)

And Asa cried to the LORD his God, 'O LORD, there is none like you to help, between the mighty and the weak. Help us, O LORD our God, for we rely on you, and in your name we have come against this multitude. O LORD, you are our God; let not man prevail against you.' So the LORD defeated the Ethiopians before Asa and before Judah, and the Ethiopians fled. (2 Chr. 14:11–12)

One king gets significantly more airplay in 2 Chronicles than in the respective sections of 2 Kings – Jehoshaphat. And whereas in Kings the emphasis is on his rather dubious connections through marriage with Ahab and Jezebel, in Chronicles Jehoshaphat is first and foremost a man of prayer. In the '2 Kings 3' version of the death of Jehoram God is at work through his word, and Jehoshaphat is portrayed as godly but intrinsically naive and foolish. In the chronicler's account Jehoshaphat is a model praying man:

Now the king of Syria had commanded the captains of his chariots, 'Fight with neither small nor great, but only with the king of Israel.' As soon as the captains of the chariots saw Jehoshaphat, they said, 'It is the king of Israel.' So they turned to fight against him. And Jehoshaphat cried out, and the LORD helped him; God drew them away from him. (2 Chr. 18:30–31)

Similarly, a couple of chapters later Jehoshaphat leads the nation beautifully in the wake of national reforms as they face an Ammonite and Moabite threat:

> O Lord, God of our fathers, are you not God in heaven? You rule over all the kingdoms of the nations. In your hand are power and might, so that none is able to withstand you. Did you not, our God, drive out the inhabitants of this land before your people Israel, and give it for ever to the descendants of Abraham your friend? And they have lived in it and have built for you in it a sanctuary for your name, saying, *'If disaster comes upon us, the sword, judgement, or pestilence, or famine, we will stand before this house and before you – for your name is in this house – and cry out to you in our affliction, and you will hear and save.'* And now behold, the men of Ammon and Moab and Mount Seir, whom you would not let Israel invade when they came from the land of Egypt, and whom they avoided and did not destroy – behold, they reward us by coming to drive us out of your possession, which you have given us to inherit. O our God, will you not execute judgement on them? For we are powerless against this great horde that is coming against us. We do not know what to do, but our eyes are on you. (2 Chr. 20:6–12)

This prayer, which has no parallel in Kings, is one of the clearest indicators that Chronicles is an invitation to pray to God's people who have made it back to the land. This is what they need to do. This is what they must do. This is the key to God's covenant – new covenant work, you could say – continuing into the future.

When Hezekiah ascends to the throne of Judah, he too is depicted from the start as a man of prayer. When a moment's carelessness threatens the success of national reforms, his instinct is to pray:

> For a majority of the people, many of them from Ephraim, Manasseh, Issachar, and Zebulun, had not cleansed themselves, yet they ate the Passover otherwise than as prescribed. For Hezekiah had prayed for them, saying, 'May the good Lord pardon everyone who sets his heart to seek God, the Lord, the God of his fathers, even though not according to the sanctuary's rules of cleanness.' And the Lord heard Hezekiah and healed the people. (2 Chr. 30:18–20)

And God responded graciously. When the people are threatened by the Assyrians, God does not abandon his people:

Then Hezekiah the king and Isaiah the prophet, the son of Amoz, prayed because of this and cried to heaven. And the LORD sent an angel, who cut off all the mighty warriors and commanders and officers in the camp of the king of Assyria. So he returned with shame of face to his own land. And when he came into the house of his god, some of his own sons struck him down there with the sword. (2 Chr. 32:20–21)

When Hezekiah was critically ill, he prayed and God preserved his messiah for a while longer:

In those days Hezekiah became sick and was at the point of death, and he prayed to the LORD, and he answered him and gave him a sign. But Hezekiah did not make return according to the benefit done to him, for his heart was proud. Therefore wrath came upon him and Judah and Jerusalem. (2 Chr. 32:24–25)

There is much to be said about Hezekiah's reforms and his final years, but it is clear that the chronicler wants to think of Hezekiah as someone who prayed and was answered by God.

Of course, having prayers answered is not simply the prerogative of kings. In 2 Chronicles 30:27 the writer helpfully slips in a reminder of this: 'Then the priests and the Levites arose and blessed the people, and their voice was heard, and their prayer came to his holy habitation in heaven.' In fact, such is Yahweh's grace in hearing and answering our prayers that *even Manasseh's prayers were heard*, although he was probably the worst king that either Judah or Israel ever had.

The prayers of Manasseh are fascinating:

The LORD spoke to Manasseh and to his people, but they paid no attention. Therefore the LORD brought upon them the commanders of the army of the king of Assyria, who captured Manasseh with hooks and bound him with chains of bronze and brought him to Babylon. And when he was in distress, he entreated the favour of the LORD his God and humbled himself greatly before the God of his fathers. He prayed to him, and God was moved by his entreaty and heard his plea and brought him again to Jerusalem into his kingdom. Then Manasseh knew that the LORD was God. (2 Chr. 33:10–13)

Now the rest of the acts of Manasseh, *and his prayer to his God*, and the words of the seers who spoke to him in the name of the

LORD, the God of Israel, behold, they are in the Chronicles of the Kings of Israel. *And his prayer, and how God was moved by his entreaty, and all his sin* and his faithlessness, and the sites on which he built high places and set up the Asherim and the images, before he humbled himself, behold, they are written in the Chronicles of the Seers. (2 Chr. 33:18–19)

There is no other explanation for it. Manasseh cried out to Yahweh, and Yahweh in his grace answered. Now there is a reason to hope – if Yahweh could choose to listen to the prayer of Manasseh, then surely there is hope for his returned people.

Conclusion

Earlier in this chapter I advanced the suggestion that both in the wisdom literature and in the exilic and post-exilic narratives (including Daniel) there is a concerted effort to recalibrate the prayers of God's people. It has been demonstrated that this is a compelling thesis. The wisdom literature, Daniel, Ezra–Nehemiah and Chronicles all say essentially the same thing – the greatest need of the people of God is simply to call on the name of the Lord.

Chapter Five

The psalms,
the Messiah and
the church

To attempt to write a short discussion of 'prayer and the psalms' feels like the theological equivalent of trying to take close-up photos of a black hole – a fascinating challenge, but one that carries the danger of being sucked into the vortex, never to be seen again.

In recent years the study of the psalter has been an area of massive interest, both in the church and in the academy. Those longing to harness the power of the psalms for personal or community devotion stand side by side with those whose primary interest is uncovering the practice and development of the Israelite cult. Integrating the psalms into the flow of biblical theology is the aim for some. Others are locked in 'genre wars'. Others still seek to unlock the mysteries of the super-scriptions and musical notation. It will clearly not be possible in a work of this scope to engage with many of these issues – our focus must, of necessity, be much narrower.

In this chapter I will seek to answer four questions to enable us to negotiate the intricacies of the psalter without losing sight of our primary goal:

1. Are the psalms 'prayers'?
2. Whose prayers are these?
3. Does the psalter have a message?
4. How, then, does the psalter contribute to the biblical theology of prayer?

Are the psalms 'prayers'?

As is often the case in Old Testament studies, this rather simple question turns out to have a rather complex answer. At face value the text of the psalter gives an explicit (if qualified) 'yes'.

Many of the psalms are characterized by their direct, personal address to God.[1] A large number of these psalms are Davidic, and are concerned initially, at least, with the trials of God's anointed. However, it is not always easy, as we will see, to agree on either the form or the setting of these psalms. Are they personal prayers? Community songs or laments cast as personal prayers? Personal prayers, which have become community songs? These are crucial – and challenging – questions for the understanding of the psalms in general, and their teaching on prayer in particular. How are we to negotiate these challenges? The final form of the book provides us with a potentially helpful starting point that narrows our focus a little.

Five of the psalms are clearly identified in their superscription as 'A Prayer' (*tĕpillâ*).[2] The superscription of Psalm 17, for example, reads 'A Prayer of David.' Similarly, Psalm 86 (also by David), 90 (by Moses), 102 (the prayer of an afflicted one) and 142 (by David again, although this psalm is designated a *maskil* of David,[3] with the additional clarification that it is also a 'prayer'[4]). It is not entirely clear why these psalms *in particular* are identified as 'prayers' over against other psalms that share many of the same characteristics, but are not so designated. It is not even entirely clear whether this term is associated with a specific structural feature, a specific psalm genre or is a more general term.[5]

In addition to this formal 'classification' of a small group of psalms it is also clear that many other psalms satisfy the definition I have been using throughout this book – many psalms obviously 'call on the name of Yahweh'. So, for example, although neither Psalm 1 nor Psalm 2 is directly addressed to God, Psalms 3 – 8 are. This pattern continues throughout the psalter. It is also noticeable that even in psalms which are essentially declarative (e.g. Ps. 19) or pronouncing blessing (e.g. Ps. 20), 'prayer' is never far away (so 19:12–14; 20:9).

---

[1] See e.g. Pss 3, 4, 5, 6, 7, 9, 10, 12, 13, 15, 16, 17, 21, 22, 25, 26, 28, 30, 31, 35, 38, 42, 43, 51, 54, 55, 56, 57, 59, 61, 63, 64, 69, 70, 71, 84, 86, 90, 102, 109, 120, 130, 139, 140, 141, 142, 143. Even this simple exercise, however, reveals the trickiness of the task.

[2] *HALOT* 2: 1776–1777.

[3] The translation of *maskil*, usually understood as a musical term, is uncertain.

[4] The other place in the OT where this designation appears is Hab. 3:1.

[5] There is little, if any, discussion of this issue in the literature (although see Hossfeld and Zenger 2005: 370; G. H. Wilson 2002: 318, n. 4; Kraus 1993a: 26). This is in all likelihood a function of the ongoing uncertainty surrounding the role of the super-scriptions in interpretation, and the criteria used in classifying Psalms. It is interesting that Futato's excellent introduction to Psalms (2007: 145–182) does not include 'prayer' as one of the psalm categories.

Even this briefest of introductions raises the wider issue of the genre of the psalms, which in turn feeds into questions of the origins both of individual psalms and the collection as a whole.[6]

Since the end of the nineteenth and start of the twentieth century, when Hermann Gunkel pioneered what became known as the form-critical method, Psalms studies have been dominated by the search for each psalm's *Gattung* (type), and *Sitz im Leben* (situation in life). Gunkel viewed the superscriptions as irrelevant, and sought to penetrate behind the presentation of a psalm to its real-life beginnings. He identified seven types of psalms: hymns, community laments, songs of the individual, thank offering songs, laments of the individual, entrance liturgies and royal psalms.[7] Interestingly, none of these 'types' could be described as 'prayer' in the sense in which he used the term. Gunkel's lack of interest in the psalms as prayer was a consequence of his view that their function in the religious cult is the primary context for interpretation. This means that even if a particular psalm starts out as the prayer of an individual, the fact that it was incorporated into the temple liturgy is what matters.

The Norwegian Sigmund Mowinckel took Gunkel's approach a step further, arguing that the psalms were *composed* for purposes of cult worship (so none of them was ever a 'private prayer').[8] He attempted to link every psalm to a specific cultic occasion. However, perhaps the twentieth century's most careful and influential Psalms scholar, Claus Westermann,[9] primarily in his 1981 book *Praise and Lament in the Psalms*, pointed out that this focus on the supposed cult festivals is too unreliable, and suggested that *worship is a more reliable context* in which to understand Psalms.

Since then Erhard Gerstenberger has brought the discussion almost full circle by suggesting that, rather than being religious cult or public worship, the psalms had their original composition and use in a family setting, and that eventually these 'family songs' were picked up by priests and Levites and incorporated into public life.[10]

In all this debate over the origins of the psalms, irrespective of the milieu in which individual psalms were composed, and the context in which the collection was used corporately, it is important to recognize

[6] Kyu Nam Jung (1990) provides a helpful overview of prayer in Psalms, although he uses much broader categories.

[7] Gunkel 1967: 10–25; 1998.

[8] Mowinckel 1962.

[9] Westermann 1980; 1981.

[10] Gerstenberger 1988.

that *the psalter as a whole provides us with the most detailed and sustained treatment of how God's people can, should and must call on him.* And if it is legitimate to consider prayer under the rubric of 'calling on the name of Yahweh', then surely it is also acceptable (if not vital) to allow the psalms to shape our view of prayer in the Bible? The psalter is, I would argue, essentially a collection of prayers that is crucial in developing a biblical theology of prayer.[11]

The prima facie evidence for this is overwhelming, and should not be overlooked, despite the complexity of analysing the discourse of the psalms.[12] Even on the most cursory reading it is hard to escape the obvious conclusion that the psalter is dominated by direct address to God, or encouragement to engage directly with him. In other words the psalter is dominated by prayer. That, however, raises a question that was raised by Gunkel and has since been tackled by many others: Whose prayers are these? I suggest that form-critical solutions to this issue are not the most helpful (or convincing). However, help is at hand, albeit from an unexpected source.

Whose prayers are these?

Dietrich Bonhoeffer, the Confessing Church pastor executed for his part in a failed assassination plot against Hitler in 1945, suggested in a seminal work called *Psalms: The Prayerbook of the Bible*[13] that the way to read the psalter is by understanding that these psalms are not, in the first place, *our psalms.* They are first and foremost the psalms of David, and then the psalms of Jesus.[14] While Bonhoeffer's exegetical (and theological) work in his tiny volume is minimal, his suggestion offers a fruitful biblical-theological way of resolving this most basic problem of how to read the psalms, which has dogged the study of Psalms for at least two hundred years.

[11] This is hardly a new idea – see e.g. Athanasius' magisterial *Letter to Marcellinus*, which is perhaps the most powerful exhortation to read and pray the psalms ever penned. I am indebted to my colleague Tony Pyles for pointing me in the direction of this glorious piece of writing. See Gregg 1980: 101–129.

[12] The analysis of direct discourse in Psalms is a huge area of contemporary interest, and is far from straightforward. For an introduction to this field see Jacobson 2004 (and esp. his bibliography on p. 17).

[13] Bonhoeffer 1974.

[14] I am also indebted to James Hely Hutchinson, Principal of Institut biblique belge, and John Woodhouse, formerly Principal of Moore Theological College, Sydney, for first pointing out to me many years ago that the psalms are, in essence, the prayers of *the Messiah.*

It is obvious that whatever the nature of the connection between David and the psalms,[15] King David casts a long shadow over the collection. The fact that thirty-seven out of the first forty-one psalms are marked 'Of David' makes that clear.[16]

After Psalm 1 has set up a paradigm of the 'righteous' and the 'wicked' (which, incidentally, already raises questions about the reign and legacy of King David),[17] and Psalm 2 has introduced the role of Yahweh's King/Son/Messiah in overcoming the power of evil in the world,[18] Psalm 3 is the first apparent prayer of the collection.[19] Both its subject matter and its tone introduce a jarring note. We have moved from the ideal man, and a victorious king, to an all-too-human David struggling to cope in the face of opposition.

The opening statement of Psalm 3 (esp. when taken with the super-scription 'When he fled from Absalom his son') raises a very important hermeneutical point:

> O LORD, how many are my foes!
> Many are rising against me;
>   many are saying of my soul,
> there is no salvation for him in God. *Selah*
>   (Ps. 3:1–2)

It is no accident that this is how the first 'psalm proper' begins – it starts with David (the 'anointed') facing enemies who are lined up against him. These enemies are not simply political, but *theological*. At some level these foes are opposed not simply to David personally, but to *David as the chosen one of God*. Which brings us to the important hermeneutical point that, at the risk of stating the obvious, neither

[15] The significance of the lamed in the superscription to the psalms has long been debated. I remain to be convinced by the arguments against the natural reading of the lamed as ascribing authorship. However, the point I am making here does not rest on a particular view of authorship of individual psalms.

[16] See the section 'Does the psalter have a message?' below for a fuller discussion of the significance of the arrangement of the Davidic psalms.

[17] Jacobson (2004; see also deClaisse-Walford et al. 2014: 64) highlights the link between the second half of the psalm and the Davidic line, but the negative implications for David's legacy are not developed.

[18] There is much discussion concerning the subject of Ps. 2. Is it David? One of his descendants? A generic reference to all of his descendants? The matter is still hotly disputed.

[19] As I pointed out earlier, there is a sense in which it does not matter whether the 'form' of Ps. 3 is that of a 'prayer' or something quite different. Undergirding the psalm (whether it was to be prayed, read or sung) is a clear understanding of prayer.

are we God's anointed king, nor are our enemies necessarily coterminous with God's enemies.[20] And flowing from that is a strong sense in which David's prayers *cannot possibly* be our prayers. Many of us are prone to hubris, but I am not sure that any of us would say we are crucial to God's advancing his plans in our world. None of us has ever received a direct promise from God that one from our line will reign for ever. And none of us can speak so easily of those who line up against us as being God's enemies.[21]

This simple observation should sound a note of caution against assuming that the purpose of these psalms – or the theology of prayer reflected by Psalms – is completely self-evident. Both the underlying assumption of the opening Davidic psalms and the specific situational information given by the superscriptions suggest that there may be other things at work.

Could it be, for example, in the light of the anticipated conflict in Psalm 2, that Psalm 3 and those following it are to be understood primarily as reflecting the experience of *David the messiah*, who, despite his anointing, is called to suffer, and repeatedly calls on Yahweh while under pressure, *asking Yahweh to come through on his promises* (in this case the promises to David and his dynasty that are recorded in the books of Samuel)? If this is the case, it adds substantial weight to the argument I have been advancing.

Before proceeding, however, I should say a word about the implication of such a view: Does this mean that the psalms are effectively removed from the lips of God's people, as they are no longer viewed as 'our prayers'? Yes and no. It would be more accurate to say that the psalms are (largely) *first* the prayers of David the messiah. Presumably, they were then picked up and prayed (or sung) by Israel as 'the people of the Messiah'. These 'prayers of the suffering Messiah', then, find their fullest meaning when read in a biblical-theological context as 'prayers of *the* Messiah' Jesus Christ. So can we pray the prayers as Christians? Yes we can – in the same sense that we are enabled by Jesus to share in his prayers to his Father,[22] his death and resurrection enable those who follow in his steps to pray these

---

[20] I am indebted to Christopher Ash for pointing this out.

[21] That is not to say, of course, that there are no occasions where this equation works. As I write, it is a weekly occurrence that Islamic State forces identify and butcher Christians. Is it legitimate to speak of these people as 'God's enemies'? Of course. However, aside from this kind of obvious 'suffering for the gospel', our circumstances and conflicts are often significantly less clear-cut.

[22] See the discussion in chapter 6.

'messianic' prayers in a derivative sense. We do not *experience* his sufferings, but we do *share in the sufferings of Christ*, which makes it deeply appropriate for us to echo his prayers. As Bonhoeffer has said:

> David himself may once have prayed this Psalm in his own song. If so, he did this as the king, anointed by God, and therefore persecuted by men, from whom Jesus Christ would descend. He did it as the one who bore Christ in himself. But Christ himself used this prayer and for the first time gave it its full meaning. We can pray this Psalm only in the fellowship of Jesus Christ, as those who have participated in the suffering of Christ.[23]

It should be underlined, however, that this is not to say that we simply bring our experiences to Psalms, find echoes of all the challenges of life here and are then able to appropriate them as our own.[24] In fact the opposite is true. This biblical-theological perspective starts with the recognition that these prayers are very definitely *not our prayers* (in the first place, at least). They are first the prayers of the Messiah, which, in the kindness of God, become the prayers of the Messiah's people as he draws them into relationship with him. To pray the psalms, then, demands significant care and thought.

This suggestion, however, does beg a very obvious question: Can it be sustained that the psalms are *prayers of the Messiah*, in the light of the fact that a substantial number of the psalms are not Davidic?

This clearly opens a huge area of study, which cannot be dealt with adequately here. However, it may be that those psalms I identified earlier as being explicitly designated *těpillîm* (prayers) can serve as a helpful starting point.[25] This 'set of five' includes three Davidic psalms (17, 86 and 142) alongside two non-Davidic psalms (90, which is designated 'of Moses', and Ps. 102, 'of one afflicted'.) It is instructive to look at each of these psalms in turn. First, Psalm 17:

---

[23] Bonhoeffer 1974: 36–37. This also has echoes in the NT idea of our sharing in the sufferings of Christ.

[24] This perspective is expressed at a popular level, in the oft-repeated description of Psalms as the 'prayer book of the Bible', as well as at a more academic level (see e.g. Schaefer 2001, and in particular the section 'A School of Prayer', xxv–xxxii).

[25] I am aware that experts in form-critical study of Psalms may well be yelling at this point, 'But you can't do that!' All I ask for is their temporary indulgence to see if it may be possible that I *can* do that.

A Prayer of David.

Hear a just cause, O LORD; attend to my cry!
   Give ear to my prayer from lips free of deceit!
From your presence let my vindication come!
Let your eyes behold the right!
You have tried my heart, you have visited me by night,
   you have tested me, and you will find nothing;
     I have purposed that my mouth will not transgress.
With regard to the works of man, by the word of your lips
   I have avoided the ways of the violent.
My steps have held fast to your paths;
   my feet have not slipped.
I call upon you, for you will answer me, O God;
   incline your ear to me; hear my words.
Wondrously show your steadfast love,
   O Saviour of those who seek refuge
   from their adversaries at your right hand.
Keep me as the apple of your eye;[26]
   hide me in the shadow of your wings,
from the wicked who do me violence,
   my deadly enemies who surround me.
They close their hearts to pity;
   with their mouths they speak arrogantly.
They have now surrounded our steps;
   they set their eyes to cast us to the ground.[27]
He is like a lion eager to tear,
   as a young lion lurking in ambush.
Arise, O LORD! Confront him, subdue him!
   Deliver my soul from the wicked by your sword,
from men by your hand, O LORD,
   from men of the world whose portion is in this life.
You fill their womb with treasure;
   they are satisfied with children,
   and they leave their abundance to their infants.
As for me, I shall behold your face in righteousness;
   when I awake, I shall be satisfied with your likeness.

---

[26] Literally, 'the little man of the daughter of your eye', a reference to the pupil.
[27] See G. H. Wilson 2002: 324 for a helpful discussion of the translation issues in this verse.

In this psalm it is obvious that David's experience is, at the very least, slightly out of step with our own. For twenty-first-century Christians to read this psalm there are more points of discomfort than immediate comfort. So, for example, there is David's claim to have 'lips free of deceit' (17:1). He pushes things further when he claims that if God examines him, he will find nothing that deserves correction or censure (17:3). He sees himself as 'the apple of [God's] eye' (17:8); and after characterizing his enemies in suitably unflattering terms, David assumes that God will intervene on his behalf to overturn his enemies (despite their current prosperity, 17:13–14). The psalm closes with David's expressing his confidence in Yahweh's grace and blessing, and looking forward to seeing his 'likeness'.

The apparent claims to 'sinlessness' (or at the very least 'blamelessness') in many of the Davidic psalms in particular have proved extremely problematic.[28] However, this need not be so. If these psalms are viewed, in the first place, to be psalms of the Messiah, then the problems all but disappear. Protestations of innocence, purity and flawless action are then bounded within a specific frame of reference – David is not claiming to have reached a state of sinless perfection, but rather insists *he has discharged his responsibilities as God's Messiah* blamelessly. His plea for God to deal with his enemies is, then, significantly removed from personal vindictiveness. It is, then, nothing less than asking God to deal with those who line up against the divine purposes by opposing his Messiah.

At a risk of stating the obvious, this then places the first of these *tĕpillîm* squarely in the arena of requesting God to come through on his covenant promises – in this case the covenant promises focused on vindicating the Messiah.

In addition the ultimate goal of the prayer is that, like Moses in Numbers 12:8, David might see the face/likeness of Yahweh. This desire coheres well with the Messiah as the first praying person of this psalm, and may well suggest his ability to act as a mediator, bringing Yahweh's estranged people back to him. The first of the five 'prayers' is most naturally understood in the context of the ultimate work of the Messiah.

The same perspective comes through in the second of the five *tĕpillîm* in Psalm 86:

---

[28] E.g. G. H. Wilson (ibid. 320) construes 'righteousness' in terms of the legal character of *mišpāṭ*: 'The Psalmist expects to survive this divine critique for there is no condemning evil to be found.'

A Prayer of David.

> Incline your ear, O LORD, and answer me,
>> for I am poor and needy.
> Preserve my life, for I am godly;
>> save your servant, who trusts in you – you are
>>> my God.
> Be gracious to me, O Lord,
>> for to you do I cry all the day.
> Gladden the soul of your servant,
>> for to you, O Lord, do I lift up my soul.
> For you, O Lord, are good and forgiving,
>> abounding in steadfast love to all who call upon you.
> Give ear, O LORD, to my prayer;
>> listen to my plea for grace.
> In the day of my trouble I call upon you,
>> for you answer me.
> There is none like you among the gods, O Lord,
>> nor are there any works like yours.
> All the nations you have made shall come
>> and worship before you, O Lord,
>> and shall glorify your name.
> For you are great and do wondrous things;
>> you alone are God.
> Teach me your way, O LORD,
>> that I may walk in your truth;
>> unite my heart to fear your name.
> I give thanks to you, O Lord my God, with my
>>> whole heart,
>> and I will glorify your name for ever.
> For great is your steadfast love towards me;
>> you have delivered my soul from the depths of Sheol.
> O God, insolent men have risen up against me;
>> a band of ruthless men seeks my life,
>> and they do not set you before them.
> But you, O Lord, are a God merciful and gracious,
>> slow to anger and abounding in steadfast love
>>> and faithfulness.
> Turn to me and be gracious to me;
>> give your strength to your servant,
>> and save the son of your maidservant.

> Show me a sign of your favour,
>> that those who hate me may see and be put to shame
>> because you, LORD, have helped me and comforted me.

In this case, although there are significant similarities with Psalm 17,[29] there is a higher degree of resonance with general human experience. David's assertion that he is 'pure and needy' is, on the face of it, much easier to identify with than his insistence that God will not be able to find anything in his life with which to take issue. It quickly becomes clear, however, that this prayer too is about much more than David's own interior spiritual journey. The language of verse 2, where David self-designates as the 'servant' of the Lord and clearly asserts 'you are my God' is probably best taken as a statement of allegiance from the king rather than primarily as one of personal piety.[30] As the psalm continues, it becomes obvious that in some way the fate of the psalmist is bound up with God's covenant purposes. Verses 9–10 take us far beyond the ability of Yahweh to intervene on behalf of his struggling servant. More is at stake than the deliverance of an individual. This is the very *telos* (end) of the covenant.[31]

This, then, allows us to make sense of the requests of verses 11–13. These are not simply prayers for growth in theological understanding or depth of affection. These petitions are most naturally taken to be the prayers of the king, who asks for wisdom in the face of significant anti-covenantal opposition, which is depicted in verses 14 and 17. Once that is acknowledged, it seems most natural to view this psalm as essentially a cry to Yahweh to act in covenant faithfulness and uphold his promises to his Messiah and people.[32]

This brings us to what seems to be a slightly puzzling inclusion in the list of *tĕpillîm* – the prayer of Moses, the man of God in Psalm 90:

[29] Zenger (Hossfeld and Zenger 2005: 369) argues that Ps. 86 is a creative summary of all the Davidic psalms to this point. It also has significant connection with Ps. 102, strengthening the case for seeing a strong link between these 'prayers'.

[30] Although, of course, this is not to be excluded.

[31] See the comments of Hossfeld and Zenger (2005: 366). Also in a discussion on Psalms P. D. Miller (1994: 125) comments, 'The covenantal bond and their history with God have given them every reason to see their relationship with God as their whole reason for being and a particular purpose that God has with them. . . . In these prayers, they remind God of that fact in various ways in order to claim God's present protection and help.'

[32] Kraus (1993b: 182), who would in no sense see this psalm as a psalm of the Messiah, nonetheless acknowledges the scope of what is being asked for, arguing that the writer 'sees Yahweh's salvific power in a universal and eschatological light'.

A Prayer of Moses, the man of God.

Lord, you have been our dwelling place
    in all generations.
Before the mountains were brought forth,
    or ever you had formed the earth and the world,
    from everlasting to everlasting you are God.
You return man to dust
    and say, 'Return, O children of man!'
For a thousand years in your sight
    are but as yesterday when it is past,
    or as a watch in the night.
You sweep them away as with a flood; they are like a dream,
    like grass that is renewed in the morning:
in the morning it flourishes and is renewed;
    in the evening it fades and withers.
For we are brought to an end by your anger;
    by your wrath we are dismayed.
You have set our iniquities before you,
    our secret sins in the light of your presence.
For all our days pass away under your wrath;
    we bring our years to an end like a sigh.
The years of our life are seventy,
    or even by reason of strength eighty;
yet their span is but toil and trouble;
    they are soon gone, and we fly away.
Who considers the power of your anger,
    and your wrath according to the fear of you?
So teach us to number our days
    that we may get a heart of wisdom.
Return, O Lord! How long?
    Have pity on your servants!
Satisfy us in the morning with your steadfast love,
    that we may rejoice and be glad all our days.
Make us glad for as many days as you have afflicted us,
    and for as many years as we have seen evil.
Let your work be shown to your servants,
    and your glorious power to their children.
Let the favour of the Lord our God be upon us,
    and establish the work of our hands upon us;
    yes, establish the work of our hands!

This ancient prayer, which begins with the pre-existence of God and rehearses several key Pentateuchal themes,[33] makes it clear that the plight of humanity is desperate, and our greatest need as a race is divine intervention (see e.g. 90:11). However, for our purposes it is the final section of the psalm that is most striking. The request for God to teach us to 'number our days' is bound up with viewing history from a covenantal perspective: 'Verse 12 is not a plea for God to teach the humans wisdom, but a plea for the humans to accurately tally the days of God's wrath so that there is an end to it.'[34]

The cry for God to 'return' cannot be understood any other way than as an appeal for him to keep his covenant promises, and the longing that he might 'satisfy us in the morning' with his 'steadfast love' is again intrinsically covenantal. In verses 15–17 this prayer is underlined repeatedly – the plaintive cry to God to let his 'work be shown' to his 'servants' and the accompanying plea that he might 'establish the work of our hands' through the gift of his favour is yet more evidence that at the heart of this Mosaic prayer is the desire that God will do what he has promised.

The overall effect, then, of Psalm 90 is to detach the plea for God to work from the immediate 'Davidic' context, to underline that the work of God is greater than David, and that his failure and the virtual death of a Davidic hope can be reignited by the mercy of God in providing 'great David's greater son'.

It seems plausible, then, that these *těpillîm* have been placed carefully in the psalter in a way which shows that the view of prayer in Psalms is completely in keeping with what we have observed elsewhere in the Old Testament. But is this understanding borne out by the last two *těpillîm*? First, Psalm 102:

A Prayer of one afflicted, when he is faint and pours out his complaint before the LORD.

> Hear my prayer, O LORD;
> let my cry come to you!
> Do not hide your face from me
> in the day of my distress!

---

[33] Note the references to creation, fall and judgment (by flood) in vv. 1–10. See also the comments of Tanner (deClaisse-Walford et al. 2014: 690–691) on the 'Mosaic' atmosphere of the psalm.

[34] Ibid. 694. Tanner also argues that there is a parallel to Exod. 32 – 34 here.

Incline your ear to me;
    answer me speedily in the day when I call!
For my days pass away like smoke,
    and my bones burn like a furnace.
My heart is struck down like grass and has withered;
    I forget to eat my bread.
Because of my loud groaning
    my bones cling to my flesh.
I am like a desert owl of the wilderness,
    like an owl of the waste places;
I lie awake;
    I am like a lonely sparrow on the housetop.
All the day my enemies taunt me;
    those who deride me use my name for a curse.
For I eat ashes like bread
    and mingle tears with my drink,
because of your indignation and anger;
    for you have taken me up and thrown me down.
My days are like an evening shadow;
    I wither away like grass.
But you, O LORD, are enthroned for ever;
    you are remembered throughout all generations.
You will arise and have pity on Zion;
    it is the time to favour her;
    the appointed time has come.
For your servants hold her stones dear
    and have pity on her dust.
Nations will fear the name of the LORD,
    and all the kings of the earth will fear your glory.
For the LORD builds up Zion;
    he appears in his glory;
he regards the prayer of the destitute
    and does not despise their prayer.
Let this be recorded for a generation to come,
    so that a people yet to be created may praise the LORD:
that he looked down from his holy height;
    from heaven the LORD looked at the earth,
to hear the groans of the prisoners,
    to set free those who were doomed to die,
that they may declare in Zion the name of the LORD,
    and in Jerusalem his praise,

> when peoples gather together,
>> and kingdoms, to worship the LORD.
> He has broken my strength in midcourse;
>> he has shortened my days.
> 'O my God,' I say, 'take me not away
>> in the midst of my days –
> you whose years endure
>> throughout all generations!'
> Of old you laid the foundation of the earth,
>> and the heavens are the work of your hands.
> They will perish, but you will remain;
>> they will all wear out like a garment.
> You will change them like a robe, and they will pass away,
>> but you are the same, and your years have no end.
> The children of your servants shall dwell secure;
>> their offspring shall be established before you.

In many ways this psalm is the crucial test case for my suggestion that the fundamental view of prayer in the psalter coheres with that of the earlier parts of the Old Testament. As with a large number of psalms, there is no explicit reference to David (or any other king), although there is obvious contact with Psalm 86, as noted above.[35]

The title seems to imply that the individual who wrote this psalm is just that – an individual, with no particular role to play in the key movements of salvation history. Although his suffering seems extreme (102:4–6), his significance is simply derived from his membership of the people of God (see vv. 14, 17). Unlike the Davidic *tĕpillîm*, there is no direct identification of his enemies with God's enemies.[36] This is a different kind of prayer, which becomes obvious when we differentiate what the psalmist prays for himself from what he asks Yahweh to do in general.

When praying for himself, after the initial request that Yahweh listen to his cry (102:1–2), the only specific request the psalmist makes comes in verses 24–25:

---

[35] This, however, does not in itself rule out the possibility that the king is speaking. See Goldingay 2008: 149.

[36] It is striking that his enemies are clearly depicted as attacking him without cause, but there seems a distinct reticence when it comes to calling on God to act directly against them. Rather, he simply calls on God to do what he is already committed to doing.

'O my God,' I say, 'take me not away
    in the midst of my days –
you whose years endure
    throughout all generations!'

It is quite striking that in the middle of all the theological richness of
the psalm the sole petition is a very understandable appeal that Yahweh
will not allow the psalmist to be cut short in his prime. But why is this?
And how is this request coloured by the surrounding material in Psalm
102? Once again, we see that the key to understanding the psalm is to
allow this cry to rest on an undergirding framework where prayer is
calling on Yahweh to come through on his covenant promises.[37]

The contrast between the psalmist's limited prayer for himself and
sweeping statements concerning God's work in the world is quite
dramatic. After a pain-ridden explication of his own circumstances,
suddenly there is a change of gear in verses 12–13:

But you, O LORD, are enthroned for ever;
    you are remembered throughout all generations.
You will arise and have pity on Zion;
    it is the time to favour her;
    the appointed time has come.

Psalms featuring 'the enthronement of Yahweh' and/or 'Zion
theology' have received significant attention since the 1920s. However,
in this context it suffices simply to point out that the psalmist is much
more concerned with what we might call 'covenantal matters' than
his own individual circumstances. It is the progress of Yahweh's
agenda in the world that brings perspective and ultimately meaning
to his own personal sufferings. This becomes increasingly clear as the
psalm progresses.

After the eschatological claim of verse 15 (which also occurred in
86:9), the psalmist makes it clear that he sees any possible answer to
his own personal prayer in the context of Yahweh's work to bring
glory to himself in the world:

For the LORD builds up Zion;
    he appears in his glory;

---

[37] The use of 'my God' firmly roots the psalm in a covenantal perspective (Hossfeld
and Zenger 2011: 26; see also deClaisse-Walford et al. 2014: 756).

> he regards the prayer of the destitute
> and does not despise their prayer.
> (Ps. 102:16–17)

Even the commitment to answer prayer must be understood in the wider context of God's agenda for our world (see also vv. 18–22).

All this, then, has the effect of relativizing the psalmist's own prayer in 102:24. Does he want to live on? Of course he does. But that desire is deliberately submitted to a greater concern, and even subsumed in a greater prayer – that Yahweh's will be done on earth. The climax of the psalm brings both a conviction of the ultimate security of God's people and a clear appreciation that the prayers of his people should be centred not on their own individual fate but on the progress of his covenantal agenda.

Somewhat surprisingly, then, even the prayer of the non-anointed, unknown psalmist bolsters the case for seeing prayer in Psalms as essentially calling on God to fulfil his promises, whether to the Messiah, or to the people of the Messiah, as he continues to bring his will to reality in our world.[38] This brings us to the final 'prayer' of the psalter, Psalm 142:

A Maskil of David, when he was in the cave. A Prayer.

> With my voice I cry out to the LORD;
> with my voice I plead for mercy to the LORD.
> I pour out my complaint before him;
> I tell my trouble before him.
> When my spirit faints within me,
> you know my way!
> In the path where I walk
> they have hidden a trap for me.
> Look to the right and see:
> there is none who takes notice of me;
> no refuge remains to me;
> no one cares for my soul.
> I cry to you, O LORD;
> I say, 'You are my refuge,

---

[38] See also the suggestion of Hossfeld (Hossfeld and Zenger 2011: 28), building on the work of Erbele-Kuster, that the context of Ps. 102 between Davidic psalms (101, 103) has the effect of investing Ps. 102 with Davidic meaning.

my portion in the land of the living.'
Attend to my cry,
for I am brought very low!
Deliver me from my persecutors,
for they are too strong for me!
Bring me out of prison,
that I may give thanks to your name!
The righteous will surround me,
for you will deal bountifully with me.

The last of the *tĕpillîm* in the psalter makes its appearance as Psalm 142. It is a relatively straightforward psalm, which has been held back deliberately, as the psalter ends with a crescendo of Davidic material.[39] The superscription places us squarely back in the world of David's conflict with Saul, which hinges on the tension over who, in fact, is the Lord's true 'anointed'. By the time of the 'publication' of the psalter the answer to that question is obvious. However, for David it is clear that if he is to survive he needs God to deliver him in line with the commitments made to him at the time of anointing. This prayer is once more essentially a Davidic cry to Yahweh to act in line with his promises. Hossfeld comments helpfully:

> The superscription as a whole throws a particular light on David, the one who prays the fifth David Psalter. The historicizing perspective confirms the interest in the 'historical' David, primarily as he is described in the books of Samuel. The genre terms point to the proptotypical David the wise teacher and the poor petitioner in distress . . .[40]

The answer to the question 'Whose prayers are these?' is clearly not a simple one. A large number of psalms are ascribed to 'David'. However this ascription is to be construed, a persuasive case can be made for the fact that many of these prayers should be considered 'prayers of the Messiah', as he calls on Yahweh to act on his promises. This goes some way towards confirming that the understanding of prayer as calling on the name of Yahweh observed elsewhere is also reflected here in Psalms. But there is more to be said.

---

[39] See the discussion of the structure of the psalter below.
[40] Hossfeld and Zenger 2011: 565.

Using the five *tĕpillîm* as a test case demonstrates that there is an essential continuity between the prayers of those who have gone before (in the case of Ps. 90, Moses), the prayers of the Messiah (David) and the prayers of faithful Israelites after David, who are still longing for *the* Messiah. In each case the focus remains on the work of Yahweh in rolling out his covenant agenda, and to pray is simply to ask God to do what he has already committed to. We will return to this in due course.

At this point it is worth taking a moment to reflect on the implications of this relatively straightforward observation for the way in which we read the rest of the psalms (and in particular those that do not fit into the limited definition of prayer as 'calling on the name of Yahweh').[41]

It seems reasonable to say with Westermann et al. that most of the psalms fall into the broad categories of 'Thanksgiving', 'Praise' and 'Lament'.[42] Others would add distinct categories including wisdom psalms and royal psalms.[43] The question before us is, how do these genres (and any related subgenres) relate to the distinct category of 'prayer', where prayer is calling on God to deliver on his promises?

Attempts to discover the original setting of individual psalms (and/ or their literary form) have tended to blind us to the fairly simple observation that there is an intrinsic connection between each of the broad categories of psalms laid out above and the prayer addressed to Yahweh, in which the God of the covenant is called upon to act.

Psalms of thanksgiving, almost without exception, offer thanks for God's doing what he had already committed to do, rescuing or protecting his messianic king, or for the people's belonging to that king. So, for example, the general exhortation at the start of Psalm 95 to give thanks inevitably flows into the call of verses 6–7, which is based on the election of Israel:

> Oh come, let us worship and bow down;
>> let us kneel before the LORD, our Maker!
> For he is our God,
>> and we are the people of his pasture,
>> and the sheep of his hand.

[41] Of course, in a general work like this even to dip a toe into the murky waters of genre studies in Psalms is a perilous exercise. However, while this study cannot devote significant space to the huge amount of work done in this area, it would be inappropriate simply to sidestep the issues involved.

[42] See David M. Howard's (2005: 23–40) excellent summary of the debate.

[43] See the excellent collection of papers *Interpreting the Psalms* (Johnston and Firth 2005) for a good summary of the variations.

Even the briefest glance at a psalm of praise like, for example, Psalm 18, shows that there is an intrinsic link between calling on Yahweh to rescue in accordance with his promise (in this case, to his Messiah), and then praising God for coming through on what he is asked to do (or, on occasion, presumably acting even before he is asked). It is not always easy to distinguish between thanksgiving and praise (and psalms often contain both), but what is clear is the link to prayer as crying out to God to act.

Psalms of lament are again, almost without exception, lamenting the fact that the current state of Israel (or occasionally individual Israelites or the Messiah) does not appear to fit with Yahweh's covenantal commitment to bless. In that one could argue that the psalms of lament are the mirror image of the prayers we have been considering – complaining because God has not acted, rather than calling on him to do so.[44] So Psalm 44, usually regarded as the first communal lament in the psalter, begins like this:

> O God, we have heard with our ears,
>> our fathers have told us,
> what deeds you performed in their days,
>> in the days of old:
> you with your own hand drove out the nations,
>> but them you planted;
> you afflicted the peoples,
>> but them you set free;
> for not by their own sword did they win the land,
>> nor did their own arm save them,
> but your right hand and your arm,
>> and the light of your face,
>> for you delighted in them.

(Ps. 44:1–3)

The interesting thing is that by the end of Psalm 44 lament has turned into exactly the kind of prayer I have been discussing:

> Awake! Why are you sleeping, O Lord?
>> Rouse yourself! Do not reject us for ever!
> Why do you hide your face?
>> Why do you forget our affliction and oppression?

---

[44] The classic treatment of lament remains Westermann 1987.

> For our soul is bowed down to the dust;
>> our belly clings to the ground.
> Rise up; come to our help!
>> Redeem us for the sake of your steadfast love!
>
> (Ps. 44:23–26)

A similar feature is evident in the wisdom psalms. In Psalm 37, a Davidic wisdom psalm, as we move through the psalm both 'promise' and 'salvation' categories become increasingly obvious (see e.g. the repeated references to inheriting the land, and the salvific emphasis in the climax of the psalm):

> The salvation of the righteous is from the LORD;
>> he is their stronghold in the time of trouble.
> The LORD helps them and delivers them;
>> he delivers them from the wicked and saves them,
>> because they take refuge in him.
>
> (Ps. 37:39–40)

In this case the truth stated in the psalm logically precedes prayer, in that a proper understanding of the truth will lead faithful Israelites to call out to Yahweh.

There is evidence, then, that prayer in Psalms is rather more sharply defined than one might think. Of course, in a brief treatment like this it would be easy to imply that *there is nothing more to be said about prayer* than it is 'calling on the name of the Lord to fulfil his promises'. That would be reductionist. However, it is also true that across the range of prayers in the psalter (esp. those that are essentially personal, heart-cry prayers) this emphasis on asking God to fulfil his promises to his people (corporately and individually) never quite disappears.

This is easily illustrated from some of the best-known (and best-loved) prayers in the psalter.

Example 1: Psalm 51

Psalm 51, which is associated with the aftermath of David's adultery with Bathsheba, is 'surely the greatest of the penitential psalms'.[45] Over the years it has provided both the keenest insight to the nature of sin and a powerful template for those wishing to confess sin. How

---

[45] Kidner 1973: 189.

is a psalm like this affected by the suggestion that prayer is essentially calling on the name of Yahweh to deliver on his promises?

In the first place it should be noted that one of the blessings of the covenant, as explicated at great length in Leviticus, for example, is that the God of Israel is committed to providing a way for sin to be forgiven. This is reflected by the opening lines of the psalm:

> Have mercy on me, O God,
>> according to your steadfast love;
> according to your abundant mercy
>> blot out my transgressions.
> Wash me thoroughly from my iniquity,
>> and cleanse me from my sin!
>>> (Ps. 51:1–2)

David both appeals to Yahweh's covenant love and draws on his commitments to show mercy to his people as he prays. Of course, it would be highly misleading to suggest that prayer is *limited to asking God to honour his promises.* The richness of the rest of the prayer makes clear that other things-can and must be said to Yahweh, but the entire prayer is shaped by the expectation that God is a promise-making and promise-keeping God who can be expected to forgive.

David's reflections on his own sinful actions (51:3–4), nature (51:5–6) and extended plea for forgiveness (51:7–9) all take place in this context. As does the most striking request of the psalm, which comes in verses 10–12:

> Create in me a clean heart, O God,
>> and renew a right spirit within me.
> Cast me not away from your presence,
>> and take not your Holy Spirit from me.
> Restore to me the joy of your salvation,
>> and uphold me with a willing spirit.
>>> (Ps. 51:10–12)

Although it is far from clear that David intended his words to be read this way, at a biblical-theological (or canonical) level it is hard not to see an anticipation of the new covenant here. David, God's anointed king, asks that, unlike Saul, the Spirit not be withdrawn. A later Davidide, rather than fearing the Spirit's removal, would pour him out on all flesh. While it is true that the words of verse 12 can be echoed by any struggling, downcast believer, in the first place they are the words of David the king. This is underlined by the link between forgiveness and a restored teaching function in 51:13.

After a final plaintive appeal and reiteration of the terms on which God offers his people forgiveness (51:13–17), the psalm finishes in a way that again lifts it beyond the individual concerns of David or the readers who follow:

> Do good to Zion in your good pleasure;
>> build up the walls of Jerusalem;
> then will you delight in right sacrifices,
>> in burnt offerings and whole burnt offerings;
>> then bulls will be offered on your altar.
>
> (Ps. 51:18–19)

Ultimately, what is at stake here is not simply the guilt of one man, but the progress of the plan of God.

Reading the psalm in this way (in the light of all that we have seen about prayer so far) does not significantly complicate things, nor does it wrench precious prayers from the hands of those who have used them for countless generations. However, it does shed fresh light on the fact that at the heart of prayer is calling on God to do his work, the work he has already committed himself to do.

Example 2: Psalm 73

Psalm 73 is one of the psalms of Asaph, and therefore clearly not a Davidic, royal or messianic psalm in any sense. So does Psalm 73 fit with the view of prayer being suggested? Perhaps surprisingly, it does.

Again, the opening lines of the psalm highlight the covenantal context:

> Truly God is good to Israel,
>> to those who are pure in heart.
>
> (Ps. 73:1)

This is a psalm about *doubting God's promises to his people*, and the psalmist's journey back to faith. Unusually, a large part of the psalm is taken up with a narration of Asaph's past struggles (see 73:2–16), and in particular his wrong attitude to the arrogant. Things change, however, when he goes to the 'sanctuary':

But when I thought how to understand this,
   it seemed to me a wearisome task,
until I went into the sanctuary of God;
   then I discerned their end.

(Ps. 73:16–17)

As the psalmist begins to address God directly, it is clear that his prayer flows from the realization that God does indeed keep his word – in this case, he realizes that the wicked will be judged:

Truly you set them in slippery places;
   you make them fall to ruin.
How they are destroyed in a moment,
   swept away utterly by terrors!
Like a dream when one awakes,
     O Lord, when you rouse yourself, you despise them
       as phantoms.
When my soul was embittered,
   when I was pricked in heart,
I was brutish and ignorant;
   I was like a beast towards you.
Nevertheless, I am continually with you;
   you hold my right hand.
You guide me with your counsel,
   and afterwards you will receive me to glory.
Whom have I in heaven but you?
   And there is nothing on earth that I desire besides you.
My flesh and my heart may fail,
   but God is the strength of my heart and my portion
     for ever.
For behold, those who are far from you shall perish;
   you put an end to everyone who is unfaithful to you.
But for me it is good to be near God;
   I have made the Lord GOD my refuge,
   that I may tell of all your works.

(Ps. 73:18–28)

In this prayer – and it clearly is a prayer – strictly speaking, Asaph does not 'call on the name of the Lord'. However, this is an assertion of confidence in Yahweh, rather than a request for him to act, and in that it is a helpful warning against being too restrictive in our definition of prayer. However, it is equally clear that the underlying conception of prayer is very similar to what we have seen already.

Example 3: Psalm 123

It is also helpful to examine a shorter song, for example Psalm 123, one of the psalms of ascent, which is clearly designed to be sung or prayed in community:

> To you I lift up my eyes,
>   O you who are enthroned in the heavens!
> Behold, as the eyes of servants
>   look to the hand of their master,
> as the eyes of a maidservant
>   to the hand of her mistress,
> *so our eyes look to the* LORD *our God,*
>   *till he has mercy upon us.*
> *Have mercy upon us, O* LORD, *have mercy upon us,*
>   *for we have had more than enough of contempt.*
> *Our soul has had more than enough*
>   *of the scorn of those who are at ease,*
>   *of the contempt of the proud.*

The central petition of the psalm (which starts in verse 2b) is very simple – God's people look to him to come through on his promises. Of course, the prayer is couched in highly emotive and creative language, but the theological premise of the psalm fits exactly with what we have observed repeatedly – to pray is to call on a promise-making God. In this case, as in Psalm 51, the preoccupation is with God's promise to have mercy on his people, and, as in Psalm 73, to judge the wicked. It is interesting that this view of prayer is broad enough to accommodate Yahweh's commitment to both mercy and judgment.

Example 4: Psalm 139

Like Psalm 51, Psalm 139 is a Davidic psalm whose expressions and sentiments have shaped Christian piety in profound ways over the centuries. The question is, does our understanding of prayer cohere with that of the psalm?

The majority of the psalm is taken up with assertions of Yahweh's omnipotence, and in particular his intimate knowledge of the psalmist and his ways. So, for example:

> O LORD, you have searched me and known me!
> You know when I sit down and when I rise up;
>   you discern my thoughts from afar.
> You search out my path and my lying down
>   and are acquainted with all my ways.
> Even before a word is on my tongue,
>   behold, O LORD, you know it altogether. . . .
> My frame was not hidden from you,
> when I was being made in secret,
>   intricately woven in the depths of the earth.
> Your eyes saw my unformed substance;
> in your book were written, every one of them,
>   the days that were formed for me,
>   when as yet there was none of them.
>   (Ps. 139:1–4, 15–16)

However, this discussion turns out not to be a meditation on the nature of the work of Yahweh in the individual, but rather an agonized appeal to God to do what he has promised by judging the wicked (as in Ps. 73):

> How precious to me are your thoughts, O God!
>   How vast is the sum of them!
> If I would count them, they are more than the sand.
>   I awake, and I am still with you.
> Oh that you would slay the wicked, O God!
>   O men of blood, depart from me!
> They speak against you with malicious intent;
>   your enemies take your name in vain!
> Do I not hate those who hate you, O LORD?
>   And do I not loathe those who rise up
>   against you?
> I hate them with complete hatred;
>   I count them my enemies.
>   (Ps. 139:17–22)

David is quick to underline that his enemies are, in fact, demonstrably enemies of Yahweh also (and perhaps even *primarily* Yahweh's enemies). His concern, then, is not simply that his life be made easier, but that he be given wisdom and discernment in discharging his responsibilities in a God-honouring way:

> Search me, O God, and know my heart!
>> Try me and know my thoughts!
> And see if there be any grievous way in me,
>> and lead me in the way everlasting!
>>> (Ps. 139:23–24)

It turns out that even Psalm 139 is, in the first place, a prayer of the king, who asks God to keep his promises and work according to his declared agenda. Yes, it is much more than a simple cry to God to act. Yes, it also touches some deep chords of human existence. But it is, like the other examples we have looked at, a prayer framed by the commitment of God to work for his glory among his people.

These four brief examples do, I hope, highlight the importance of seeing prayer primarily (although not exhaustively) as asking Yahweh to keep his promises to his king and his people. Prayer in Psalms may often be more than this, but it is never less.

At one level this is an extremely cursory treatment of the issue of genre in Psalms, but at another it demonstrates the strong prima facie case for seeing the psalter as *supporting the understanding of prayer we have already observed in the Pentateuch and in both the Former and Latter Prophets.* This case has been strengthened by recent work on the structure of the book of Psalms, to which we now turn briefly.

Does the psalter have a message?

Since the publication of Gerald H. Wilson's seminal work *The Editing of the Hebrew Psalter*,[46] there has been a dramatic shift in the way in which the book of Psalms has been read. Not since the patristic period has there been such an emphasis on reading the psalter *as a whole.* Building on the work of his mentor, Brevard Childs, Wilson carefully highlighted the canonical shape of the psalter, pointing out the clear evidence that the collection did not simply grow organically, but was deliberately and purposefully arranged. While his thesis has not been accepted universally, it has changed the nature of the discussion concerning the shape of the psalter.

Post-Wilson, although interpreters differ wildly in some aspects of their understanding of the psalter it is widely accepted that the book displays the following key structural features:

---

[46] G. H. Wilson 1985.

163

A. The psalter is divided into five books:

1. Book 1: Pss 2 – 41
2. Book 2: Pss 42 – 72
3. Book 3: Pss 73 – 89
4. Book 4: Pss 90 – 106
5. Book 5: Pss 107 – 150

B. These five books are demarcated by similar doxologies:

1. Ps. 41:13: 'Blessed be the LORD, the God of Israel, / from everlasting to everlasting! / Amen and Amen.'
2. Ps. 72:19: 'Blessed be his glorious name for ever; / may the whole earth be filled with his glory! / Amen and Amen!'
3. Ps. 89:52: 'Blessed be the LORD for ever! / Amen and Amen.'
4. Ps. 106:48: 'Blessed be the LORD, the God of Israel, / from everlasting to everlasting! / And let all the people say, "Amen!"'
5. Pss 146 – 150 all begin with 'Praise the LORD!'

C. Royal psalms occur prominently at many of the 'seams' between Books 1–5

It is at this point that consensus breaks down. Wilson argues that royal psalms mark the seams in Books 1–3, to be replaced by wisdom psalms in Books 4–5. This is the result of a loss of hope in and emphasis on the Davidic monarchy, with the resultant substitution of wisdom for the here and now replacing any messianic hope. David Mitchell has, however, argued persuasively in a very different direction.[47] He suggests that rather than downplaying the Davidic hope, the psalter develops an increasingly strong eschatological hope centred on the Davidic Messiah in books 4 and 5.[48]

At one level it is extremely tempting to engage further with this stimulating discussion. However, whether the day is won by Wilson's more pessimistic approach or the hopeful messianic eschatology of

---

[47] Mitchell 1997.

[48] This is an extremely fertile and stimulating area in Psalms studies; see e.g. the work of Grant 2004; Hossfeld and Zenger 2005. See also the work of my colleague Doug Green on the psalms as prophecy, e.g. https://www.academia.edu/5130978/The_Lord_is_Christs_Shepherd._Psalm_23_as_Messianic_Prophecy, accessed 31 May 2015.

Mitchell, for our purposes it is enough to observe that they have shown that the *psalter has a message* and that the message concerns top-level, theological concerns, rather than simply speaking to the everyday piety of exilic and post-exilic Judeans. It is this recognition that lays the foundation for expressing the contribution of Psalms to a biblical theology of prayer in a fresh way.

How does the psalter contribute to a biblical theology of prayer?

The psalter is often spoken of in terms like 'the prayer book of the Bible', and as validating all kinds of expressions to God ('we can bring our deepest emotions to God – he can handle them'). There is, of course, some truth in this. But we must not rush to such conclusions without dealing faithfully with the text in front of us.

In the first place the psalter is dominated by psalms of the Messiah – that is, the prayers, thanksgiving, lament and even wisdom of God's anointed king (generally but not universally David). Where any given Davidic psalm is a prayer, it is first and foremost his prayer. On close examination both David's experiences and the way he reacts to these experiences *are not* intended to capture the generalities of life on planet earth for human beings – this is the intense reality of life as God's Messiah, the one who stands at the centre of God's plans on earth, and as a result is the focus of God's enemies. To attempt to pray the psalms without recognizing this is a sure road to self-aggrandizement! But this is not the end of the story.

Within the psalter itself, while there is a definite focus on the prayers of the Messiah, there is also a progression to prayers prayed by the people of the Messiah, who cry to God to do what he has promised both the patriarchs and his anointed king. In that sense, then, the prayers of the Messiah become the prayers of the people of the Messiah. This seems to be a foreshadowing of the New Testament concept of the incorporative sonship of Jesus the Messiah, where his people are able to pray 'Abba, Father' on the basis of his life and work.[49] This dynamic also lends support to Mitchell's contention that the psalter itself presents an eschatological hope of a Davidic Messiah to come.

The psalter's 'teaching' on prayer, then, is both more complex than is often realized, but also more integrated with the rest of the Old

---

[49] See the discussion in chapter 6.

Testament's teaching on prayer than one might think. The essential understanding of prayer in Psalms is reflected by the way in which the king/Messiah prays – it is calling on Yahweh to deliver on his promises. This conception of prayer spills over into the prayers of the people of the Messiah, who continue to cry for God to work by sending the ultimate Davidic King, establishing his kingdom and drawing the nations to him.

The richness of other material in the psalter – thanksgiving, praise, lament and even wisdom – flows from this fundamental understanding that our most urgent need is to plead with God to deliver what he has already committed to. To pray in the psalter, then, is to call on the name of Yahweh, as the psalms fill out the conviction that has shaped the other material in the Old Testament.

Chapter Six

Jesus and prayer: prayer in the Gospels

Of the many enormously valuable discussions on prayer (both those dealing explicitly with the biblical material and those focusing more on the theology and/or practice of prayer), a very large proportion focus their attention on the teaching and practice of Jesus himself.[1] However, very few of these make any attempt to ground Jesus' attitude to and teaching on prayer in the flow of biblical theology. That is the distinctive contribution of this chapter, and the subsequent material on the rest of the New Testament.

The purpose of this section will be limited – I will not make a concerted attempt to root Jesus' practice in the normal patterns of piety in first-century Judaism,[2] nor will I be able to offer detailed exegeses of all Jesus' teaching on prayer. Instead, I will attempt to make a more modest contribution to discussion of this area by pointing out how Jesus' teaching on prayer is clearly a development of the Old Testament material. This is true both at the level of Jesus' understanding of prayer as response to the word (and action) of Yahweh and viewing prayer as asking God to establish the new covenant (and ultimately bring in the new creation). In other words I will show how the Gospels present Jesus as 'calling on the name of Yahweh' in the long tradition of the Old Testament, while at the same time transforming prayer, as he invites us to join in his prayers as the eternal Son.[3]

---

[1] With, not surprisingly, the 'Lord's Prayer' demanding most attention. Prayer in Luke's Gospel has also been regularly discussed – see e.g. O'Brien 1973.

[2] For a discussion on prayer in Jewish life in the first century see Finkel 2001: 43–65. Also see the excellent article by David Crump (2013: 684–692). Crump provides a succinct summary not simply of the background but of the full range of material on prayer in the Gospels.

[3] Max Turner, my former teacher at Aberdeen, has provided us (1990) with what remains the outstanding short work on prayer in the Gospels (his article also covers Acts). Much of my understanding of the material has been shaped by him.

The simplest way of handling the material is, I think, to take a broadly thematic approach to the material in the Gospels.[4] First, we will examine the role of prayer in the infancy narratives of Matthew and Luke, before discussing Jesus' explicit teaching on prayer, followed by parables on prayer and finally, offering some comment on Jesus' own practice of prayer.

The birth of Jesus and prayer

The importance of prayer in Luke's Gospel has been pointed out many times.[5] From the outset Luke depicts God's faithful people looking to him to fulfil his promises. That is made obvious as early as Luke 1:10–11, when the angel appears to Zechariah as the people of God are praying: 'And the whole multitude of the people were praying outside at the hour of incense. And there appeared to him an angel of the Lord standing on the right side of the altar of incense.'

Even though the 'songs' of both Mary and Zechariah are strictly speaking not prayers,[6] they exhibit the mindset apparent throughout the Gospel. After Mary expresses a mixture of both praise and gratitude for the way in which God has dealt with her, she uses language strongly reminiscent of the prayer of Hannah in 1 Samuel 2. The focus of her song shifts from the specific way in which God has favoured her to the language of covenant fulfilment:

> And his mercy is for those who fear him
> from generation to generation.
> He has shown strength with his arm;
> he has scattered the proud in the thoughts of
> their hearts;
> he has brought down the mighty from their thrones
> and exalted those of humble estate;
> he has filled the hungry with good things,
> and the rich he has sent away empty.

---

[4] I am aware that this cuts across the almost universal convention of treating John as something 'other', but in this case the nature of the material warrants the approach. For a specific discussion of the teaching of the fourth Gospel on prayer see Turner 1990: 75–83.

[5] Ibid. 58; O'Brien 1973: 112–121.

[6] As we have already seen, it is important to allow biblical usage to shape our understanding of what 'prayer' is, while also realizing that it is not always possible to operate with hard and fast categories. See also Farris 2001.

He has helped his servant Israel,
   in remembrance of his mercy,
as he spoke to our fathers,
   to Abraham and to his offspring for ever.
                                    (Luke 1:50–55)

This essentially covenantal framework also dominates Zechariah's 'prophecy', uttered when God returns his ability to speak:

Blessed be the Lord God of Israel,
   for he has visited and redeemed his people
and has raised up a horn of salvation for us
   in the house of his servant David,
as he spoke by the mouth of his holy prophets from of old,
that we should be saved from our enemies
   and from the hand of all who hate us;
to show the mercy promised to our fathers
   and to remember his holy covenant,
the oath that he swore to our father Abraham, to grant us
   that we, being delivered from the hand of our enemies,
might serve him without fear,
   in holiness and righteousness before him all our days.
                                    (Luke 1:68–75)

Having established this conceptual framework, it comes as no surprise when Simeon prays like this on encountering the child:

Lord, now you are letting your servant depart in peace,
   according to your word;
for my eyes have seen your salvation
   that you have prepared in the presence of all peoples,
a light for revelation to the Gentiles,
   and for glory to your people Israel.
                                    (Luke 2:29–32)

Jesus' true identity is recognized by one who epitomizes faithful Israel – someone who has been 'waiting for the kingdom of God', which for Luke clearly entails 'calling on the name of Yahweh to deliver his people'. This is confirmed by the parallel account of the aged prophetess Anna, where prayer is mentioned in the narrative for the first time:

And there was a prophetess, Anna, the daughter of Phanuel, of the tribe of Asher. She was advanced in years, having lived with her husband seven years from when she was a virgin, and then as a widow until she was eighty-four. She did not depart from the temple, worshipping with fasting and prayer night and day. And coming up at that very hour she began to give thanks to God and to speak of him to all who were waiting for the redemption of Jerusalem. (Luke 2:36–38)

Again, given the wider context, the most natural reading of 2:37 is that Anna, like Simeon, was waiting – and praying – for God to come through for his people, remembering the promises to Abraham, Isaac and Jacob.

Right at the beginning of Luke's Gospel, then, the coming of Jesus is linked to faithful Israelites calling on the name of Yahweh to keep his promises, which he is now evidently doing before their very eyes. What is interesting, however, is that in Matthew's Gospel the infancy narratives contain no reference to prayer at all.

The absence of any of this material in Matthew's account of the birth of Jesus is quite surprising. As we will see, a substantial amount of space in the Gospel is devoted to Jesus' teaching on prayer, and yet there is no reference at all to prayer in the infancy narratives. Why might this be?[7] It is hard to say definitively, but it is probably the case that Matthew's sole intention in the opening chapters is to establish Jesus' identity as God's rescuing King. As a result, Matthew's presentation has a significantly narrower focus than that of Luke, presumably because Luke's purpose is to demonstrate that the coming of Jesus is the fulfilment of the Old Testament at multiple levels (including fulfilling the promises to the patriarchs and the promise of the Spirit).

The teaching of Jesus and prayer

Jesus' teaching on prayer is not as extensive as one might think. Apart from the Sermon on the Mount in Matthew (and/or the Sermon on the Plain in Luke), explicit discourse on prayer is limited to several virtually 'throwaway' statements, and a series of parables in Luke.[8]

---

[7] One of the drawbacks of commentaries is often a failure to answer intriguing questions arising from the *absence* of material rather than its presence – this is one of those occasions.

[8] These parables, as we will see in the next section, are trickier and less relevant to the question of prayer than might at first appear.

In Matthew's Gospel the two key passages on prayer come in 6:5–15 and 7:7–11. Again, I cannot here do justice to the richness of scholarship even on these two sections, nor offer a complete exegesis – my concern is simply to ask if (or how) these passages cohere with the understanding of prayer as 'calling on the name of Yahweh', which is ubiquitous in the Old Testament.

In the Sermon on the Mount Jesus' most famous utterance on prayer (the 'Lord's Prayer') is prefaced by a warning against showy, hypocritical public prayers:

> And when you pray, you must not be like the hypocrites. For they love to stand and pray in the synagogues and at the street corners, that they may be seen by others. Truly, I say to you, they have received their reward. But when you pray, go into your room and shut the door and pray to your Father who is in secret. And your Father who sees in secret will reward you.
>
> And when you pray, do not heap up empty phrases as the Gentiles do, for they think that they will be heard for their many words. Do not be like them, for your Father knows what you need before you ask him. (Matt. 6:5–8)

Perhaps reflecting on contemporary Jewish practice, inspired by Ecclesiastes 5:2,[9] Jesus insists that succinct, private prayers are to be the order of the day for his followers.[10] This is based on the omniscient generosity of God. However, to stop there would be to miss the key element in Jesus' teaching here – his deliberate linking of 'prayer' with 'reward' (*misthos*). What exactly is Jesus thinking of? In the context of the Sermon on the Mount 'reward' can mean only one thing (see Matt. 5:12, 46; 6:1–2, 4–6, 16, 18) – to enjoy the promised, covenantal blessings of God, or, to use a favourite Matthean phrase, to share in the kingdom of heaven.

When due weight is given to this, Jesus' teaching is seen to be remarkably similar to the pattern of much of the Old Testament. It is possible, according to Jesus as well as the prophets who went before him, to pray essentially orthodox prayers, but not to be heard (and thus, by extension, not to enjoy the blessings of the covenant) because of the 'noise' of one's life.

[9] See Bruner 2004: 289.

[10] There is obviously a myriad of discussions of this passage in the literature. For a concise explanation of the issues and force of Jesus' teaching see Carson 1995: 162–169; also France 2007: 231–241.

The continuity of Jesus' teaching with the Old Testament is confirmed instantly by the positive corollary offered in Matthew 6:9–13:

Pray then like this:

> 'Our Father in heaven,
> hallowed be your name.
> Your kingdom come,
> your will be done,
>> on earth as it is in heaven.
> Give us this day our daily bread,
> and forgive us our debts,
>> as we also have forgiven our debtors.
> And lead us not into temptation,
>> but deliver us from evil.'

N. T. Wright sums up his discussion of this passage by describing the Lord's Prayer as 'the heart of the New Covenant charter'.[11] Irrespective of whether or not his exegesis of the prayer is correct at every point, this statement surely takes us to the core of Jesus' concern. The very use of 'Father' language is both unique and suggestive of a new intimacy, which only the new covenant, adumbrated in for example Jeremiah 31:31–34, can bring.[12] This emphasis is only strengthened by the Ezekiel-like concern for the honour of the name of God (that it may be recognized as holy[13]).

Jesus then urges his disciples to pray:

> Your kingdom come,
> your will be done
>> on earth as it is in heaven.

The envisaged inbreaking of the eschatological rule of God[14] is to be understood as the ultimate fulfilment of all God's promises and

---

[11] Wright 2001: 147. For an excellent overview of this prayer see Crump 2006: 95–157.

[12] See Carson 1995: 169–170 for a succinct and helpful discussion. This of course is not built simply on Jesus' vocabulary, but on the much wider place of sonship in his teaching (see Crump 2013). Marshall (2001: 129) points out that the king in this kingdom is a father.

[13] Ezek. 36:21–23; 39:7. Wright (2001: 140–141) argues that the background to this statement is found in Exod. 3:13–16, but this is unpersuasive.

[14] See O'Donnell 2013: 168. Also Wright 1997: 24–25.

creative purposes. In other words to pray for the 'kingdom' to come is the ultimate extension of 'calling on the name of Yahweh':

> All three [requests] are primarily a plea that God will act so decisively in judgment and salvation that his glory will be unveiled, and all (as a result) enabled to see him as the holy, almighty King he truly is. It is thus a prayer for the End, for the consummation of the kingdom of God, and for the bringing into being of the new earth and the heavens that the End entails.[15]

It is also argued by some that the remaining petitions in the prayer – for the provision of 'daily bread', the forgiveness of 'debts', strengthening in temptation and the (ultimate) defeat of evil – are also 'eschatological' prayers. The tricky phrase 'daily bread' (*ton epiousion dos hēmin sēmeron*) is understood as 'the bread we will receive on the Day' (and therefore a participation in the eschatological messianic feast). Similarly, forgiveness is end-time forgiveness, and the prayer concerning temptation either seeks strength to continue in faithfulness until the last day, or, according to Wright,[16] is dealing with our testing of God. (For Wright these ideas all reflect the new exodus paradigm that shapes the whole prayer.) This reading would further strengthen the case presented here, but interpreters are still divided on this approach, and on balance a more literal reading of the prayer is to be preferred.[17]

Jesus then returns to the subject of 'asking' in Matthew 7:7–11.[18] While it is not made explicit that Jesus is speaking about prayer, there is no other satisfactory explanation:

> Ask, and it will be given to you; seek, and you will find; knock, and it will be opened to you. For everyone who asks receives, and the one who seeks finds, and to the one who knocks it will be opened. Or which one of you, if his son asks him for bread, will give him a stone? Or if he asks for a fish, will give him a serpent? If you then, who are evil, know how to give good gifts to your children, how much more will your Father who is in heaven give good things to those who ask him!

---

[15] Turner 1990: 65.
[16] Wright 2001: 145.
[17] See the judicious treatment of France (2007: 241–254).
[18] The parallel passage in Luke 11 also makes the link to prayer explicit.

CALLING ON THE NAME OF THE LORD

As with the 'reward' promised in chapter 6, the trickiest exegetical issue in this section concerns what Jesus' followers are to ask *for*. Once again, the context yields the answer fairly easily.

The reference to 'dogs' and 'pigs' trampling truth underfoot in 7:6 grounds the injunctions of 7:7–11 in the overwhelming concern of the sermon that Jesus' followers should choose his way rather than that of the 'hypocrites' (which is further expounded as the section moves to a close in terms of entering by the right gate, eating from the right tree and building on the right foundation). The 'asking' in view here, then, is most naturally understood as asking God to pour out what he has promised *through Jesus*. One could summarize it as asking to be welcomed into the kingdom and to be included in the blessings of the new covenant. There seems to be strong continuity between Jesus' teaching on prayer and what we have seen up to this point.

Even though no sustained attention is paid to prayer in the remainder of the Gospel, towards the end of Matthew's writing are several short (but nonetheless important) passages in which Jesus appears to address the subject of prayer. The first is the oft-quoted assurance of Jesus' presence when 'two or three are gathered': 'Again I say to you, if two of you agree on earth about anything they ask, it will be done for them by my Father in heaven. For where two or three are gathered in my name, there am I among them' (Matt. 18:19–20). There is some suggestion that these verses break the flow of the argument from the previous section,[19] but it is more natural to take these statements on prayer in the context of the actions recommended in verses 15–18. This means that, rather than a general statement about the involvement of Jesus in small-group prayer, it is an assurance that prayers for wisdom by those involved in 'discipline' will be heard and answered by Yahweh. And why is this so? Such prayers can be prayed with confidence on the grounds that 'where two or three are gathered in my name, there am I among them'. The Lord Jesus, it seems, maintains that he is present and involved in the proper exercise of discipline in the 'gathering' that is his church.

This means that, on the one hand, it does not seem that Jesus is saying anything about the value of prayer meetings, or reassuring the hardy few that they need not be discouraged by the poor turn out.

[19] E.g. Leon Morris (1992: 469) states unequivocally that this is a fresh section not linked to what has gone before, but on balance it is better to see what Jesus says as an extension of the discussion of what could be loosely called 'church discipline'; see also O'Donnell 2013: 509–519; France 1985: 274–276.

174

But on the other, Jesus is saying that prayers that cry to Yahweh for the good of his church at key moments can be offered secure in the knowledge that God will answer, presumably because he has already made it clear that he is committed to protecting and growing his people.

This leads neatly on to the second passage where Jesus alludes to prayer. It turns out that he repeats the same point:

> In the morning, as he was returning to the city, he became hungry. And seeing a fig tree by the wayside, he went to it and found nothing on it but only leaves. And he said to it, 'May no fruit ever come from you again!' And the fig tree withered at once.
>
> When the disciples saw it, they marvelled, saying, 'How did the fig tree wither at once?' And Jesus answered them, 'Truly, I say to you, if you have faith and do not doubt, you will not only do what has been done to the fig tree, but even if you say to this mountain, "Be taken up and thrown into the sea", it will happen. And whatever you ask in prayer, you will receive, if you have faith.' (Matt. 21:18–22)

This is one of the most hotly disputed passages in Matthew's Gospel. It is not even agreed, for example, whether verse 21 is simply colourful language (a play on the universally common phrase 'moving mountains') or a direct citation of an Old Testament text (usually Zech. 14:4).[20] But that need not divert us, because the points of verse 21 and then the ensuing statement of verse 22 are quite clear. Jesus seems to be drawing on Micah 7 in this symbolic action, and making the point that Israel, God's chosen one, has chosen the path of curse, rather than blessing. However, now that the kingdom has arrived, the disciples' association with Jesus the King will mean that they will be an intrinsic part of God's realizing his promises, both in blessing and curse in the world. Jesus' teaching on prayer here, then (which, admittedly, is not the central concern of the unit), continues to reflect the same concerns. Prayer in Matthew is linked to God's continuing to bring to fruition his plans for his people and universe.[21]

---

[20] See the helpful discussion of Crump (2006: 31–33).
[21] The other reference to prayer in Matthew comes in the temple discourse of Matt. 24:15–20: 'So when you see the abomination of desolation spoken of by the prophet Daniel, standing in the holy place (let the reader understand), then let those who are in Judea flee to the mountains. Let the one who is on the housetop not go down to take what is in his house, and let the one who is in the field not turn back to take his cloak.

Andrew Lincoln sums up the burden of Jesus' teaching on prayer helpfully:

> Prayer, then, is one of the primary means for co-operation in God's mission in the world. And requests supporting the essentials of Jesus' prayer will be answered because they conform to God's purposes for this world in making known the divine name through Jesus.[22]

While Jesus' teaching on prayer is not entirely without innovation, it shares and builds on the fundamental Old Testament framework I have highlighted.

Is this contention supported by the other Gospels? It seems so. There is very limited teaching material on prayer in Mark, but the single instance does seem to cohere well with such an understanding. It comes in the context of Jesus' inner circle failing to cast out a spirit from a boy, whose father memorably announced, 'I believe; help my unbelief!' (Mark 9:24). The climax to this narrative comes in Mark 9:28–29: 'And when he had entered the house, his disciples asked him privately, "Why could we not cast it out?" And he said to them, "*This kind cannot be driven out by anything but prayer.*"'[23] A myriad of possibilities has been advanced to account for this statement.[24]

For some the issue is fairly simple – the disciples' method of exorcism proves deficient. Jesus' instruction is, then, a simple rebuke; and in future when they come up against this particularly tough kind of evil spirit, they will need to pray (with the unfortunate implication that for common or garden exorcisms they can simply use their new-found special powers). However, nothing in Mark's Gospel (or anywhere else for that matter) implies that some 'works' can be performed 'solo' while others require additional help from Yahweh. Despite attempts to argue to the contrary, it does seem that the key

---

(footnote 21 *cont.*)
And alas for women who are pregnant and for those who are nursing infants in those days! *Pray that your flight may not be in winter or on a Sabbath.*' This is a little unusual, in that it is a prayer for safety in the middle of turmoil. Yet even here the context is that of a definitive moment in salvation history, which imbues this desperate prayer with a certain theological weight. With most commentators I hold that the original version of Matt. 17:14–21 did not contain any reference to prayer.

[22] Lincoln 2001: 177.

[23] For a helpful discussion of possible ways to interpret this verse see Gundry 1993: 492–493.

[24] See Crump 2006: 40–53.

PRAYER IN THE GOSPELS

to understanding the passage comes in the phrase 'this kind' (*touto to genos*). The only distinguishing feature of 'this kind' of spirit is that it made the boy both deaf and mute. It is possible, then, that, drawing on passages like Isaiah 35:1–6, Jesus understands the significance of this particular kind of evil spirit as mounting a direct assault on the messianic mission.[25] If this is so, then the reference to prayer here is entirely comprehensible (and perhaps even to be expected), as from the beginning the realization of God's purposes on earth has been linked to his people calling on him in prayer.

A similar association of ideas is visible in Luke's Gospel, when the following statement of Jesus is recorded: 'But I say to you who hear, Love your enemies, do good to those who hate you, bless those who curse you, pray for those who abuse you' (Luke 6:27–28). The language of blessing and curse, so closely associated with the idea of prayer (in this case praying for 'enemies'), deliberately encourages followers of Jesus to act in a way that may lead to the opponent's being 'won over', and so, ideally, to experience the blessing of being part of the kingdom rather than the curse of being excluded from it. To pray for those who abuse, then, could be construed as an example of calling on the name of the Lord.

The Lucan version of the Lord's Prayer is slightly shorter than the Matthean equivalent, but there is not a significant difference in emphasis.[26] However, Jesus' exposition of the principles undergirding prayer is much longer in Luke 11 than in Matthew 7:7–11, and ends with a completely different reassurance:

> And he said to them, 'Which of you who has a friend will go to him at midnight and say to him, "Friend, lend me three loaves, for a friend of mine has arrived on a journey, and I have nothing to set before him"; and he will answer from within, "Do not bother me; the door is now shut, and my children are with me in bed. I cannot get up and give you anything"? I tell you, though he will not get up and give him anything because he is his friend, yet because of his impudence he will rise and give him whatever he needs. And I tell you, ask, and it will be given to you; seek, and you will find; knock, and it will be opened to you. For everyone who asks receives, and the one who seeks finds, and to the one who knocks it will be opened. What father among you, if his son asks for a fish, will

---

[25] Admittedly, this idea finds little support in the literature.
[26] See Crump 2013: 687–689.

instead of a fish give him a serpent; or if he asks for an egg, will give him a scorpion? If you then, who are evil, know how to give good gifts to your children, how much more will the heavenly Father give the *Holy Spirit* to those who ask him!' (Luke 11:5–13)

The story of the reluctant friend,[27] despite giving rise to plenty of confusion and not a few slightly bizarre interpretations over the years,[28] is straightforward. Social convention in the first century demanded that a neighbour got out of bed quickly to offer the help a friend needed. The humour in the story is based on the reluctance of the friend to get out of bed. And Jesus' point? *If even a terrible friend like this responds to requests from a neighbour, how much more readily can we expect God to answer us when we ask him?*[29] This, of course, does beg the question what are we to ask God for? Jesus' answer in Luke is simple – we are to ask the heavenly Father *for the Holy Spirit*. This is clearly a new covenant kind of prayer. It confirms that for Jesus in Luke prayer is essentially calling on the name of Yahweh. This is borne out in Jesus' parables that deal with prayer, to which we will return in a moment.

Before moving on, however, we need to take some time to examine the apostle John's perspective on Jesus' teaching on prayer.

As one might expect, Jesus' emphasis appears to be slightly different in the Johannine material on prayer, which is contained within the Farewell Discourse. The first passage we need to consider is John 14:8–14:

Philip said to him, 'Lord, show us the Father, and it is enough for us.' Jesus said to him, 'Have I been with you so long, and you still do not know me, Philip? Whoever has seen me has seen the Father. How can you say, "Show us the Father"? Do you not believe that I am in the Father and the Father is in me? The words that I say to you I do not speak on my own authority, but the Father who dwells in me does his works. Believe me that I am in the Father and the Father is in me, or else believe on account of the works themselves.

---

[27] There is some discussion over whether or not this is, in fact, a parable. Lenski (1946: 625) calls it an illustration, but does not give much discussion. Marshall (1978: 465) refers to two 'sayings'. As the story lacks many of the formal features of parables in Luke, it seems better simply to take this as a developed narrative illustration.

[28] See e.g. Metzger 2010: 33–57.

[29] Crump (2006: 64–76) provides a balanced discussion of this unit.

'Truly, truly, I say to you, whoever believes in me will also do the works that I do; and greater works than these will he do, because I am going to the Father. *Whatever you ask in my name, this I will do, that the Father may be glorified in the Son. If you ask me for anything in my name, I will do it.*'

The double reassurance that *whatever is asked in Jesus' name* will be granted is quite remarkable.[30] But the content of this guarantee is clearly defined by the context. Jesus' discussion with Philip concerns Jesus' revelation of his Father (which, according to Jer. 31:34, is a key part of the blessing of the new covenant). Philip is gently rebuked by Jesus for his inability to grasp the purpose of Jesus' coming or the goal of his ministry to date. However, Jesus goes straight on to announce that whoever believes in him will do the works that he does and will go on to do greater works still. It is to this end that people are to ask anything in his name.

So what are these works?[31] From the beginning of the Gospel of John Jesus has made it clear that 'My food is to do the will of him who sent me and to accomplish his work' (John 4:34). This work is nothing more and nothing less than to accomplish what God has already committed to doing in the Old Testament, which is to bring about the fulfilment of the promise of Genesis 3:15. In what sense can the works of the followers be greater than those of the master? Presumably, they will be in a position to do 'greater works' because they are able to point back to what Jesus has accomplished in his death and resurrection.[32]

This raises a fascinating suggestion – it seems that 'praying in the name of Jesus' is the New Testament equivalent of 'calling on the name of the Lord'. In both cases prayer is construed as asking God to do what he has promised – in the Old Testament to send the Messiah and establish his kingdom; in the New Testament to continue to build the church of the Lord Jesus Christ until he returns.[33]

This perspective is confirmed in the next chapter: 'You did not choose me, but I chose you and appointed you that you should go

[30] Although, there are obvious similarities with much of the Matthean material on prayer.

[31] See John 4:34; 5:17; 10:25, 37; 14:10; 15:24.

[32] Barrett 1978: 460; Carson 1991: 496; Köstenberger 2004: 433. Bruce (1983: 300) and Morris (1995: 574) hold that 'greater works' makes reference to the larger influence of Jesus' followers in terms of number of people and geography.

[33] Typically, writers pay very little heed to any OT background to this idea; see e.g. the otherwise excellent discussion of Crump (2006: 164–169).

and bear fruit and that your fruit should abide, so that whatever you ask the Father in my name, he may give it to you' (John 15:16). In the context of John 15 the 'fruit' envisaged is people being added to the covenant family of God. Jesus' followers are to 'ask the Father in Jesus' name' to do precisely what he has already promised. They are to call on the name of the Lord, the striking development being that they now know the name of the Lord to be 'Jesus Christ'.

Similarly in chapter 16 Jesus confirms that when he speaks of prayer, he does so from the perspective of asking God to keep his promises in a fallen world:

> In that day you will ask nothing of me. Truly, truly, I say to you, whatever you ask of the Father in my name, he will give it to you. Until now you have asked nothing in my name. Ask, and you will receive, that your joy may be full.
>
> I have said these things to you in figures of speech. The hour is coming when I will no longer speak to you in figures of speech but will tell you plainly about the Father. In that day you will ask in my name, and I do not say to you that I will ask the Father on your behalf; for the Father himself loves you, because you have loved me and have believed that I came from God. (John 16:23–27)

For Jesus, to pray in his name is to ask the Father to do what he has already promised (in the case of 16:24 a promise Jesus himself has just made in 15:11).

The theological richness of this vein of thought runs right through the most important passage on prayer in the Gospels – Jesus' long recorded prayer in John 17. While this is clearly quite different from any other prayer in the Gospels, the theological underpinnings remain the same.[34]

In the first section of the so-called High Priestly Prayer Jesus' focus is firmly on the purpose and completion of his mission. This mission was not only planned and initiated by the Father but will result in the Father's being glorified:

---

[34] As this recorded prayer is technically a prayer of Jesus rather than a straight-forward 'teaching exercise' (like the Lord's Prayer), one could discuss this under the section 'The life of Jesus and prayer' below. However, given the uniqueness of the prayer, and its teaching role in John's Gospel, it is equally appropriate to discuss it in the context of Jesus' explicit teaching on prayer.

When Jesus had spoken these words, he lifted up his eyes to heaven, and said, 'Father, the hour has come; glorify your Son that the Son may glorify you, since you have given him authority over all flesh, to give eternal life to all whom you have given him. And this is eternal life, that they know you the only true God, and Jesus Christ whom you have sent. I glorified you on earth, having accomplished the work that you gave me to do. And now, Father, glorify me in your own presence with the glory that I had with you before the world existed.' (John 17:1–5)

The terms in which the work of Jesus are described here are different to anything else we have seen, but, theologically speaking, Jesus is simply doing what he, standing on the shoulders of many who have gone before, does repeatedly in the Gospels – he is calling on his Father to complete what he has started; in this case the work of salvation viewed from the divine perspective.

The emphasis on the work of the Son as fulfilling both the promises and intentions of the Father continues unabated throughout the next section of the prayer:

I have manifested your name to the people whom you gave me out of the world. Yours they were, and you gave them to me, and they have kept your word. Now they know that everything that you have given me is from you. For I have given them the words that you gave me, and they have received them and have come to know in truth that I came from you; and they have believed that you sent me. (John 17:6–8)

It is, however, when Jesus begins to pray specifically for his 'own' that it becomes undeniable that his concern for them centres on God's fulfilling his purposes in and for them:

I am praying for them. I am not praying for the world but for those whom you have given me, for they are yours. . . . Holy Father, keep them in your name, which you have given me, that they may be one, even as we are one. While I was with them, I kept them in your name, which you have given me. I have guarded them, and not one of them has been lost except the son of destruction, that the Scripture might be fulfilled. But now I am coming to you, and these things I speak in the world, that they may have my joy fulfilled in themselves. . . . Sanctify them in the truth; your word is truth. As

181

you sent me into the world, so I have sent them into the world. (John 17:9, 11–13, 17–18)[35]

Obviously, it would take a much larger study to begin to unpack the full implications of this prayer.[36] For our purposes, however, it is sufficient simply to highlight the fact that Jesus' prayer here dovetails beautifully with the concerns so apparent in the other Gospels and in the Old Testament before that. It is highly appropriate, and consonant with all we have seen, that Jesus' longest and richest recorded prayer focuses on 'the work of the gospel' – it is a thoroughly salvation-historically motivated cry to his Father to continue to work out his purposes through Jesus.

If we need confirmation of this, then the closing verses of the prayer provide it. In John 17:20–23 Jesus prays for the continuation of this great covenantal work by praying for those who in the future will believe:

I do not ask for these only, but also for those who will believe in me through their word, that they may all be one, just as you, Father, are in me, and I in you, that they also may be in us, so that the world may believe that you have sent me. The glory that you have given me I have given to them, that they may be one even as we are one, I in them and you in me, that they may become perfectly one, so that the world may know that you sent me and loved them even as you loved me. (John 17:20–23)

His concern here is not for unity per se but rather that those who will hear the word of the apostles in future will be caught up in the sweeping work of God, which finds its fulfilment not in visible unity on earth but in the perfected unity of God and his reconciled people, presumably in the renewed universe.[37]

This, in turn, is underlined by the closing stanza:

Father, I desire that they also, whom you have given me, may be with me where I am, to see my glory that you have given me because you loved me before the foundation of the world. O righteous

---

[35] For a nuanced account of the full import of these verses see Köstenberger 2008: 166–179.

[36] Even at a non-technical level it would take several volumes to even approach doing justice to this chapter (see Lloyd-Jones 2000; Boice 1975).

[37] See Köstenberger 2004: 497–498; Barrett 1978: 512; Carson 1991: 568.

Father, even though the world does not know you, I know you, and these know that you have sent me. I made known to them your name, and I will continue to make it known, that the love with which you have loved me may be in them, and I in them. (John 17:24–26)

As is usual in John, there is an emphasis on the 'name', which, as I have argued, is a strong link to the Old Testament tradition of calling on the name of the Lord. This means that Jesus in effect both models 'calling on the name of Yahweh' and reconfigures it, as with his Father the Son answers the prayers of the saints, making it possible for God's people to know the God of the covenant in previously unimagined ways through Jesus' death and resurrection.

On examining Jesus' explicit teaching on prayer across the Gospels, it is impossible to miss the consistency in the biblical witness. Whether in his own extended prayer or in engaging with his disciples, prayer for Jesus is inextricably bound up with the work of God in the world. To pray is, at heart, to ask God to do what he has promised.

That is not to say, however, that Jesus simply adopts some ancient patterns and passes them on unaltered. By encouraging his disciples to pray specifically to God as 'Abba', thus joining in his filial conversations, Jesus' model of 'new covenant' prayer is more intimate than anything previously envisaged. He also makes the bold step of inviting his followers to pray 'in his name', rather than simply 'calling on the name of Yahweh'. This unthinkable development is an important step in the first disciples coming to the point where they recognize Jesus Christ as God incarnate.

The parables of Jesus and prayer

At this point it is helpful to examine briefly Jesus' teaching on prayer (or touching on prayer) in the parables of Luke.

It is often stated that Luke has a particular interest in prayer, and that his parables show this.[38] However, on closer inspection, prayer is an explicit theme in very few of the parables. One could argue that the parable of the two sons in Luke 15 has powerful implications for the way in which we pray (particularly in repentance), but *within the parable itself no one prays*. Similarly, the parable of the rich man and

[38] Turner (1990: 58) notes that there are three additional parables on prayer in Matthew. See also O'Brien 1973: 118–119.

Lazarus, which often causes all kinds of theological problems with its imaginary *post mortem* conversations, has little bearing on the nature or practice of biblical prayer. The exceptions are the two parables that occur back to back in Luke 18.

In an unusually explicit piece of editorial Luke explains the purpose of the parable of the unjust judge or persistent widow like this: 'And he told them a parable to the effect that they ought always to pray and not lose heart' (Luke 18:1). Luke's wording is interesting – Jesus clearly tells the parable to ensure that people keep praying in a particular way for the long haul. But how are they to pray? The parable explains:

> He said, 'In a certain city there was a judge who neither feared God nor respected man. And there was a widow in that city who kept coming to him and saying, "Give me justice against my adversary." For a while he refused, but afterwards he said to himself, "Though I neither fear God nor respect man, yet because this widow keeps bothering me, I will give her justice, so that she will not beat me down by her continual coming."' And the Lord said, 'Hear what the unrighteous judge says. And will not God give justice to his elect, who cry to him day and night? Will he delay long over them? I tell you, he will give justice to them speedily. Nevertheless, when the Son of Man comes, will he find faith on earth?' (Luke 18:2–8)

Jesus presents a simple contrast between the unjust judge, who gives justice simply because he is worn down by the widow's pleas, and the one and only God, who will readily and swiftly give justice to his people in due time. And the point? *Keep calling out to God, asking him to do exactly what he has promised.* This parable is, in essence, an exposition of the Old Testament view of prayer.

The second parable in Luke 18, while not focusing on prayer, does provide some insight into Jesus' view of what real prayer involves. In this case Jesus expounds on what it means to 'call on the name of the Lord':

> He also told this parable to some who trusted in themselves that they were righteous, and treated others with contempt: 'Two men went up into the temple to pray, one a Pharisee and the other a tax collector. The Pharisee, standing by himself, prayed thus: "God, I thank you that I am not like other men, extortioners, unjust, adulterers, or even like this tax collector. I fast twice a week; I give

tithes of all that I get." But the tax collector, standing far off, would not even lift up his eyes to heaven, but beat his breast, saying, "God, be merciful to me, a sinner!" I tell you, this man went down to his house justified, rather than the other. For everyone who exalts himself will be humbled, but the one who humbles himself will be exalted.' (Luke 18:9–14)

Jesus' point is not complex – to *pray* is to accept the fact that one cannot help oneself, has no grounds for boasting and has no other hope but to call on the name of the Lord who has promised to be merciful. This is the only kind of prayer that will be heard.

Luke 18 demonstrates that Jesus' view of prayer as reflected in his teaching is built squarely on the Old Testament. In particular Jesus likens the Pharisees to the people of Israel, whose prayers were not heard because of their arrogance and self-reliance. He also encourages his contemporaries to keep praying, confident in the knowledge that God keeps his promises and will act to vindicate his people. This, for Jesus, as for the Old Testament, is what it means to pray.

The life of Jesus and prayer

The final piece of the 'puzzle' that is the view of prayer in the Gospels is Jesus' own commitment to prayer. It quickly becomes obvious that for both Jesus and the Gospel writers prayer is not simply a pious practice followed by Jesus as an observant Jew. Prayer is a vital part of Jesus' fulfilling his mission, as Jesus himself *calls on the name of Yahweh.*

It is often noted that Jesus regularly makes times to pray, usually alone.[39] On occasion this seems to be an opportunity for spiritual 'recovery' after dramatic events. So, for example, Jesus goes off to pray after the initial launch of his mission (Mark 1:35; Luke 4:42), after feeding the five thousand (Matt. 14:23; Mark 6:46; Luke 9:18) and after the initial forays of the 'seventy-two' (Luke 10:1). Luke 5:15–16 provides a summary statement of this practice: 'But now even more the report about him went abroad, and great crowds gathered to hear him and to be healed of their infirmities. But he would withdraw to desolate places and pray.'

What is commented on less frequently, however, is the way in which the Gospels very clearly underline the fact that Jesus prays *at key points in his mission.*

[39] See Turner 1990: 60–64.

When the Father authenticates Jesus' ministry at his baptism, Luke states that the voice from heaven is heard while Jesus is praying:

> Now when all the people were baptized, and when Jesus also had been baptized and was praying, the heavens were opened, and the Holy Spirit descended on him in bodily form, like a dove; and a voice came from heaven, 'You are my beloved Son; with you I am well pleased.' (Luke 3:21–22)

Before he chooses the disciples, Jesus spends the whole night in prayer: 'In these days he went out to the mountain to pray, and all night he continued in prayer to God. And when day came, he called his disciples and chose from them twelve, whom he named apostles' (Luke 6:12–13). Similarly, at the transfiguration while Jesus is praying his true nature is revealed: 'Now about eight days after these sayings he took with him Peter and John and James and went up on the mountain to pray. And as he was praying, the appearance of his face was altered, and his clothing became dazzling white' (Luke 9:28–29).[40]

It is interesting that John only records Jesus' praying once before the Farewell Discourse:

> And Jesus lifted up his eyes and said, 'Father, I thank you that you have heard me. I knew that you always hear me, but I said this on account of the people standing around, that they may believe that you sent me.' When he had said these things, he cried out with a loud voice, 'Lazarus, come out.' The man who had died came out, his hands and feet bound with linen strips, and his face wrapped with a cloth. Jesus said to them, 'Unbind him, and let him go.' (John 11:41–44)

As Jesus performs his most powerful sign yet, preparing us for the ultimate sign of his death and resurrection, John deliberately ties this action to Jesus' prior request to God to defeat death.

For Jesus there seems to be an integral link between fulfilling his mission and prayer. At each turning point of his ministry he takes time to ask his Father to work. This is more than an example of piety – it is a recognition that the work of the gospel begins with 'calling on the name of the Lord'.

---

[40] Neither Matthew nor Mark includes the fact that Jesus was praying.

It is no accident that virtually all of the recorded prayers of Jesus (rather than a simple mention of the *fact* that he prayed) come at significant moments in the progress of his mission. Jesus is recorded as praying for his disciples as they begin to join him in proclaiming the good news of the kingdom, and for others to join in this task:

> When he saw the crowds, he had compassion for them, because they were harassed and helpless, like sheep without a shepherd. Then he said to his disciples, 'The harvest is plentiful, but the labourers are few; therefore pray earnestly to the Lord of the harvest to send out labourers into his harvest.' (Matt. 9:36–38)

He also gives thanks when people grasp the message of the kingdom: 'At that time Jesus declared, "I thank you, Father, Lord of heaven and earth, that you have hidden these things from the wise and understanding and revealed them to little children; yes, Father, for such was your gracious will"' (Matt. 11:25–26; see also Luke 10:21). But it is as we approach the crucifixion that the connection between Jesus' mission and prayer becomes unmissable.

All four Gospels highlight the fact that Jesus prayed intensely before the onset of the events that would lead to his death:

> Then Jesus went with them to a place called Gethsemane, and he said to his disciples, 'Sit here, while I go over there and pray.' And taking with him Peter and the two sons of Zebedee, he began to be sorrowful and troubled. Then he said to them, 'My soul is very sorrowful, even to death; remain here, and watch with me.' And going a little farther he fell on his face and prayed, saying, 'My Father, if it be possible, let this cup pass from me; nevertheless, not as I will, but as you will.' And he came to the disciples and found them sleeping. And he said to Peter, 'So, could you not watch with me one hour? Watch and pray that you may not enter into temptation. The spirit indeed is willing, but the flesh is weak.' Again, for the second time, he went away and prayed, 'My Father, if this cannot pass unless I drink it, your will be done.' And again he came and found them sleeping, for their eyes were heavy. So, leaving them again, he went away and prayed for the third time, saying the same words again. Then he came to the disciples and said to them, 'Sleep and take your rest later on. See, the hour is at hand, and the Son of Man is betrayed into the hands of sinners. Rise, let us be going; see, my betrayer is at hand.' (Matt. 26:36–46; see also Mark 14:32–42)

And he came out and went, as was his custom, to the Mount of Olives, and the disciples followed him. And when he came to the place, he said to them, 'Pray that you may not enter into temptation.' And he withdrew from them about a stone's throw, and knelt down and prayed, saying, 'Father, if you are willing, remove this cup from me. Nevertheless, not my will, but yours, be done.' And there appeared to him an angel from heaven, strengthening him. And being in an agony he prayed more earnestly; and his sweat became like great drops of blood falling down to the ground. And when he rose from prayer, he came to the disciples and found them sleeping for sorrow, and he said to them, 'Why are you sleeping? Rise and pray that you may not enter into temptation.' (Luke 22:39–46)

While the Matthean/Marcan account differs slightly in some details from the Lucan version, the prayer of Jesus varies only very slightly in wording. The prayer Jesus prays (which incidentally adds substantial weight to my interpretation of the Lord's Prayer as asking God to establish the new covenant) focuses squarely on the fulfilment of the mission adumbrated in the Old Testament. Jesus knows it now falls to him to drain the cup of God's wrath through his substitutionary death. His prayer is a request to God to ask his Father to enable him to carry out the unspeakable task before him, *so that the promises of God may be fulfilled.*[41]

Exactly the same perspective is reflected in Jesus' prayer in John 12:27–28:

'Now is my soul troubled. And what shall I say? "Father, save me from this hour"? But for this purpose I have come to this hour. Father, glorify your name.' Then a voice came from heaven: 'I have glorified it, and I will glorify it again.'

This prayer, prayed earlier in the piece, uses different vocabulary to portray the same reality. Jesus is asking his Father to glorify his name (calling on the name of Yahweh), by enacting his plans. This is the focus of Jesus' prayers in the run-up to his death. And he maintains that focus even during his execution.

[41] This perspective also shapes the way Jesus prays for Simon Peter in Luke 22:31–32: 'Simon, Simon, behold, Satan demanded to have you, that he might sift you like wheat, but I have prayed for you that your faith may not fail. And when you have turned again, strengthen your brothers.'

Each of the Synoptics records prayers uttered by Jesus from the cross:

> And about the ninth hour Jesus cried out with a loud voice, saying, 'Eli, Eli, lema sabachthani?' that is, 'My God, my God, why have you forsaken me?' . . . And Jesus cried out again with a loud voice and yielded up his spirit. (Matt. 27:46, 50; see also Mark 15:34, 37)

> And when they came to the place that is called The Skull, there they crucified him, and the criminals, one on his right and one on his left. And Jesus said, 'Father, forgive them, for they know not what they do.' . . . Then Jesus, calling out with a loud voice, said, 'Father, into your hands I commit my spirit!' And having said this he breathed his last. (Luke 23:33–34, 46)

Jesus' prayers – whether drawn from Psalm 22, or crying to the God of mercy to forgive, the defiant 'Into your hands I commit my spirit' and even the inchoate shout of Matthew 27:50 – all share one thing: they are focused on his mission. His prayers are not for himself. Right to the end he continues to call on the name of the Lord, not to deliver him, but to work out his purposes through him. Jesus' prayers offer a vibrant and moving example of the biblical theology of prayer I have been tracing through this book.

Chapter Seven

The church at prayer: prayer in the book of Acts

We have seen that in the Gospels Jesus affirms the Old Testament understanding of prayer – calling out to Yahweh to come through on his covenant promises. At the start of the New Testament Jesus also insists that he transforms prayer. Part of the answer to the prayers of the Old Testament saints is that One comes who invites to us pray 'Abba Father' with him – to pray in *his* name. So the Gospels urge us to pray to the Father in the name of Jesus to build his kingdom. But is this the dominant understanding of prayer all through the New Testament? Is this played out in the life of the early church? We turn first to the book of Acts.[1]

Prayer in Jerusalem

In the immediate aftermath of Jesus' death and resurrection one of the things that dominates the life of the new community of Jesus' followers is prayer. Luke describes the scene after the ascension in Acts 1 like this:

> Then they returned to Jerusalem from the mount called Olivet, which is near Jerusalem, a Sabbath day's journey away. And when they had entered, they went up to the upper room, where they were staying, Peter and John and James and Andrew, Philip and Thomas, Bartholomew and Matthew, James the son of Alphaeus and Simon the Zealot and Judas the son of James. All these with one accord were devoting themselves to prayer, together with the women and Mary the mother of Jesus, and his brothers. (Acts 1:12–14)

It would be easy to pass over this as a routinely pious description of the life of an emergent religious community, but there is surely something more to this. In Luke's Gospel, as we have already seen, prayer is not simply a general expression of dependence on God.

[1] Peter O'Brien (1973) provides an excellent brief overview of the subject.

To pray is to call on God to advance his agenda and deliver on his promises. That is surely the sense here. This is supported both by what the disciples do and the language Luke uses.

For first-century Jews who have been convinced by Jesus' death and resurrection that the Messiah has come, and have heard him announce that the kingdom has arrived, it is compellingly obvious that God is in the process of building a 'new Israel' from the remnant of his people.[2] That is why they put such importance on finding a replacement for Judas – only when they are 'twelve' does the new Israel symbolism work.[3]

After identifying two suitable candidates who have witnessed the events of Jesus' death and resurrection, Luke tells us:

> And they prayed and said, 'You, Lord, who know the hearts of all, show which one of these two you have chosen to take the place in this ministry and apostleship from which Judas turned aside to go to his own place.' And they cast lots for them, and the lot fell on Matthias, and he was numbered with the eleven apostles. (Acts 1:24–26)

As Jesus did, from the outset, the apostles are keen to pray for help at key moments in the life of the incipient church family in Jerusalem.

This is probably reflected in the summary statement concerning the post-Pentecost church in Acts 2:42 'And they devoted themselves to the apostles' teaching and the fellowship, to the breaking of bread *and the prayers*.'[4] 'The prayers' may refer to the times of set temple prayer[5] or to a more general commitment to prayer.[6] If the latter is in view, it is likely, as in chapter 1, that the prayer Luke has in mind concerns the inbreaking of the kingdom in Jesus Christ. The first

---

[2] Making statements like this instantly poses some massive theological questions. Did the first Christians see themselves as the new Israel *replacing* ethnic Israel? Was the new Israel for everyone or just for Jews? And so on. I strongly suspect that at this point in the narrative the disciples themselves have not got that one worked out, so it is unwise for us to expend huge amounts of energy trying to resolve it here.

[3] This goes some way to explaining both the fact that Matthias fades out of the narrative as soon as he enters, and the use of 'lots': they can select one 'randomly' because (1) there is nothing between the two candidates, for either of them would have done, and (2) the purpose of the appointment is not primarily personal but *symbolic*. What matters is that 'number twelve' (whoever he is) is added as soon as possible.

[4] The phrase is *kai tais proseuchais*.

[5] This finds some support in 3:1 (although the reference is not decisive). See Peterson 2009: 162.

[6] Keener 2012: 1011; Schnabel 2012: 180.

recorded prayer in the life of the Jerusalem church goes some way to confirming this.

After Peter and John are released by the Sanhedrin in the wake of the healing of the lame man in the temple courts, Luke describes how the church

> lifted their voices together to God and said, 'Sovereign Lord, who made the heaven and the earth and the sea and everything in them, who through the mouth of our father David, your servant, said by the Holy Spirit,
>
> > "Why did the Gentiles rage,
> >   and the peoples plot in vain?
> > The kings of the earth set themselves,
> >   and the rulers were gathered together,
> >   against the Lord and against his Anointed" –
>
> for truly in this city there were gathered together against your holy servant Jesus, whom you anointed, both Herod and Pontius Pilate, along with the Gentiles and the peoples of Israel, to do whatever your hand and your plan had predestined to take place.' (Acts 4:24–28)

The main observation to make is that this initial prayer of the Jerusalem church focuses on *God himself working out his plans*.[7] Psalm 2 is the lens through which the early church views this encounter with the Jewish authorities. As a result, their prayer is framed by the conviction that the events surrounding Jesus' death and resurrection were ordained by God himself. This, then, means that everything else they pray for is conditioned by the fact that God is continuing to work out his purposes. That becomes plain in Acts 4:29–30:

> And now, Lord, look upon their threats and grant to your servants to continue to speak your word with all boldness, while you stretch out your hand to heal, and signs and wonders are performed through the name of your holy servant Jesus.

In this prayer the earliest church continues to 'call on the name of the Lord' to act in power, revealing Jesus through the eyewitness message

---

[7] E.g. Crump 2006: 183.

of the apostles. Interestingly, there is no direct appeal for safety or protection – their main concern is for the spread of the gospel. God clearly answers their prayers, which is made obvious in 4:31: 'And when they had prayed, the place in which they were gathered together was shaken, and they were all filled with the Holy Spirit and continued to speak the word of God with boldness.'

There is significant continuity in the understanding of prayer in the minds of the Jerusalem church and the Old Testament. Joel Green goes so far as to say:

> One of the names given to Jesus' disciples in Acts is 'those who call upon the name of the Lord' (9:14, 21). Rooted exegetically in the citation of Joel 2:32 in Acts 2:21, this descriptive label identifies those who believe in the name of Jesus . . . By using this designation for followers of Jesus, Luke thus indicates how fundamental prayer is to Christian experience, for it marks the beginning of one's incorporation into the messianic community and designates one of the practices that speak of faithfulness within that community.[8]

The main preoccupation of our prayers should be the outworking of the promises of God, which all through the Scriptures is linked to God's working through his Word, which is now written on the hearts of these new covenant believers.

This collocation of prayer and the word of God recurs at the beginning of Acts 6:

> Now in these days when the disciples were increasing in number, a complaint by the Hellenists arose against the Hebrews because their widows were being neglected in the daily distribution. And the twelve summoned the full number of the disciples and said, 'It is not right that we should give up preaching the word of God to serve tables. Therefore, brothers, pick out from among you seven men of good repute, full of the Spirit and of wisdom, whom we will appoint to this duty. But we will devote *ourselves to prayer and to the ministry of the word.*' (Acts 6:1–4)

It is important to understand that these are not completely separate activities (it is not envisaged e.g. that the apostles were freed up to divide all their time between these two equally vital but unrelated activities).

---

[8] Green 2001: 194–195.

It is also vital, as we have seen in several other contexts, to ask what the apostles have in mind when they specify prayer here. It would be easy to use this verse as a proof text for much needed encouragement to church leaders to make sure they pray for those in their care, for world mission and world events, but I think the apostles had something else in mind. In the context of Acts the only kind of prayer we have encountered so far is prayer for God to advance the work of the kingdom through the risen, reigning Jesus. In that case this prayer can only be prayer for God to do what he has promised, and to establish the new covenant through the preaching of the word. As David Peterson says:

> Prayer was a necessary accompaniment because it expresses dependence on the Lord, to give boldness in speaking the word, to protect its agents and to provide opportunities for the word to be heard and believed.[9]

The apostles then devote themselves to proclamation and praying for the impact of that proclamation. It is prayer for the preaching of the Word. The connection between prayer (calling on God to come through on his covenant promises) and the gospel (in this case represented by the Word) is unbreakable.

The final reference to prayer in the opening section of Acts dealing purely with events in Jerusalem comes at the end of chapter 7, as Stephen is stoned to death. As Stephen dies, he (consciously or unconsciously) echoes the words of the Lord Jesus as he prays:

> And as they were stoning Stephen, he called out, 'Lord Jesus, receive my spirit.' And falling to his knees he cried out with a loud voice, 'Lord, do not hold this sin against them.' And when he had said this, he fell asleep. (7:59–60)

Once again, the subject of his prayers, even at the point of death, is guilt, forgiveness and acceptance as part of the people of God.

Prayer in Judea and Samaria

As the action in the book moves beyond Jerusalem (as anticipated by 1:8), we find a consistent emphasis on prayer as a key factor in the work of God advancing. When the gospel spreads to Samaria, raising

[9] Peterson 2009: 234.

the question of whether or not the Samaritans have received the gift of the Spirit, the gift is given through apostles from Jerusalem 'calling on the name of the Lord':

> Now when the apostles at Jerusalem heard that Samaria had received the word of God, they sent to them Peter and John, who came down and prayed for them that they might receive the Holy Spirit, for he had not yet fallen on any of them, but they had only been baptized in the name of the Lord Jesus. Then they laid their hands on them and they received the Holy Spirit. (Acts 8:14–17)

The fascinating feature of this narrative in the context of our study is that being 'baptized in the name of the Lord Jesus' does not appear to be enough. However, when Peter and John come and 'call on the name of the Lord', asking the Father to pour out the Spirit in the name of the Lord Jesus, the gift is given and the unity of the new 'movement' is preserved across ethnic boundaries.

What follows provides an interesting contrast between the kind of gospel-shaped prayer that flows from the mission of Jesus and the general view of prayer in the pagan world. A well-known local mystic or sorcerer recognizes real power when he sees it, and makes the apostles an offer he thinks they cannot refuse:

> Now when Simon saw that the Spirit was given through the laying on of the apostles' hands, he offered them money, saying, 'Give me this power also, so that anyone on whom I lay my hands may receive the Holy Spirit.' But Peter said to him, 'May your silver perish with you, because you thought you could obtain the gift of God with money! You have neither part nor lot in this matter, for your heart is not right before God. Repent, therefore, of this wickedness of yours, and pray to the Lord that, if possible, the intent of your heart may be forgiven you. For I see that you are in the gall of bitterness and in the bond of iniquity.' And Simon answered, 'Pray for me to the Lord, that nothing of what you have said may come upon me.' (Acts 8:18–24)

Prayer here, as in the Old Testament (see e.g. Joel 2:32), is 'calling on the name of the Lord', specifically to ask for mercy in the face of our obvious guilt.

A similar use is found in the story of Saul's conversion in Acts 9. When the unsuspecting Ananias is enlisted by God to disciple the new convert, what marks this transformed man is simply that 'he is praying': 'And the Lord said to him, "Rise and go to the street called Straight, and at the house of Judas look for a man of Tarsus named Saul, for behold, he is praying"' (Acts 9:11). In context this does not simply imply that Saul is engaged in general religious activity (which, of course, had been part of his life for many years as an observant Jew). This must mean that he is 'calling on the name of the Lord', asking for mercy in the face of his recent actions and lifelong pride.

Meanwhile, back in Judea events are unfolding which make clear that God is continuing to roll out his plans. As he worked through the prayers of Elijah and Elisha (and the prayers of Jesus in John 11), God works through Peter outside Jerusalem (in Joppa) to raise a little girl from the dead.[10]

The pattern in Acts, then, seems to be similar to what we have observed elsewhere. Prayer is essentially calling on God to act in line with his promises. In the light of the coming of Jesus this can be sharpened to praying for God to do what he has promised in the gospel – whether that means to forgive us on the basis of Jesus or build his kingdom through the power of the Spirit and the Word. As the gospel steadily spreads outwards towards the Gentile world, this pattern is constantly repeated.

The Cornelius narrative, which leads to Peter's welcoming Gentile God-fearers into the fledgling Christian community, starts with prayer, both in Cornelius' house and in Peter's lodgings in the house of Simon the tanner:

> At Caesarea there was a man named Cornelius, a centurion of what was known as the Italian Cohort, a devout man who feared God with all his household, gave alms generously to the people, and *prayed continually to God*. About the ninth hour of the day he saw clearly in a vision an angel of God come in and say to him, 'Cornelius.' And he stared at him in terror and said, 'What is it, Lord?' And he said to him, '*Your prayers and your alms have ascended as a memorial before God*. And now send men to Joppa and bring one Simon who is called Peter.' . . . The next day, as they were on their journey and approaching the city, Peter went up on the housetop about the sixth hour *to pray*. (Acts 10:1–5, 9)

---

[10] Acts 9:40: 'But Peter put them all outside, and knelt down and prayed; and turning to the body he said, "Tabitha, arise." And she opened her eyes, and when she saw Peter she sat up.'

At another key moment in salvation history, as a Gentile (albeit a Gentile 'insider') receives both the gospel and the Holy Spirit, the catalyst appears to be that both Cornelius and Peter are 'calling on the name of the Lord'.

In chapter 12 the focus of the narrative returns to Jerusalem, where the latest Herod is the most recent to seek to suppress the newly established church. What does the church do to ensure that the gospel project stays on track in these fragile early days? The church prays: 'So Peter was kept in prison, but earnest prayer for him was made to God by the church' (Acts 12:5). After Peter has walked free from jail, he goes to find the rest of the community: 'he went to the house of Mary, the mother of John whose other name was Mark, where many were gathered together and were praying' (Acts 12:12). Little did they know that their prayers had already been answered – God would continue to build his church.

From chapter 13 onward, as the Gentile mission gathers pace, Luke notes that when new workers are appointed to take the gospel forward, the church prays (and fasts):

> Now there were in the church at Antioch prophets and teachers, Barnabas, Simeon who was called Niger, Lucius of Cyrene, Manaen a member of the court of Herod the tetrarch, and Saul. While they were worshipping the Lord and fasting, the Holy Spirit said, 'Set apart for me Barnabas and Saul for the work to which I have called them.' Then after fasting and praying they laid their hands on them and sent them off. (Acts 13:1–3)

And similarly: 'And when they had appointed elders for them in every church, with prayer and fasting they committed them to the Lord in whom they had believed' (14:23).

As the church spreads, so does the emphasis on prayer as the means by which God does the work of the gospel and continues to build the church. The events in Philippi are a typically vivid illustration of this:

> About midnight Paul and Silas were praying and singing hymns to God, and the prisoners were listening to them, and suddenly there was a great earthquake, so that the foundations of the prison were shaken. And immediately all the doors were opened, and everyone's bonds were unfastened. (Acts 16:25–26)

As he did for Peter in Acts 12, God now does for Paul and Silas, and the mission to the Gentiles can continue. Which takes us to the final movement of the book.

Prayer at the ends of the earth

As Paul makes his way deliberately and strategically towards Rome, and the interim fulfilment of Acts 1:8,[11] at several stages mention is made of the church praying (notably in the multistage departure from Ephesus in chs. 20–21):

> And when he had said these things, he knelt down and prayed with them all. And there was much weeping on the part of all; they embraced Paul and kissed him, being sorrowful most of all because of the word he had spoken, that they would not see his face again. And they accompanied him to the ship. (Acts 20:36–38)

> When our days there were ended, we departed and went on our journey, and they all, with wives and children, accompanied us until we were outside the city. And kneeling down on the beach, we prayed and said farewell to one another. Then we went on board the ship, and they returned home. (Acts 21:5–6)

To heighten the sense of gospel significance in Paul's saying his goodbyes to the converts of Asia Minor, Luke notes that they pray together. The gospel is moving beyond the immediate proximity of Palestine. And, as always, such major gospel movements are accompanied by prayer.

Paul's brief stop on Malta sees the final instance of prayer in Acts: 'It happened that the father of Publius lay sick with fever and dysentery. And Paul visited him and prayed, and putting his hands on him healed him' (28:8). As happened earlier with Peter, God acts through Paul to vindicate his message, namely the message of Jesus Christ.

So Acts ends with the gospel's being proclaimed at the centre of the known world, as God continues to listen to the pleas of his people to do what he has promised in the gospel.

Conclusion

The idea and practice of prayer are not central to the book of Acts, but nor are they absent. Prayer runs through the book like an

---

[11] Cf. Keener 2012: 703.

ever-present yet inconspicuous thread – not hard to find, yet at the same time, easy to overlook. When one does look closely, Acts provides a fascinating snapshot of the church at prayer in the earliest days of Christianity. And what can we see from Acts of how the church prayed? The church's praying, in a way, fitted with both the life and ministry of Jesus, and the centuries of Old Testament teaching before that.

The prayers in Acts are centred on and shaped by the gospel. The overwhelming matter prayed about is the promised progress of the gospel. Prayer is asking God to continue to work through the gospel of Jesus by his Spirit.

Chapter Eight

Church planting and prayer: prayer in Paul's letters

If any of the New Testament writers can lay claim to being the 'theologian of prayer', it is the apostle Paul. Paul talks more about his own prayers, encourages his readers to pray more and includes more prayer in his letters than anyone else. Paul, more than anyone else, shaped the theology and practice of prayer in the church of the Lord Jesus, as he spearheaded the church-planting movement across the Mediterranean.[1]

For Paul the gospel shapes the prayers of the church. In this chapter I will highlight the ways in which this plays out in Paul's own prayers for new churches, his teaching on prayer and his injunctions to pray, which are embedded in many of his letters.[2] We will examine each of these in turn.

Praying for others with Paul

Perhaps surprisingly, the majority of Pauline material dealing with prayer is taken up with either actual or reported prayers for others. This is a new development in the biblical material – up to this point there has been a large amount of intercession for those opposing the work of God, but minimal prayer offered for God's people. Now all that changes.

Although atypical in some ways (arising from the fact that Paul has not visited Rome), his introductory assurance of his prayerful concern for them contains the key elements of his prayers for others:[3]

---

[1] The material discussed in this chapter has, of course, generated a massive amount of literature over the years. Even to attempt to discuss the Pauline view of prayer is an enormous challenge. Given the constraints of this book, this chapter must of necessity focus on tracing the continuity of the Pauline materials and what has gone before. For a more general starting point, and a helpful introduction to the material, see e.g. Peterson 1990b.

[2] I am convinced of the case for Pauline authorship of all the letters in the traditionally ascribed Pauline corpus.

[3] There are, of course, many more substantial and rigorous treatments of these prayers, most notably O'Brien 1982. See also Carson 1993.

First, I thank my God through Jesus Christ for all of you, because your faith is proclaimed in all the world. For God is my witness, whom I serve with my spirit in the gospel of his Son, that without ceasing I mention you always in my prayers, asking that somehow by God's will I may now at last succeed in coming to you. For I long to see you, that I may impart to you some spiritual gift to strengthen you – that is, that we may be mutually encouraged by each other's faith, both yours and mine. I want you to know, brothers, that I have often intended to come to you (but thus far have been prevented), in order that I may reap some harvest among you as well as among the rest of the Gentiles. I am under obligation both to Greeks and to barbarians, both to the wise and to the foolish. (Rom. 1:8–14)

Paul begins with thanksgiving, which, although strictly speaking is a separate activity to prayer, takes place in the context of prayer. However, it is important to notice the content of Paul's thanksgiving, which always coheres with the content of his prayers. In this case Paul thanks God that their 'faith' (*pistis*) is being reported all over the world. As is fitting in the context of Romans, Paul's main concern and prayer for the Romans is simply that they *trust God*, as he has revealed himself to them in the gospel.

His expressed desire to visit them in Rome is equally shaped by the gospel – he longs to encourage the Romans through imparting some 'spiritual gift' to strengthen them. In this context, rather than referring to a Spirit-imbued ability, Paul seems to have in mind the strengthening that comes by the Spirit through the word as the gospel is explained.[4] In addition he wants to reap a harvest among them, which is most naturally understood as wanting to do some evangelism in Rome and see people come to know Christ through his ministry there. This 'gospel-heartedness' is also apparent in the middle of the emotionally charged discussion of the fate of the Jewish people when Paul breaks off to say, 'Brothers, my heart's desire and prayer to God for them is that they may be saved' (Rom. 10:1).

It is fair to say, then, that Paul's overwhelming concern as he both writes to and prays for the churches of the Mediterranean is that they embrace, live and proclaim the gospel. This is what dominates his

---

[4] See e.g. the discussions of Schreiner 1998: 52–53; Moo 1996: 59–60.

prayers for others. Reading through the rest of Paul's letters provides compelling evidence that this is the case.[5]

Paul's letter to the Ephesians provides the greatest amount of evidence for the content of and driving force behind his prayers. Unusually, both in the introductory section and the body of the letter itself Paul includes long reports of the way in which he prays for the church in Ephesus, which are among the richest in the Bible. The first is found in Ephesians 1:15–23:

> For this reason, because I have heard of your faith in the Lord Jesus and your love towards all the saints, I do not cease to give thanks for you, remembering you in my prayers, that the God of our Lord Jesus Christ, the Father of glory, may give you a Spirit of wisdom and of revelation in the knowledge of him, having the eyes of your hearts enlightened, that you may know what is the hope to which he has called you, what are the riches of his glorious inheritance in the saints, and what is the immeasurable greatness of his power towards us who believe, according to the working of his great might that he worked in Christ when he raised him from the dead and seated him at his right hand in the heavenly places, far above all rule and authority and power and dominion, and above every name that is named, not only in this age but also in the one to come. And he put all things under his feet and gave him as head over all things to the church, which is his body, the fullness of him who fills all in all.

Paul's opening thanksgiving for the *faith* of the church in Ephesus is similar to that in Romans. However, what follows is virtually unmatched in the Scriptures. At the core of Paul's request is the prayer 'that you may know what is the hope to which he has called you, what are the riches of his glorious inheritance in the saints, and what is the immeasurable greatness of his power towards us who believe'. Paul's desire is that the Ephesians grasp the hope of the gospel, the incredible effect of the gospel (in creating a people for God) and the power of the gospel, which is exerted and displayed in the death and

---

[5] The exceptions to this are Galatians, 1 Timothy and Titus (and to a lesser extent, the Corinthian correspondence). But in each of these cases there is a pressing matter at hand to which Paul turns straight away, thus skipping his usual 'prayer report' section. In 1 Corinthians he expresses thankfulness, but does not then turn to prayer. Similarly, in 2 Cor. 1 Paul moves quickly to his 'defence', omitting any comment on his prayers for them.

resurrection of Jesus, and in drawing this people to himself.[6] In other words Paul's prayer is profoundly gospel shaped. And how will this prayer be answered? He knows that this can come about only through the work of the Spirit, as he brings us to a greater knowledge of God, who is both the Father of the Lord Jesus and the God of glory revealed in the Old Testament through the gospel.

It is interesting that at the end of his prayer Paul appends this statement: 'And he put all things under his feet and gave him as head over all things to the church, which is his body, the fullness of him who fills all in all' (Eph. 1:22–23). The church here is the gathering of all God's people in heaven, of which every local gathering is an anticipation. But notice the two startling things Paul says:

- The ruling risen Christ is given *to the church*.
- The ruling risen Christ *fills the church*.

The implications of this are profound, but from the perspective of this study the most important thing to notice is that the work of Jesus Christ has already put all that Paul prays for within our grasp. All that remains is for Paul to ask God to do what he has promised in the gospel – to call on the name of the Lord.

This same perspective, that God has already done all things for us in Christ, and holds out all this to us in the gospel, also undergirds the prayer in Ephesians 3:14–21:

For this reason I bow my knees before the Father, from whom every family in heaven and on earth is named, that according to the riches of his glory he may grant you to be strengthened with power through his Spirit in your inner being, so that Christ may dwell in your hearts through faith – that you, being rooted and grounded in love, may have strength to comprehend with all the saints what is the breadth and length and height and depth, and to know the love of Christ that surpasses knowledge, that you may be filled with all the fullness of God. Now to him who is able to do far more abundantly than all that we ask or think, according to the power at work within us, to him be glory in the church and in Christ Jesus throughout all generations, for ever and ever. Amen.

---

[6] See the helpful explanation of Lincoln (1990: 78–79) and O'Brien (1999), where hope is clearly the central idea, contra Arnold (2010: 98–99), who argues that the end of the prayer is power.

As with the prayer in Ephesians 1, the sentence structure is somewhat complex here,[7] but the following observations can be made about the theological underpinnings of Paul's prayer:

1. He prays to the God who is the maker of all, and yet makes it possible through Jesus for us to call him 'Father'.
2. Paul prays that God will supply us with strength in a way that is commensurate with the riches of his glory. In other words his request is shaped by his understanding of what God has already done for us in the gospel.
3. The first main request of this prayer is that the Ephesians will be 'strengthened with power through his Spirit in your inner being, so that Christ may dwell in your hearts through faith'. Paul prays that God will work by the Spirit to help them to grasp the gospel and so trust him.
4. He then goes on to make a second request – that they be enabled to grasp the full extent of the love that God has shown us in the Lord Jesus Christ.[8]
5. In the final clause of the prayer he adds the plea that they 'may be filled with all the fullness of God'.[9] In praying that, Paul is talking about *Christian maturity*. Back in 1:23 he said that as the body of Christ, we the church *already share in the fullness of Christ*. He prays for power to be godly, and the ability to grasp the love of Christ, so that we may 'become who we already are', as Martyn Lloyd-Jones used to put it, so that we will be all that God wants us to be: *spiritually mature*.

Of course, there is much more to be said on this chapter, but for now it suffices to point out that *everything Paul prays for* has already been achieved for us, and is held out to us in the gospel. Paul's incredibly rich prayers ask God to do what he has already done for us and holds out to us in the gospel. And this position is reflected over and over again through his letters.

---

[7] See the discussion of the syntax in O'Brien (1999: 252–253).

[8] Vv. 18–19 function like a rhetorical drum roll – I pray that you will grasp how broad and long and high and deep the love of Christ is, and that you will *know this love that surpasses knowledge*.

[9] O'Brien (1999: 253) states that this 'has been viewed as the third and climactic request, or the summarizing request in which the two preceding petitions are realized'. Carson (1993: 195) suggests that it is simply clarifying the second request. However, these syntactical issues do not substantially affect my discussion.

In Philippians we find the same pattern:

> I thank my God in all my remembrance of you, always in every prayer of mine for you all making my prayer with joy, because of your partnership in the gospel from the first day until now. *And I am sure of this, that he who began a good work in you will bring it to completion at the day of Jesus Christ.* . . . And it is my prayer that your love may abound more and more, with knowledge and all discernment, so that you may approve what is excellent, and so be pure and blameless for the day of Christ, filled with the fruit of righteousness that comes through Jesus Christ, to the glory and praise of God. (Phil. 1:3–6, 9–11)

Paul's prayer for them is based on the fact that he is convinced that God is committed to finishing his work in them through the gospel. His prayer is doing nothing more than asking God to do that to which he is already committed. That is reiterated in Philippians 1:9–11, where Paul reports that he prays for their love to grow, for God to enable them to think like Christ, becoming more like him. However, elsewhere in the Pauline corpus he states that God has already committed to doing exactly these things in the life of the believer.[10]

This pattern of requesting what God has already committed to delivering through the Lord Jesus by the Spirit is, if anything, even clearer in Colossians:

> We always thank God, the Father of our Lord Jesus Christ, when we pray for you, since we heard of your faith in Christ Jesus and of the love that you have for all the saints, because of the hope laid up for you in heaven. . . .
>
> And so, from the day we heard, we have not ceased to pray for you, asking that you may be filled with the knowledge of his will in all spiritual wisdom and understanding, so as to walk in a manner worthy of the Lord, fully pleasing to him, bearing fruit in every good work and increasing in the knowledge of God. May you be strengthened with all power, according to his glorious might, for all endurance and patience with joy, giving thanks to the Father, who has qualified you to share in the inheritance of the saints in light. He has delivered us from the domain of darkness and

---

[10] See e.g. Eph. 1:22–23. The discussion of O'Brien (1991: 72–83) is immensely helpful.

transferred us to the kingdom of his beloved Son, in whom we have redemption, the forgiveness of sins. (Col. 1:3–5, 9–14)

In this case, after conventionally giving thanks for their trust in Christ (and in Colossians, also their love), Paul states unambiguously that he does so on the basis of the 'hope laid up for you in heaven'. His prayers are informed by God's commitment to them in the gospel. This is made clearer still by the addition of verses 13–14 at the end of the prayer. Paul simply states what is now true of them because of the work of Christ – they have been delivered, transferred and given redemption, the forgiveness of sins. What he prays for in verses 9–12, then, can simply be understood as the outworking of the gospel – that the gospel they have already believed would continue to penetrate their hearts and minds so that they will know how to obey God in every way, growing in effectiveness and the knowledge of him. Again he prays that God will supply his promised power, enabling them to live steadily, joyfully and thankfully for Christ. But once again there is nothing new here – Paul is just praying home God's commitments in the gospel.[11]

The Thessalonian correspondence does not deviate from what emerges as Paul's practice – he thanks God for their faith, and in this case also the outworking of their trust in Jesus in both love and hope (qualities that clearly flow from the gospel): 'We give thanks to God always for all of you, constantly mentioning you in our prayers, remembering before our God and Father your work of faith and labour of love and steadfastness of hope in our Lord Jesus Christ' (1 Thess. 1:2–3). When he moves on to pray specifically for the church in Thessalonica, the subject of his prayer is that God will enable him (and other members of his team?) to strengthen their faith in Christ (in a similar way that he prays for the Romans). But once again his prayers are focused on the impact of the gospel in their lives.

Later in his correspondence this is confirmed when Paul writes:

To this end we always pray for you, that our God may make you worthy of his calling and may fulfil every resolve for good and every work of faith by his power, so that the name of our Lord Jesus may be glorified in you, and you in him, according to the grace of our God and the Lord Jesus Christ. (2 Thess. 1:11–12)

---

[11] Cf. the comments of Moo (2008: 100–101), including 'Paul's intended meaning is clear enough: God the Father has himself provided what sinners need to be considered worthy to join the people of God.'

When Paul prays for the churches he has planted (or, in the case of Rome, hopes to visit), his unremitting concern is the work of the gospel in their lives. As he prays, he simply asks God to do what he has already committed to do in the gospel, as he works out the implications of Jesus' death and resurrection in the lives of his people. For Paul to pray is simply to ask God to do the work of the gospel through him and in the lives of others. This is clearly an advance on the Old Testament idea of 'calling on the name of the Lord', but it is a natural development rather than a fundamental change.

This finds further confirmation in the letters Paul writes to individuals, notably Timothy and Philemon. In both these epistles Paul thanks God for his work of God in their lives, and in the case of Philemon goes on to pray that he will 'do the work of the gospel' and grow in the knowledge of Christ through the gospel:[12]

> I thank my God always when I remember you in my prayers, because I hear of your love and of the faith that you have towards the Lord Jesus and for all the saints, and I pray that the sharing of your faith may become effective for the full knowledge of every good thing that is in us for the sake of Christ. (Phlm. 4–6)[13]

It is appropriate to include at this point one of the few places where Paul speaks of praying for himself. He is facing some acute but unspecified suffering. While Paul does pray that the suffering be relieved, he does so within a framework which makes clear that his great concern in all this is the progress of the gospel in and through him:

> So to keep me from becoming conceited because of the surpassing greatness of the revelations, a thorn was given me in the flesh, a messenger of Satan to harass me, to keep me from becoming conceited. Three times I pleaded with the Lord about this, that it should leave me. But he said to me, 'My grace is sufficient for you, for my power is made perfect in weakness.' Therefore I will boast all the more gladly of my weaknesses, so that the power of Christ may rest upon me. For the sake of Christ, then, I am content with weaknesses, insults, hardships, persecutions, and calamities. For when I am weak, then I am strong. (2 Cor. 12:7–10)

---

[12] 2 Tim. 1:3: 'I thank God whom I serve, as did my ancestors, with a clear conscience, as I remember you constantly in my prayers night and day.'

[13] See O'Brien 1982: 47–58 for a much fuller discussion of these verses.

In summary, then, when Paul prays for others, whether individuals or churches, and even when he prays for himself, he prays for God to do his work in their lives by the Spirit through the gospel. He prays that God may apply the benefits of Jesus' death and resurrection to their lives, and continue his work of perfecting them until the day when all things are brought together under Christ. He prays gospel-driven, gospel-centred prayers.

Paul's teaching on prayer

Alongside the prayers Paul prays for others, we also need to consider his teaching on prayer. Interestingly, there is very little discussion of prayer, detached from the prayers I have already discussed. A little material is presented in Romans, the least 'personal' of Paul's letters. Elsewhere Paul's 'teaching' on prayer is largely restricted to presenting the importance of praying for him and others involved in evangelism and church planting.

In Romans Paul makes several comments pertinent to our discussion:

> For you did not receive the spirit of slavery to fall back into fear, but you have received the Spirit of adoption as sons, by whom we cry, 'Abba! Father!' . . . Likewise the Spirit helps us in our weakness. For we do not know what to pray for as we ought, but the Spirit himself intercedes for us with groanings too deep for words. (Rom. 8:15, 26)[14]

Paul draws on Jesus' own teaching to emphasize that the gift of the Spirit draws us into Jesus' own relationship with his Father, enabling us to pray to his Father as our own, using the title 'Abba'. For Paul our prayers are made possible and informed at every level by the gospel. I would also tentatively suggest that the use of the word 'cry' here echoes the Old Testament injunctions to call on the name of Yahweh – but now, through the Spirit, we are empowered to call out 'Father' with and through the Lord Jesus.

The note Paul sounds in Romans 8:26, however, is intriguing. In the face of the brokenness, suffering and disappointment we can take

---

[14] The intervening material in Rom. 8 does not directly relate to prayer in any conventional sense, but to the role of the Spirit, which is beyond the purview of our discussion.

comfort in the fact that even when our words fail us, the Spirit continues to pray for us. However, we must be careful here, for verses 23–25 make it clear that Paul has a specific situation in mind:

> And not only the creation, but we ourselves, who have the firstfruits of the Spirit, groan inwardly as we wait eagerly for adoption as sons, the redemption of our bodies. For in this hope we were saved. Now hope that is seen is not hope. For who hopes for what he sees? But if we hope for what we do not see, we wait for it with patience. (Rom. 8:23–25)

The angst envisaged is 'gospel angst', not simply struggling to make sense of life in our messy world. Paul anticipates a situation where the tension between what we are now and what we will be brings us to the end of ourselves (or, at least, to the end of our words).[15] At this point he is quick to assure us that the Spirit not only brings about this gospel work in us, but 'oils the wheels' of this work in our lives by facilitating our prayers.

Aside from this, Paul's other reference to prayer in Romans, which I think reflects his attitude to prayer, is embedded in a list of 'Christian basics' in chapter 12:

> Let love be genuine. Abhor what is evil; hold fast to what is good. Love one another with brotherly affection. Outdo one another in showing honour. Do not be slothful in zeal, be fervent in spirit, serve the Lord. Rejoice in hope, be patient in tribulation, be constant in prayer. Contribute to the needs of the saints and seek to show hospitality. (Rom. 12:9–13)

The other passages that demand our attention in this context are both highly contentious, although not because of the material on prayer. First, in 1 Timothy 2, Paul urges Timothy to make prayer a priority:

> First of all, then, I urge that supplications, prayers, intercessions, and thanksgivings be made for all people, for kings and all who are in high positions, that we may lead a peaceful and quiet life, godly and dignified in every way. This is good, and it is pleasing in the sight of God our Saviour, who desires all people to be saved and to come to the knowledge of the truth. . . .

---

[15] See Schreiner 1998: 442–447 for a nuanced account of Paul's argument.

> I desire then that in every place the men should pray, lifting holy hands without anger or quarrelling . . . (1 Tim. 2:1–4, 8)[16]

The logic of Paul's exhortation here is crucial – the point of his prayers is not simply that we might be free to live a quiet life, minding our own business. He deliberately ties our prayers to the fact that God 'desires all people to be saved and to come to the knowledge of the truth'. In other words the prayers of verse 3 are designed to bring about the growth of the gospel in verse 4. Similarly, his injunction to men to devote their energies to prayer, rather than struggling for power, is undoubtedly a gospel injunction.[17]

The only remaining Pauline passage that touches on prayer which requires comment is the equally problematic section in 1 Corinthians:

> But I want you to understand that the head of every man is Christ, the head of a wife is her husband, and the head of Christ is God. Every man who prays or prophesies with his head covered dishonours his head, but every wife who prays or prophesies with her head uncovered dishonours her head, since it is the same as if her head were shaven. For if a wife will not cover her head, then she should cut her hair short. But since it is disgraceful for a wife to cut off her hair or shave her head, let her cover her head. For a man ought not to cover his head, since he is the image and glory of God, but woman is the glory of man. For man was not made from woman, but woman from man. Neither was man created for woman, but woman for man. That is why a wife ought to have a symbol of authority on her head, because of the angels. Nevertheless, in the Lord woman is not independent of man nor man of woman; for as woman was made from man, so man is now born of woman. And all things are from God. Judge for yourselves: is it proper for a wife to pray to God with her head uncovered? Does not nature itself teach you that if a man wears long hair it is a disgrace for him, but if a woman has long hair, it is her glory? For her hair is given to her for a covering. If anyone is inclined to be contentious, we have no such practice, nor do the churches of God. (1 Cor. 11:3–16)

---

[16] As the rest of the material in this passage does not impinge directly on the issue of prayer, I make no comment, but simply refer interested readers to Köstenberger and Schreiner 2005 (for a different perspective see Towner 2006).

[17] See Towner (2006: 202–203), who suggests that a concern for God's global purposes may lie behind the use of 'everywhere'.

The key question here is the extent to which this has any bearing on Paul's understanding of prayer.[18]

The fact that both 'praying' and 'prophesying' are subject to the condition of a woman having her head covered suggests that the issues at play here do not flow from Paul's understanding of prayer. The apparent disgrace being brought on the church in Corinth was coming from outsiders, who had little or no appreciation of a biblical theology of prayer (or prophecy for that matter). The question is not 'What is it in the nature of prayer that caused this problem?' but rather 'What was the nature of the behaviour that was causing opprobrium to be heaped on the church in Corinth?' The answer, according to Winter, is that the Corinthian women had chosen to display their freedom in a scandalous way, which was dragging the gospel into disrepute. The issue is ultimately about marriage (and authority in marriage), rather than prayer per se.[19]

Overall, there is a surprising paucity of direct teaching material on prayer in Paul. It seems that when it comes to prayer, the apostle would rather do than talk (or write) about it.

Paul's exhortations to pray

The relative lack of explicit teaching on prayer is more than made up for by Paul's repeated exhortations *to pray*. These exhortations fall into two categories: (1) appeals to pray for Paul and his mission, and (2) general encouragement to pray (which, in context, is also primarily to pray for the spread of the gospel).

Paul includes, with striking regularity, requests for prayer for his own church-planting endeavours. Even when the presenting issue is his own safety and/or freedom, the ultimate reason Paul is asking for prayer is that the gospel may flourish:

> I appeal to you, brothers, by our Lord Jesus Christ and by the love of the Spirit, to strive together with me in your prayers to God on my behalf, that I may be delivered from the unbelievers in Judea, and that my service for Jerusalem may be acceptable to the saints, so that by God's will I may come to you with joy and be refreshed in your company. May the God of peace be with you all. Amen. (Rom. 15:30–33)

---

[18] See the discussion in Winter (2001: 121–140).
[19] For an exhaustive overview of the issues involved in interpreting this chapter see Thiselton 2001: 799–848.

You also must help us by prayer, so that many will give thanks on our behalf for the blessing granted us through the prayers of many. (2 Cor. 1:11)

To that end keep alert with all perseverance, making supplication for all the saints, and also for me, that words may be given to me in opening my mouth boldly to proclaim the mystery of the gospel, for which I am an ambassador in chains, that I may declare it boldly, as I ought to speak. (Eph. 6:18–20)

At the same time, pray also for us, that God may open to us a door for the word, to declare the mystery of Christ, on account of which I am in prison – that I may make it clear, which is how I ought to speak. (Col. 4:3–4)

Finally, brothers, pray for us, that the word of the Lord may speed ahead and be honoured, as happened among you, and that we may be delivered from wicked and evil men. For not all have faith. (2 Thess. 3:1–2)

It is instructive that the apostle is so insistent on his own need for prayer as he carries out the work of the gospel. Therefore it is reasonable to see his regular injunctions to others as flowing from this commitment. When Paul urges people to pray, it is not simply to engage in meditation, or to be more reflective – it is to cry to God to do what he has committed to do through the death and resurrection of the Lord Jesus through the gospel. That becomes clear when we examine his general exhortations in context.

Paul's global instruction in Ephesians 6 to pray 'at all times in the Spirit, with all prayer and supplication' encompasses all of the previous statements concerning the 'armour of God':

Stand therefore, having fastened on the belt of truth, and having put on the breastplate of righteousness, and, as shoes for your feet, having put on the readiness given by the gospel of peace. In all circumstances take up the shield of faith, with which you can extinguish all the flaming darts of the evil one; and take the helmet of salvation, and the sword of the Spirit, which is the word of God, praying at all times in the Spirit, with all prayer and supplication. (Eph. 6:14–18)

It is clear, however, that this armour, drawing on the 'armour of the servant' in Isaiah 11:4–5 and 59:17, has been 'redesigned' by Paul in the light of the gospel. 'Righteousness', 'readiness' (which explicitly flows from the gospel), 'faith', 'salvation' and the 'word of God' are all instrinsically linked to the proclamation of the gospel in Paul. Prayer here, then, cannot be anything other than prayer to continue to live and speak the gospel in the middle of the raging spiritual conflict. Prayer, once more, is intrinsically linked to gospel proclamation.

Similarly, in Philippians 4, a classic passage dealing with facing anxiety, the appeal to prayer simply cannot be excised from a 'gospel' context:

> Rejoice in the Lord always; again I will say, Rejoice. Let your reasonableness be known to everyone. The Lord is at hand; do not be anxious about anything, but in everything by prayer and supplication with thanksgiving let your requests be made known to God. And the peace of God, which surpasses all understanding, will guard your hearts and your minds in Christ Jesus. (Phil. 4:4–7)

The double appeal to 'rejoice' is a common New Testament device, which is virtually always linked to what God has done and will do for us in the Lord Jesus Christ.[20] It is this foundation that enables us to be reasonable and gentle. Whether 'the Lord is at hand' is taken to mean proximity or about to return,[21] in either case it gives us reason to continue to commit everything to him, knowing that he is already committed to doing the work of the gospel in and through us, and once again is tantamount to 'calling on the name of Yahweh to do the work of the gospel'.

In a passage to which I have already referred, Paul also links general prayer with specific prayer for him in his church-planting and teaching ministry:

> Continue steadfastly in prayer, being watchful in it with thanksgiving. At the same time, pray also for us, that God may open to us a door for the word, to declare the mystery of Christ, on account of which I am in prison – that I may make it clear, which is how I ought to speak. (Col. 4:2–4)

---

[20] E.g. Rom. 5:2, 11; 12:12; 1 Cor. 7:30; 2 Cor. 6:10; Gal. 4:27; Phil. 1:18; 2:17; Col. 1:24.
[21] See O'Brien 1991: 488–489 for the arguments each way.

The assumption behind these statements is that there will be a continuity in their general prayers (presumably for themselves and their own churches) and their prayers for Paul's gospel work.

Later in the same passage Paul shows that this is his default understanding of prayer, when commending Epaphras: 'Epaphras, who is one of you, a servant of Christ Jesus, greets you, always struggling on your behalf in his prayers, that you may stand mature and fully assured in all the will of God' (Col. 4:12). In the context of the letter (and ch. 4 in particular) Epaphras can only be praying for them to grasp the truth of the gospel in a deeper way, so that they may continue to live and proclaim the gospel faithfully in Colossae.

Finally, in 1 Thessalonians 5:16–18 Paul makes a similar statement: 'Rejoice always, pray without ceasing, give thanks in all circumstances; for this is the will of God in Christ Jesus for you.' The pattern of thought is the same. It is the gospel that is the ground of our joy and our thanksgiving. It is the gospel that embodies God's will for us. For Paul it is also the gospel that grounds both the content and practice of our prayers.

Paul and corporate prayer? An aside

One intriguing aspect of the material we have looked at is that it is, with the exception of the Pastoral Epistles and Philemon, embedded in letters written to groups of individuals – all these injunctions are addressed to *churches*. Given the fact that the prayers in Acts are predominantly prayers of the gathered church, and the encouragements to pray in the Pauline epistles seem to be largely addressed to the gathered church, it seems that the present practice of prayer largely being relegated to the private sphere is out of step with the practice of the New Testament.[22]

Conclusion

The most prominent feature of the Pauline material on prayer, whether Paul's own appeals for prayer or injunctions to pray, is the almost universal focus on prayers for the gospel to take root in people's lives through his ministry and the ministry of the church. This is clearly a development of earlier biblical material on prayer, but it builds on what has gone before rather than seeking radically to reinterpret the understanding of the prophets, Jesus and the early church. For Paul

---

[22] See further in the afterword below.

prayer is still calling on the name of God to do what he has promised – however, Paul's great contribution to the biblical theology of prayer is that it articulates what God has promised in terms of the gospel of the Lord Jesus Christ.

Chapter Nine

The end of prayer: prayer in the later New Testament

The closing books of the New Testament are a fascinating witness to the challenges faced by the church of Jesus Christ as the foundational, apostolic generation of eyewitnesses to the resurrection of Jesus gives way to those who would take the lead in the post-apostolic church. As the trajectory is set for the future of Christianity, do we see the same theology and practice when it comes to prayer? In this final chapter this crucial question will be to the fore.[1]

Prayer and Hebrews

Given both the subject matter of Hebrews and the intended audience, one might expect Hebrews to be a rich source for material on prayer. However, relatively little space is devoted to prayer in the book. Presumably, this is because the focus is on the issue of *access to God* through Jesus, our great high priest and substitute.

Although an Old Testament prayer is quoted in Hebrews 1:10–12, one has to read to chapter 4 to find the first possible reference to prayer. The wording here is interesting: 'Let us then with confidence draw near to the throne of grace, that we may receive mercy and find grace to help in time of need' (Heb. 4:16). The 'throne of grace' is a unique phrase, although almost certainly influenced by Old Testament imagery.[2] Is 'draw near to the throne of grace' a circumlocution for prayer? It has usually been interpreted like this over the years, perhaps under the influence of 7:25 (see below).[3] However, there are a couple of reasons why this may not be the most obvious interpretation. First,

---

[1] Peterson 1990a also provides a helpful overview of this material.

[2] O'Brien (2010: 184–186) has a detailed explanation of the background of the throne as the place from which God both rules and dispenses grace. However, he does not account for the absence of any prayer language. Ellingworth's (1993: 269–271) slightly more nuanced treatment is, on balance, to be preferred.

[3] So e.g. Peterson (1990a: 105–106), although following the argument set out above, sets his discussion in a section entitled 'The Prayers of Christians'.

there is the fact that prayer is not mentioned up to this point in the letter – it seems a large jump to expect readers to make the connection with prayer, when the phrase itself seems to be without precedent, and there is nothing in chapters 1–4 to point in this direction. Secondly, it is highly unusual for the word 'confidence' to be linked to prayer (this is not impossible, just not the normal vocabulary). In addition prayer is not often presented as the means by which to receive 'mercy and grace'. Of course, none of this is decisive – and in a sense should it refer to prayer, it would further strengthen the case I have been making that prayer is essentially asking God to do what he has promised (and he has promised mercy and grace to all those who call); but nonetheless, given the concerns of the book of Hebrews, it seems more likely that rather than thinking of prayer *specifically*, the writer is simply making the point that the way is now open for us to approach our open-handed God freely.

There is no such ambiguity, however, when we come to Hebrews 5:7: 'In the days of his flesh, Jesus offered up prayers and supplications, with loud cries and tears, to him who was able to save him from death, and he was heard because of his reverence.' In context this is presented by the writer as evidence that Jesus was truly human (as well as divine), and is therefore properly equipped to be the ultimate mediator. But in arguing like this the text confirms what I argued concerning Jesus and prayer in chapter 6. On the one hand, Jesus, like those who had gone before him in the Old Testament, viewed prayer (in this case 'prayer and supplication', which I take to be synonyms[4]), as crying out to Yahweh as the one who is committed to rescuing his people. On the other, it is another example of the 'prophetic' understanding of how God will ultimately refuse to hear those who are impenitent. Hebrews 5:7, then, provides significant evidence that the writer to the Hebrews has a similar view of prayer to the rest of the biblical writers.

Jesus' work of intercession is the focus of the next possible reference to prayer in 7:23–25, but once more it is not entirely clear whether prayer is the central concern of the writer:

The former priests were many in number, because they were prevented by death from continuing in office, but he holds his priesthood permanently, because he continues for ever. Consequently, he is able to save to the uttermost those who draw near

---

[4] With O'Brien (2010: 198), who cites the classical background of the phrase.

to God through him, since he always lives to make intercession for them. (Heb. 7:23–25)

There are two separate issues here: (1) what does the writer have in mind when he speaks of Jesus' 'intercession', and (2) what is he describing when he uses the term 'draw near' (*proserchomai*)? Neither of these problems has a clear-cut solution.

While it is *possible* that Jesus' ministry of intercession is, in part at least, one of *intercessory prayer*, that is not made explicit in this text, or in any other text in Hebrews. Jesus' intercession is a fundamental part of his high priestly ministry – he *brings us to his Father* rather than simply speaking to his Father on our behalf.[5] In any case, as I am referring to Jesus' post-ascension activity, it is hard to see how this can be considered 'prayer' in any normal sense of the word. However, the second problem is more significant for our discussion: Does 'draw near' to God here mean to pray? There is nothing in the semantic range of this word to suggest that it means anything other than to 'move closer' to God relationally. If that is the case, then this text may have little to contribute to a biblical theology of prayer.

The final reference to prayer in Hebrews comes right at the end of the letter, when the writer (Apollos?[6]), in a very Paul-like fashion, requests prayer for himself and his group that they may conduct themselves in a godly way, thus somehow enabling them to return to their brothers more quickly: 'Pray for us, for we are sure that we have a clear conscience, desiring to act honourably in all things. I urge you the more earnestly to do this in order that I may be restored to you the sooner' (Heb. 13:18–19).

Despite the unique subject material in Hebrews, there is nothing to suggest that the writer diverges from Paul's understanding of Christian prayer. But can the same be said for the work of Jesus' half-brother James, who is not slow to express things in an obviously un-Pauline way?

Prayer and James

Despite both the relative brevity of his letter, and the relative rarity of his statements on prayer, James has managed to provide us with some of the most striking statements on prayer in the whole Bible.

---

[5] Although against this, *entynchanein* may well refer to speaking to the Father on our behalf. But even so this is a case of Jesus' reminding the Father of what has already been paid for us rather than praying for us in any sense.

[6] I find the case made by Witherington 2007 to be quite convincing.

One of his opening comments enshrines an important, enduring and misunderstood principle:

> If any of you lacks wisdom, let him ask God, who gives generously to all without reproach, and it will be given him. But let him ask in faith, with no doubting, for the one who doubts is like a wave of the sea that is driven and tossed by the wind. For that person must not suppose that he will receive anything from the Lord; he is a double-minded man, unstable in all his ways. (Jas 1:5–8)

The first thing to note is that this promise is specific. The condition of verse 6 is not a general principle that applies to all prayer.[7] This is not a guarantee, though, that all our prayers and wishes will be met if only we ask 'hard enough'. The only thing on offer is 'wisdom'. James is clearly heavily influenced by the wisdom literature, but has also given much thought to the way in which Jesus Christ is our wisdom, and has both embodied the fear of the Lord and put godly living within our grasp in the gospel. Now all we need to do to receive this Christ-shaped wisdom is to ask – to 'call on the name of the Lord', as it were.

What is interesting is the way in which James insists that any such asking must be done in 'faith'. It is very hard to imagine (esp. given the strong view of 'faith' James expounds in the next chapter; i.e. a faith that shows itself in actions) that James's understanding of faith is any different to that of the rest of the apostles – faith is trusting in Jesus. It is believing the gospel. Which in turn means that the issue that gave rise to verse 7, and the strong condemnation of verse 8, is much more than a lack of confidence. This 'doubt' calls the gospel itself into question. *And as played out countless times in the Old Testament, where there is no trust in Yahweh, sooner or later prayer is not heard.* And that must be the case here in James too. When we pray, we call on God to give us what he has already procured for and offered us in Jesus Christ – to fail to ask, or to question whether we will receive (in this case wisdom) is not a matter of anaemic trust; it is refusing to believe the gospel, which is a serious thing.

James is dealing with some highly emotive issues in this letter. In fact when he returns to the subject of prayer in chapter 4, it is in the context of complete breakdown of community life in the churches to which he writes. Even allowing for some hyperbole, the situation is

---

[7] E.g. Davids (1982: 72–73) sees the promise to hold specifically in the context of testing. So also Martin (1988: 19).

grave: 'You desire and do not have, so you murder. You covet and cannot obtain, so you fight and quarrel. You do not have, because you do not ask. You ask and do not receive, because you ask wrongly, to spend it on your passions. You adulterous people!' (Jas 4:2–4). James deliberately parallels the situation in the church(es) to which he writes with that of the people of God in the Old Testament. At the heart of their issues is self-reliance – they refuse to call on the name of the Lord, asking him to do for them what they cannot do for themselves. Or, to be more accurate, like the people of Israel they ask for the wrong things in the wrong way at the wrong time! This leads James to call on God's people to humble themselves and come back to God before it is too late (Jas 4:7–10). The continuity with the theology of prayer we have seen emerging through the preceding pages is striking.

This takes us, then, to the longest passage in James, and the most contentious. It is worth reproducing the text in full, before jumping into the minefield that is interpreting James 5:

> Is anyone among you suffering? Let him pray. Is anyone cheerful? Let him sing praise. Is anyone among you sick? Let him call for the elders of the church, and let them pray over him, anointing him with oil in the name of the Lord. And the prayer of faith will save the one who is sick, and the Lord will raise him up. And if he has committed sins, he will be forgiven. Therefore, confess your sins to one another and pray for one another, that you may be healed. The prayer of a righteous person has great power as it is working. Elijah was a man with a nature like ours, and he prayed fervently that it might not rain, and for three years and six months it did not rain on the earth. Then he prayed again, and heaven gave rain, and the earth bore its fruit. (Jas 5:13–18)

The first intriguing phrase in this section is, not surprisingly, the first phrase. It is the key to unlocking this whole section. 'Is anyone among you suffering? Let him pray [*proseuchomai*].' The word for 'suffering', *kakopathō*, is an unusual one. Judging from the context (it is used in 5:10 of the prophets), it has in mind a specific context where one is suffering 'evil' either as a result of other people's wrong actions or one's own.[8]

---

[8] We can see the ambiguity in the term in 2 Tim. 2:9, where Paul is 'suffering as a criminal'. In other words there is a reason for his suffering; it is just that in his situation the suffering is not deserved.

This explains why we have the unusual instruction to pray.[9] Already, then, we are in an unusual situation – some non-typical (judicial?) evil has come upon an individual, and he is to call on the name of the Lord in the hope that he will rescue him.

The logic of the passage flows like this:

suffering → prayer; cheerful → praise; 'sick' → call the elders

The middle pair of the progression (cheerful, praise) is self-evident, and underlines that each of these responses is similarly normal and obvious. The problem is, of course, that the responses on either side are not so obvious. Praying when suffering? Perhaps. But calling the elders when one is 'sick'? That seems strange. But all may not be as it seems. Although the word 'sick' (*astheneō*) can mean 'ill' (e.g. Luke 4:40), it can also mean 'weak' (so Rom. 14:1, where the phrase is 'weak in faith'). There is a strong case for preferring the latter translation, particularly in the light of James 5:15.[10]

It has often been assumed that the 'prayer of faith' here is a prayer offered with a remarkable degree of confidence (a kind of 'souped up' version of the prayer of Jas 1), which, as a result, has a dramatic impact on the sick person.[11] But there is a more natural and straight-forward way of reading the text. If the person concerned is not ill, but rather 'weak in faith' (or even 'weak in the faith'), and as a result has sinned spectacularly, it may well be that he is in a state of deep despair and personal disintegration. If that is the case, what is needed most? People like this need to be reminded of the gospel, and to be reassured of their forgiveness in Christ, and even that the Spirit lives in them and that they are secure in Christ. They need to be encouraged to come back to Christ in repentance, and taste again that he is good. Could that be what James 5:15 is describing? 'And the prayer of faith will save the one who is sick, and the Lord will raise him up. And if he has committed sins, he will be forgiven.'

This finds some confirmation in James 5:16 – rather than a celebration of physical healing per se, James seems to encourage

---

[9] It may be easily understandable, but that does not change the fact that it is not a common biblical connection.

[10] Contra e.g. Davids (1982: 192), who acknowledges that the word can mean 'weak', but then argues from the context that it must mean 'sick'. His argument seems circular.

[11] Davids (ibid.) also discusses a possible Hellenistic background for the phrase. This is unconvincing.

confession and repentance in order that we experience the healing that comes through the gospel: 'Therefore, confess your sins to one another and pray for one another, that you may be healed.' This reading of James 5 solves several exegetical conundra, and also shows how James's view of prayer neatly coheres with everything else we have seen. It even explains the puzzling allusion to Elijah at the end of the section.

James continues in 5:16 like this: 'The prayer of a righteous person has great power as it is working.' At first glance it looks as if James is establishing a new category of particularly effective prayers. On this view these 'mighty prayer warriors' are so effective because they are 'righteous'. However, such an understanding of the text comes with an aroma of works righteousness that is impossible to dispel. But if we take 'righteous' here as simply designating someone who is 'righteous by faith', then it may be that James's point is much more straightforward – those who are wobbling will do well to seek out those who are trusting Christ, and ask for their help, because not only will they pray for them, but they will pray with them, knowing the importance of leading the wanderers back to repentance.[12]

The example of Elijah confirms that the interpretation I have suggested is almost certainly the right one. The point is not that we are to seek out any other mediators, for 'Elijah was a man with a nature like ours', 5:17, but he prayed, and knew the seriousness of sinning against God. In the context of 1 Kings Elijah announces that the drought has come from Yahweh and is part of the curse of the covenant now falling upon disobedient Israel. But after confronting the prophets of Baal on Mount Carmel, and the people (begrudgingly) admitting 'the Lord, he is God', that covenant curse is lifted. Now in a situation where sin, it seems, has brought down temporal judgment from God, when people are experiencing God's displeasure and discipline, what is necessary? We simply need someone who is justified to lead them back to repentance – because in the gospel God has made clear that he will forgive those who run to him, a fact made even clearer in James 5:19–20.

As the New Testament continues, it throws up a series of fascinating passages teaching about prayer. They enrich and shape our previous understanding, but there is still a strongly observed continuity – prayer

---

[12] See the excellent discussion of Tim Chester (2003: 82–83, developed in concert with Steve Timmis), which presents a broadly similar interpretation.

is to call on God to do what he has promised in the gospel; it is calling on the name of Yahweh refreshed.

Prayer and Peter

Before I come to the writings of John,[13] for the sake of completeness I should say a word about the letters of Peter and Jude, both of which make only passing reference to prayer.

In Peter's first letter in the course of his discussion on the roles of husbands and wives (in particular, when one partner has been converted) he reminds his readers of the Old Testament principle that living in contradiction to the commands of God will prevent one's prayers being heard. He applies this principle to boorish husbands like this: 'Likewise, husbands, live with your wives in an understanding way, showing honour to the woman as the weaker vessel, since they are heirs with you of the grace of life, so that your prayers may not be hindered' (1 Peter 3:7).

A few verses later, quoting the Hebrew Scriptures directly this time, he says:

> For the eyes of the Lord are on the righteous,
>   and his ears are open to their prayer.
> But the face of the Lord is against those who do evil.
>   (1 Peter 3:12)[14]

A similar note is sounded in chapter 4, where Peter insists that living in the light of all that Christ has done and will do is essential – it will shape our lives and, in turn, will enable us to play our part in God's work in the world, as we pray gospel-shaped prayers, waiting for God to intervene decisively at the end of history: 'The end of all things is at hand; therefore be self-controlled and sober-minded for the sake of your prayers' (1 Peter 4:7).

Prayer and Jude

Jude's single comment on the subject of prayer is this: 'But you, beloved, building yourselves up in your most holy faith and praying in the Holy Spirit, keep yourselves in the love of God, waiting for

---

[13] Assuming that the same John (presumably the Beloved) is responsible for both the Johannine letters and the Apocalypse.
[14] Cf. Ps. 34:13–17.

the mercy of our Lord Jesus Christ that leads to eternal life' (Jude 20–21). Jude shows a similar concern to maintain a future focus, but expresses himself differently, talking of 'praying in the Holy Spirit'. This has, of course, been understood in a variety of ways.[15] However, it is highly probable that Jude simply uses the phrase as a shorthand to mean, 'as people who are indwelled by the Spirit, guided by the Spirit, used by the Spirit and changed by the Spirit', rather than creating any experiential expectation, or encouraging ecstatic prayer.[16]

These short comments on prayer, however, pale into insignificance beside the Johannine material that brings the canon, and our theological journey, to a close.

Prayer and John

Two significant passages in 1 John build on and develop the biblical theology of prayer, bringing a new clarity to a specific part of the biblical witness. The passages are 1 John 1:8–10 and 1 John 5:13–17. And they bring a new freshness to the idea of prayers for forgiveness:

> If we say we have no sin, we deceive ourselves, and the truth is not in us. If we confess our sins, he is faithful and just to forgive us our sins and to cleanse us from all unrighteousness. If we say we have not sinned, we make him a liar, and his word is not in us. (1 John 1:8–10)[17]

And the second is this:

> I write these things to you who believe in the name of the Son of God that you may know that you have eternal life. And this is the confidence that we have towards him, that if we ask anything according to his will he hears us. And if we know that he hears us in whatever we ask, we know that we have the requests that we have asked of him.
>
> If anyone sees his brother committing a sin not leading to death, he shall ask, and God will give him life – to those who commit sins

---

[15] See Bauckham 1983: 113–114 and Davids 2006: 94–95 for the various options.

[16] In this context Chester's (2003: 62–73) excellent discussion of what it means to pray in the Spirit is extremely helpful.

[17] As with some other key NT passages, there is no explicit mention of prayer here. However, in this case, as it is obviously dealing with direct address to God, it is hard to see how one could exclude it from any list of biblical prayer material.

that do not lead to death. There is sin that leads to death; I do not say that one should pray for that. All wrongdoing is sin, but there is sin that does not lead to death. (1 John 5:13–17)

Building on the teaching of Jesus in John's Gospel in particular (see chapter 6 above), the apostle spells out that because of the gospel of the Lord Jesus Christ forgiveness is now a divine obligation for those who have entrusted themselves to Jesus. It is a matter of justice (1 John 5:9). Forgiveness, then, is one of those things covered in 1 John 5:13–17. Verse 14 says, 'if we ask anything according to his will he hears us'. Of course, what is 'according to his will' is what he has already made possible for us in the gospel. Interestingly, God will even hear us as we pray for our brothers and sisters, unless they reject the gospel, which I take to be the 'sin that leads to death'.[18]

Presumably, this gospel-rich perspective also lies behind the simple assurance given to Gaius in 3 John:

The elder to the beloved Gaius, whom I love in truth.

Beloved, I pray that all may go well with you and that you may be in good health, as it goes well with your soul. For I rejoiced greatly when the brothers came and testified to your truth, as indeed you are walking in the truth. I have no greater joy than to hear that my children are walking in the truth. (3 John 1–4)

Once more, a biblical prayer finishes with the ultimate priority of living and proclaiming the truth. This is what matters. And that is demonstrated powerfully in the final book of the Bible, which leads us on to the place where prayer is no longer necessary.

John's vision in the book of Revelation is punctuated by scenes of people, both in heaven and on earth, both right now and in the future, praying in the light of the gospel of Jesus Christ.[19]

We first encounter the 'prayers of the saints' in 5:8–10:

And when he had taken the scroll, the four living creatures and the twenty-four elders fell down before the Lamb, each holding a harp, and golden bowls full of incense, which are the prayers of the saints. And they sang a new song, saying,

[18] See the excellent discussion by Jobes (2014: 232–237).
[19] See the helpful overview of Ng (1990: 119–135).

> 'Worthy are you to take the scroll
>   and to open its seals,
> for you were slain, and by your blood you ransomed
>   people for God
>   from every tribe and language and people and nation,
> and you have made them a kingdom and priests to
>   our God,
>   and they shall reign on the earth.'

The prayers of the saints are filling the bowls of incense. It is clear from the song of the twenty-four elders and the living creatures that the prayers of the saints concern one thing: the progress of the gospel on earth.[20] These are gospel-shaped prayers, which focus on God's work on earth in salvation and judgment. This is confirmed by the prayer of the martyrs in chapter 6:

> When he opened the fifth seal, I saw under the altar the souls of those who had been slain for the word of God and for the witness they had borne. They cried out with a loud voice, 'O Sovereign Lord, holy and true, how long before you will judge and avenge our blood on those who dwell on the earth?' Then they were each given a white robe and told to rest a little longer, until the number of their fellow servants and their brothers should be complete, who were to be killed as they themselves had been. (Rev. 6:9–11)

It is frankly unmissable that the main subject of the prayers of the saints, both those who died of natural causes and have gone to be with Christ, and the prayers of the martyrs, is the progress of the gospel. They are preoccupied with the victory of God, and the outcome of the battles along the way. This leads Bauckham to comment:

> All the prayers in the book of Revelation are fully eschatological – that is, they are prayers for the coming of God's Kingdom, for the completion of God's purposes for his creation, for the fulfilment of all that God has promised, for everything that is finally to come, and in the end, for God himself to come to his creation to perfect it by his own presence throughout eternity.[21]

---

[20] And in particular the righteous judgment of the ungodly. See Beale 1998: 357; Mounce 1997: 34.
[21] Bauckham 2001: 252–253.

This is reiterated in Revelation 8:

> And another angel came and stood at the altar with a golden censer, and he was given much incense to offer with the prayers of all the saints on the golden altar before the throne, and the smoke of the incense, with the prayers of the saints, rose before God from the hand of the angel. Then the angel took the censer and filled it with fire from the altar and threw it on the earth, and there were peals of thunder, rumblings, flashes of lightning, and an earthquake. (8:3–5)

There is no question that God is listening to these prayers, the prayers of the saints. Their prayers for judgment and salvation will be answered. As the great movement of salvation history draws to a close, it is plain that, if anything, the gospel-centred nature of prayer intensifies. As it has been from the beginning, prayer is essentially salvation-historical – calling on God to do what he has promised and to advance his agenda in the world.

This finds tangential support in the 'song' of Moses and the Lamb, sung by those who share in God's victory:

> Great and amazing are your deeds,
> O Lord God the Almighty!
> Just and true are your ways,
> O King of the nations!
> Who will not fear, O Lord,
> and glorify your name?
> For you alone are holy.
> All nations will come
> and worship you,
> for your righteous acts have been revealed.
> (Rev. 15:3–4)

The answer to the rhetorical question 'Who will not fear, O Lord, / and glorify your name?' is 'No one!', because God has acted decisively in both salvation and judgment, and the plaintive cries of prayer have been replaced by songs of victory and vindication.

As John's vision, the book of Revelation, and indeed the entire canon of Scripture, draws to a close, it seems that prayer is replaced by singing. The prayers of the saints are answered, and there is nothing left to ask for. All that remains is celebration. So in Revelation 19 – 22 there is much 'crying out' (see Rev. 19:1–3, 6–8), but this is not calling on the name of the Lord to act – voices join together to cry 'Hallelujah!', because all their prayers have finally and decisively been answered. All that remains is endless delight, worship and surprise at the endless magnificence of the glory of God.

Conclusion

The latter part of the New Testament adds richness to the biblical theology of prayer. James's insistence that wisdom is available simply by asking and John's clarity on the fact that God always hears and answers prayers for forgiveness from those who trust him add an extra layer to what we have already seen. However, there is no evidence that the later New Testament significantly departs from the conviction of the rest of the Bible: prayer is essentially calling on the name of God to do what he has promised in the Lord Jesus Christ.

This is why, as I suggested at the beginning, it becomes obvious at the end of the Bible that the time of prayer is coming to an end. Prayer is designed for a fallen world, and a day is coming when there will be no need to 'call on the name of Yahweh', because he has already met our every need, and in any case he is right there with us in all the fullness of his splendour. This becomes increasingly apparent as John describes what he sees at the climax of his series of visions in Revelation 21 – 22:

And I saw no temple in the city, for its temple is the Lord God the Almighty and the Lamb. And the city has no need of sun or moon to shine on it, for the glory of God gives it light, and its lamp is the Lamb. By its light will the nations walk, and the kings of the earth will bring their glory into it, and its gates will never be shut by day – and there will be no night there. (Rev. 21:22–25)

No longer will there be anything accursed, but the throne of God and of the Lamb will be in it, and his servants will worship him. They will see his face, and his name will be on their foreheads. And night will be no more. They will need no light of lamp or sun, for the Lord God will be their light, and they will reign for ever and ever. (Rev. 22:3–5)

What need could there be to cry out to God to do what he has promised? For it is finished, and we will enjoy him for ever in the ultimate Eden.[22]

---

[22] In the words of Chester (2003: 38), 'Prayer is not ultimate, but penultimate.'

But in the meantime? We pray. The final words of Revelation distil all that we have seen on this biblical-theological journey through Scripture into a single word – 'Come!' In the meantime we cry to God to do his work in our world by the Spirit through the gospel. We call on his name, asking him to do what he has promised. John captures this essential movement at the heart of prayer like this: 'The Spirit and the Bride say, "Come." And let the one who hears say, "Come"' (Rev. 22:17). 'He who testifies to these things says, "Surely I am coming soon." Amen. Come, Lord Jesus!' (Rev. 22:20). This is the heart of biblical prayer.

Afterword: why this matters – (re)learning to pray big prayers

Introduction

Given the subject matter of this book, it would be remiss not to make any effort to apply its argument to the life of the church (even in a series whose relatively narrow focus is 'biblical theology'). That need is amplified by the fact that we live at a moment in history, in the English-speaking world at least, where it is harder to pray than ever before, and we are praying less than ever before.

Praying has always been hard for Christians. I once heard John Stott say that it was his greatest struggle in the Christian life. James Houston wrote in 1989, 'Why write another book on prayer? The answer is simple – because a lack of prayer is so characteristic of today's world.'[1] A nineteenth-century English bishop wrote, 'I have come to the conclusion that the great majority of professing Christians do not pray at all.'[2] And so it goes on and on.[3] Thus it is not that the challenges we face as the church of the Lord Jesus Christ are unique, but I think there is a sense in which it is *harder for this generation to pray than those who have gone before*. And I am concerned that the evangelical church is slowly but surely giving up on prayer.

First, I want to suggest that we as evangelicals pray much less than we used to, and then to offer some analysis of why that may be. Once I have done that, I want to point out *how the observations in this book should reshape both the way in which we pray,* and *what we pray for*.

[1] Houston 1989: 11.
[2] Ryle 1998: 68.
[3] At least back to the 'Desert Fathers' in the third century, who withdrew to the wilderness to seek God in the face of the growing worldliness of the church.

Analysis: Whatever happened to evangelicals and prayer?

In my lifetime (I am 48) there has a been a shift in the way in which evangelicals *pray*. When I was a student in Belfast, Northern Ireland, and then in Aberdeen, Scotland, one of the defining features of university Christian Unions was the prayer meeting. Evangelical student groups had two main gatherings each week – one focused on Bible teaching and the other dedicated completely to prayer. Whereas in Belfast about 50% of the members came to pray, in Aberdeen the figure was around 80%. But universally, coming together to pray was a reliable index of spiritual maturity and commitment. For most students this pattern was replicated in their local church, where Sunday's teaching was accompanied by some kind of prayer gathering through the week. The vibrancy may have varied, but the understanding was that to be at the core of church life involved a commitment to prayer. That is no longer the case.[4] This is a radical departure from the way things have been in Reformed evangelical circles at least since the seventeenth century. However, this trend is not completely new.

Richard Lovelace, in his profoundly helpful book *The Dynamics of Spiritual Life*, writes:

> Ask evangelicals what the most essential condition of revival is and they are most likely to point to prayer. In much of the church's life in the 20th century, however, in both Evangelical and non-Evangelical circles, the place of prayer has become limited and almost vestigial. The proportion of horizontal communication that goes on in the church (in planning, arguing and expounding) is overwhelmingly greater than that which is vertical (in worship, thanksgiving, confession and intercession). Critically important committee meetings are begun and ended with formulary prayers, which are ritual obligations and not genuine expressions of dependence – when problems and arguments ensue, they are seldom resolved by further prayer, but are wrangled out on the battlefield of human discourse.[5]

---

[4] E.g. here in Australia, while there is still a prayer meeting on most campuses, Australian Fellowship of Evangelical Students staff say it is generally small and regarded as slightly peripheral to the 'main action' on campus. I also know of very few churches that retain a dedicated meeting for corporate prayer.

[5] Lovelace 1979: 153.

Lovelace was writing in 1979. And in the years since then, if anything, things have got worse rather than better. Corporately, prayer has slipped further down the agenda. Individually, I suspect that prayer is the great guilty secret of the evangelical church. The important question is 'Why'?

Diagnosis: Why is the church praying less?

I think at least six factors have contributed to the current weakness of prayer in the English-speaking evangelical church.

Life is easy

Relatively speaking, life is easy. Despite the impact of the global financial crisis, Western economies continue to thrive. Major conflicts have subsided. As a Northern Irishman, for example, I grew up in a small country where people were shooting at and blowing up each other, and lived on a continent where nuclear annihilation seemed a real prospect. But now peace has broken out. Where threats to our security exist, they seem to do so at a greater distance. And the effect of all this? We find it harder to pray when we can say 'No worries' and believe it.

The communications revolution

One of the challenges of this generation is to process and adapt to the radical shift in the way in which we live, which has been brought about by developments in information technology. The immediacy of the flow of information across the globe is staggering. I think nothing of having a face-to-face online meeting with colleagues spread across multiple time zones. I expect instant answers to messages during waking hours. My day is punctuated by a bewildering variety of communications from family, friends and those trying to convince me to part with my money. To be parted from one's mobile phone is a particularly modern form of torture – to be able to 'surf', read, play and 'message' anytime, anywhere, has reached the status of an inalienable human right! And all this makes it harder to pray. In the past it was still hard to pray. There were still distractions. The difference is that we can access these distractions simply by reaching into our pockets. There is no longer any need to count bricks in the church walls when, should the sermon fail to be sufficiently engaging or the prayers too long, we have *Candy Crush* to play on our smartphones.

The rise of Bible study groups

The third reason why prayer (and in particular corporate prayer) has slid down the list of priorities of the church is a little different. It is the rise of Bible study groups. These groups are given different names in different places, and may have slightly different foci, but the 'home group' has become a universal feature of the evangelical church in my lifetime. And I think this is a very good thing. I strongly suspect that the church as a whole is far better at reading and applying the text to real life than it was a generation ago. But this gain has not come without a cost.

Come with me to a Bible study group near you. Let me predict how the evening will run. People will drift in at some point after the start time (someone is always held up in traffic, with an awkward toddler or by a difficult phone call). Then we launch into the excellent and demanding study material. Inevitably, we spend more time talking than we should, and the study runs late. At this point the group leader says something like 'I think we should stop now, and I know that Jimmy has to leave soon, so we really should pray – has anyone got anything to pray for?' Depending on the group, one of two things will happen: either no one will volunteer anything (because we all know that time is short), or a couple of people will inform us of their next-door neighbour's friend's aunt who has just got bad news. Then we fulfil all righteousness, and pray and leave.[6] Over time this practice undermines the importance of prayer and its place in the local church.

The availability of good teaching

The fourth reason may seem stranger still. I think we find it harder to pray now because we have so much good teaching. Those under 40 may find it difficult to imagine, but it is not all that long ago that the only way to hear good preachers from elsewhere (unless they were on a visit to your area – which was rare) was to listen to a 'cassette'. Since cassettes were (1) expensive, and (2) hard to get, they were passed around, used, reused and abused. (In fact, I would still love to hear the end of the Martyn Lloyd-Jones talk on Rom. 11 that someone recorded ABBA's Greatest Hits over!) In the 'bad old days' Christians were reliant on their own pastor for teaching. It sounds bizarre, I

---

[6] I have loved all the home groups I have been part of over the years. However, with the glorious exception of the Howth Home Group that met from 2001 to 2007 in our house, it has always seemed much easier to study the Bible together than to pray.

know, but it is true. And that moved people to pray – in some cases, to pray very fervently!

When we are counting on our own pastor to teach us, we know that God needs to work if we are to hear his word. We see our pastor week by week. We know his weaknesses, we know when he is tired, and when he has had three funerals in the same week, or when his children are sick – and all these things drive us to pray. But if much of our teaching comes through a podcast, delivered by an apparently brilliant guy we do not know, in a place we have never been, to people we have never met, it is not quite the same. To put it bluntly, it does not matter to us if God showed up and addressed his people through his word when it was recorded. It does not matter what was going on in that church, or even in the preacher's life. The only thing that matters is that the preacher produces the goods. And we expect him to. We do not need to pray, then; we just need to press 'Play'. The connection between our prayers and the sermon is broken – and when that happens, it is not easily fixed.

The dominance of pragmatism

There are many things that I love about the church today. Here in Australia, for example, we have seen growth in biblical preaching, church planting, strategic thinking and biblical counselling. And we thank God for all that. But prayer? I do not think so. I suspect that is because we are most comfortable in skills-based settings – when we can read something, talk to someone, go to a conference that will give us the ability to fix whatever is wrong. We are instinctively pragmatic. We are more in control of our lives than any other generation. And that means we pray less. And one more thing – we are praying less because of . . .

The vacuum created by cynicism

I am *cynical*. But the biggest problem with being like me today is that I am surrounded by millions of other people, here in Australia and all over the world, who are exactly like me. The air we breathe is cynical and the people we rub shoulders with are cynical. The pressure is on not to believe. And that means I find it hard to pray. Oh, I am clear on what I will not do when I pray – I am crystal clear on what prayer is definitely not doing. So I do not pray. Lovelace again says:

> It is hard to avoid the conclusion that much of the absence of prayer in the church is due to a virtual allergy produced by

uncomfortable experience with imperfect forms of prayer or to models of the Christian life which require superhuman bouts of prayer in order to qualify at an acceptable level of saintliness.[7]

We fail to pray because there is something false or ridiculously un-realistic about much we have seen and heard. Many of us have been burned – we do not pray because we were told that prayer would fix everything and it did not. So we give up. We pray less. So what should we do?

Relearning to pray

Recalibrating how we pray in the light of the biblical theology of prayer

We pray recognizing our greatest need(s)

Once we realize that God's agenda for us is nothing less than trans-formation into the likeness of Jesus, and that God is passionate about enabling us to live wholeheartedly for him all day, every day for our whole lives, then our need to pray – and the kinds of things we need to pray for – becomes rather obvious. If we are asked to give a talk, to teach a Sunday school class, to lead a home group, to meet to pray with someone else, to visit someone who is ill, can we do those things? Yes we can. We can cut out the craft, prepare the lesson, read the passage, make the coffee, get into the car and drive to the hospital. There are things we can all do competently without being thrown into a blind panic. But can we do the work of God in our own lives or in anyone else's? You must be joking! Paul Miller so helpfully says that 'Learned desperation is at the heart of a praying life.'[8] And that desperation comes when we see the massive scope of God's plans for us and our world. When we see our inability to do anything that makes any difference to ourselves or our world. When we see past what is happening right now, and today, and tomorrow, to what God has been doing in us and our world, and to what he *will do* in us and our world. When we see how much we need God to change us by his Spirit, and to change other people by his Spirit. When we see that, then we will start to pray – and keep praying. If we get this, then it will also radically change the way in which we pray. The focus of our prayers

[7] Lovelace 1979: 154.
[8] P. E. Miller 2009: 114.

will increasingly become God's work in us, and God's work in the lives of others.

So we will pray like this, constantly, in every phase of life:

> Lord, help me to see this as part of your great work in my life and in our world.
> Lord, use this to make me more like the Lord Jesus and to bring others to know Jesus.
> Lord, strengthen me so that I might point other people to Jesus today, encouraging them to see your agenda for their lives.
> Lord, work through me to advance your agenda in the lives of my friends, and family and in our world through the gospel.

We pray realizing that it is always going to be hard work
There is a commonly accepted myth that if we are praying properly (if we are those who are spiritual), then prayer will be a breeze. This is not a new idea. It has been around for ever. The problem is, it is wrong. Paul tells the Colossians that Epaphras, who is held up in the New Testament as a model of what it means to follow Jesus, 'is always struggling on *your* behalf in his prayers' (Col. 4:12). It is hard work! A simple glance at Matthew 26 and Jesus' prayer in the garden shows beyond any doubt that prayer is not always a walk in the park. So let us make sure we do not think that if prayer is hard, that is a problem – it is supposed to be like that. It is hard because we live in a fallen world. But it is also hard because it is intricately linked to God's lifelong work of transforming our lives. So do you find praying hard? Good – you are on the right track.

We pray patiently (while looking for interim answers to big prayers)
We may not see the answers to all our prayers and the prayers of others as God's work in our lives. We will not wake up one morning to discover that, to our surprise, we are now like the Lord Jesus. We will not realize, as we lie in bed one night, that now we know all there is to know about God. We will not see the answer to many of our prayers. At points God in his kindness will give us grace-filled glimpses of what he has done in us. But more often than not we will have to wait. We know how, if we change our car we suddenly become aware that there are, in fact, far more red Toyotas on the road than we realized. We need to go through the same kind of experience when it comes to prayer. We need to learn to see what is already there. I pray regularly for our girls to grow in their love for Jesus – but sometimes

I do not see what happens next as an answer to prayer. The searching question, the sight of one of them reading the Bible in her room, the selfless action that can only be because of grace at work, the uncomplaining commitment to church this week, the hour spent talking to each other in their rooms, the opportunity to speak the gospel to their friends – these are all answers to prayer that I often miss. So we pray patient, persistent, gospel-shaped prayers. But let us get a bit more specific.

Recalibrating what we pray for in the light of the biblical theology of prayer

What we should pray for is controlled by the gospel. Over and over again in the Bible God tells us to ask, because he is delighted to give. It is no accident that all the words in the Bible for 'prayer' mean the same thing – they mean *ask*. Which fits perfectly with the gospel, does it not? *The core of the gospel is that we have nothing, contribute nothing, bring nothing to God – we are rescued by grace alone through faith – asking – alone. It should not come as a shock that prayer, which is made possible by the gospel and shaped by the gospel, works exactly the same way.* The gospel tells us that God gives to us; we do not give to him. So we need to ask. God has spoken to us. We talk back to him, which means asking. Asking for help to understand what God has done for us, to live in the light of what he has done for us, to hold on to what he has done for us, to show other people what he has done for us.

Now in one sense we do not need to get too uptight about this – in a marvellous passage in Luke 11 Jesus makes it clear that we are free to ask our Father for things, knowing that he will not give them to us if they are bad for us, or bad for his kingdom (or plain stupid). So what should we do? Get on with asking! I have learned a lot about this from Rebekah, our youngest daughter. Becky is both completely ridiculous in her asking and also completely content to take 'No' for an answer.

'Daddy, can I have a car of my own?'

'No, Rebekah.'

'That's fine, Daddy. Can we have a pet Tasmanian devil?'

'No, Rebekah.'

'That's fine, Daddy. Can I take all my sister's precious things?'

'No, Rebekah.'

'That's fine, Daddy.'

I suspect that is not far from what Jesus means when he says we must become like little children. Children have no problem asking, nor in trusting their parents to give them only what is good for them.

But that is not the burden of the New Testament when it comes to prayer. The New Testament is explicit in telling us what we should be praying for – or at least in what the focus of our prayers should be. That is because there are, of course, some prayers that God has said he will *always answer*. And I would argue that the prayers God has said he will always answer positively are those that ask him to deliver on his new covenant promises. Or, to put it more generally, God will always answer when we ask him to do his work through his word. So we should ~~pray for~~ *God to do his new covenant work through the gospel.*

I can find five prayers the New Testament encourages us to believe God will always come through on: he will always answer our prayers when we *ask him to do his new covenant work through his word by the Spirit.* And what does that look like? Here is a summary of the 'no brainer' prayers we should pray for as individuals and communities, because God has already guaranteed to answer

- when we pray for forgiveness (1 John 1:9);
- when we pray to know God better (Eph. 1:15–22; 3:18–19);
- when we pray for wisdom (to know how to live for God) (Jas 1:5–6);
- when we pray for strength to obey/love/live for God (Eph. 1:15–22; 3:14–15);
- when we pray for the spread of the gospel (Luke 10:2; Acts 5; Col. 4).

How do we know God will answer these prayers? Because, in the first place, he says he will. But more than that, because these prayers sum up the work of the gospel. This is what God has said he will do, this is what he does and this is what he will do. These are all prayers for God to do his new covenant work through his word – this is what it means to call on the name of Yahweh.

So do you want to become an 'advanced praying person'? Then you do not need a stopwatch. You do not need to learn new contemplative methods. You do not need to do knee exercises. But you do need to become an expert asker – this is gospel-driven prayer. You need to realize that you are a walking disaster who needs God every step of the way, every day, to avoid making a train wreck of your life and the lives of those around you, to realize that the gospel yells at us, 'You are weak and sinful and flawed – but he is strong and gracious and good!' So ask him to do what he has already promised to do. And, above all, pray for the spread of the gospel everywhere. God will answer, because this is how he displays his goodness and glory in our broken world. And keep doing it, until that day when we no longer need to pray, because we will see our God and King face to face.

Bibliography

Aejmelaus, A. (1986), *The Traditional Prayer in the Psalms*, BZAW 167, Berlin: de Gruyter.

Allen, L. C. (2012), 'Jeremiah: Book of', in M. J. Boda and J. G. McConville (eds.), *Dictionary of the Old Testament Prophets*, Downers Grove: IVP Academic; Nottingham: Inter-Varsity Press, 423–441.

Alter, R. (1999), *The David Story*, New York: Norton.

Arnold, C. E. (2010), *Ephesians*, ZECNT, Grand Rapids: Zondervan.

Ash, C. J. (2014), *Job: The Wisdom of the Cross*, PTW, Wheaton: Crossway.

Baker, D. W. (2003), 'God, Names of', in *DOTP*, 359–368.

Balentine, S. E. (1993), *Prayer in the Hebrew Bible: The Drama of Divine–Human Dialogue*, OBT, Minneapolis: Fortress.

—— (2006), *Job*, SHBC, Macon, Georgia: Smith & Helwys.

Baltzer, K. (1971), *The Covenant Formulary*, Oxford: Blackwell.

Barrett, C. K. (1978), *The Gospel According to John*, London: SPCK.

Bauckham, R. J. (1983), *Jude, 2 Peter*, WBC, Waco: Word.

—— (2001), 'Prayer in the Book of Revelation', in R. N. Longenecker (ed.), *Into God's Presence*, Grand Rapids: Eerdmans, 43–65.

Baumgartner, W. L. (1987), *Jeremiah's Poems of Lament*, Sheffield: Almond.

Beale, G. K. (1998), *Revelation*, NIGTC, Exeter: Paternoster.

Blenkinsopp, J. (2002), *Isaiah 40–55: A New Translation with Introduction and Commentary*, AYB, New Haven: Yale University Press.

Block, D. I. (2012), *Deuteronomy*, NIVAC, Grand Rapids: Zondervan.

—— (2014), *For the Glory of God: Recovering a Biblical Theology of Worship*, Grand Rapids: Baker.

Boice, J. M. (1975), *John: Peace in a Storm, John 13–17*, Grand Rapids: Baker.

Boling, R. G. (1975), *Judges*, AB, New York: Doubleday.

Boling, R. G., and G. E. Wright (1995), *Joshua*, AYB, New Haven: Yale University Press.

Bonhoeffer, D. (1974), *Psalms: The Prayerbook of the Bible*, Minneapolis: Augsburg Fortress.

Boyce, R. N. (1988), *The Cry to God in the Old Testament*, SBLDS 103, Atlanta: Scholars Press.

Bruce, F. F. (1983), *The Gospel of John*, Grand Rapids: Eerdmans.

────── (1993), 'Habakkuk', in T. E. McComiskey (ed.), *The Minor Prophets: An Exegetical and Expository Commentary: Obadiah, Jonah, Micah, Nahum, and Habakkuk*, Grand Rapids: Baker, 831–896.

Bruckner, J. K. (2003), 'Habakkuk, Book of', in *DOTP*, 294–301.

Brueggemann, W. (1998), *A Commentary on Jeremiah: Exile and Homecoming*, Grand Rapids: Eerdmans.

Bruner, F. D. (2004), *The Christbook: Matthew 1–12*, Grand Rapids: Eerdmans.

Bunyan, J. (1999), *Prayer*, Carlisle: Banner of Truth.

Butler, T. C. (2006), *Judges*, WBC, Waco: Word.

Calvin, J. (1847), *Genesis*, Carlisle: Banner of Truth.

────── (1960), *Institutes of the Christian Religion*, ed. J. T. McNeill, tr. F. L. Battles, vols. 1–2, Philadelphia: Westminster.

Carson, D. A. (ed.) (1990), *Teach Us to Pray: Prayer in the Bible and the World*, Grand Rapids: Baker.

────── (1991), *The Gospel According to John*, PNTC, Grand Rapids: Eerdmans; Leicester: Apollos.

────── (1992), *A Call to Spiritual Reformation: Priorities from Paul and His Prayers*, Grand Rapids: Baker; Leicester: Inter-Varsity Press.

────── (1995), *Matthew*, EBC, Grand Rapids: Zondervan.

Charlesworth, J. H., M. Harding and M. Kiley (eds.) (1994), *The Lord's Prayer and Other Prayer Texts from the Greco-Roman Era*, Valley Forge, Pa.: Trinity Press International.

Chester, T. (2003), *The Message of Prayer*, Leicester, Inter-Varsity Press.

Childs, B. S. (2001), *Isaiah: A Commentary*, OTL, Louisville: Westminster John Knox.

Clements, R. E. (1985), *The Prayers of the Bible*, London: SCM.

Clines, D. J. A. (1989), *Job 1–20*, WBC, Waco: Word.

Clowney, E. P. (1990), 'A Biblical Theology of Prayer', in D. A. Carson (ed.), *Teach Us to Pray: Prayer in the Bible and the World*, Grand Rapids: Baker, 136–173.

Collins, J. J. (1993), *Daniel*, Hermeneia, Minneapolis: Fortress.

Crump, D. M. (1992), *Jesus the Intercessor: Prayer and Christology in Luke-Acts*, Tübingen: Mohr-Siebeck.

────── (2006), *Knocking on Heaven's Door: A New Testament Theology of Petitionary Prayer*, Grand Rapids: Baker.

—— (2013), 'Prayer', in J. B. Green, S. McKnight and N. Perrin (eds.), *Dictionary of Jesus and the Gospels*, 2nd ed., Downers Grove: InterVarsity Press; Nottingham: Inter-Varsity Press, 684–692.

Cullman, O. (1995), *Prayer in the New Testament*, London: SCM.

Cumerford, B. (2015), 'In What Ways Does the Book of the Twelve Prepare for a New Movement in Salvation History?', MDiv thesis, St Lucia: Queensland Theological College.

Davids, P. H. (1982), *James*, NIGTC, Grand Rapids: Eerdmans.

—— (1990), *1 Peter*, NICNT, Grand Rapids: Eerdmans.

—— (2006), *The Letters of 2 Peter and Jude*, PNTC, Nottingham: Apollos.

Davis, D. R. (1999), *2 Samuel: Out of Every Adversity*, FOTB, Tain: Christian Focus.

—— (2000), *Judges: Such a Great Salvation*, FOTB, Tain: Christian Focus.

—— (2007), *1 Kings: The Wisdom and the Folly*, FOTB, Tain: Christian Focus.

deClaisse-Walford, N., R. A. Jacobson and B. LaNeel Tanner (2014), *Psalms*, NICOT, Grand Rapids: Eerdmans.

Dillard, R. B. (1987), *2 Chronicles*, WBC, Waco: Word.

—— (1992), 'Joel', in T. E. McComiskey (ed.), *The Minor Prophets: An Exegetical & Expository Commentary*, vol. 1, Grand Rapids: Baker Academic, 203–248.

Dozemann, T. B. (2009), *Exodus*, ECC, Grand Rapids: Eerdmans.

Dunn, J. D. G. (1992), 'Prayer', in J. B. Green, S. McKnight and I. H. Marshall (eds.), *Dictionary of Jesus and the Gospels*, Downers Grove: IVP Academic; Leicester: Inter-Varsity Press, 617–625.

Ellingworth, P. (1993), *The Epistle to the Hebrews*, NIGTC, Grand Rapids: Eerdmans.

Farris, S. (2001), 'The Canticles of Luke's Infancy Narrative as the Appropriation of a Biblical Tradition', in R. N. Longenecker (ed.), *Into God's Presence: Prayer in the New Testament*, Grand Rapids: Eerdmans, 91–112.

Finkel, A. (2001), 'Prayer in Jewish Life of the First Century as Background to Early Christianity', in R. N. Longenecker (ed.), *Into God's Presence: Prayer in the New Testament*, Grand Rapids: Eerdmans, 43–65.

Firth, D. G. (2009), *1 & 2 Samuel*, AOTC, Nottingham: Apollos; Downers Grove: InterVarsity Press.

Forsyth, P. T. (1916), *The Soul of Prayer*, London: Independent.

France, R. T. (1985), *Matthew*, TNTC, Leicester: Inter-Varsity Press.

————— (2007), *Matthew*, NICNT, Grand Rapids: Eerdmans.

Fredericks, D. C., and D. J. Estes (2010), *Ecclesiastes and the Song of Songs*, AOTC, Nottingham: Apollos; Downers Grove: InterVarsity Press.

Futato, M. D. (2007), *Interpreting the Psalms*, Grand Rapids: Kregel.

Garrett, D. A. (2012), 'Joel: Book of', in M. J. Boda and J. G. McConville (eds.), *Dictionary of the Old Testament Prophets*, Downers Grove: IVP Academic; Nottingham: Inter-Varsity Press, 449–455.

Gerstenberger, E. S. (1988), *Psalms: Part 1*, FOTL, Grand Rapids: Eerdmans.

Goldingay, J. (2008), *Psalms Volume 3: Psalms 90–150*, BCOTWP, Grand Rapids: Baker.

Goldsworthy, G. (2003), *Prayer and the Knowledge of God*, Leicester: Inter-Varsity Press.

Gordon, R. P. (1986), *1 & 2 Samuel*, Exeter: Paternoster.

Grant, J. A. (2004), *The King as Exemplar: The Function of Deuteronomy's Kingship Law in the Shaping of the Book of Psalms*, AcBib 17, Atlanta: Society of Biblical Literature.

Green, J. B. (2001), 'Persevering Together in Prayer – the Significance of Prayer in the Acts of the Apostles', in R. N. Longenecker (ed.), *Into God's Presence: Prayer in the New Testament*, Grand Rapids: Eerdmans, 183–202.

Greenberg, M. (1983), *Biblical Prose Prayer: As a Window to the Popular Religion of Ancient Israel*, Berkeley: University of California.

Gregg, R. C. (1980), *Athanasius: The Life of Anthony and the Letter to Marcellinus*, Mahwah, N.J.: Paulist Press.

Gundry, R. H. (1993), *Mark: A Commentary for His Apology for the Cross*, Grand Rapids: Eerdmans.

Gunkel, H. (1967), *The Psalms – a Form Critical Introduction*, Minneapolis: Fortress.

————— (1998), *Introduction to Psalms: The Genres of the Religious Lyric of Israel*, MLBS, Macon, Ga.: Mercer University Press.

Gunn, D. M. (1980), *The Fate of King Saul*, Sheffield: Sheffield Academic Press.

Hallesby, O. (1948), *Prayer*, Leicester: Inter-Varsity Press.

Harrison, R. K. (1973), *Jeremiah and Lamentations*, TOTC, Leicester: Inter-Varsity Press.

Hobbs, T. R. (1986), *2 Kings*, WBC, Waco: Word.

Hossfeld, F.-L., and E. Zenger (2005), *Psalms 2: A Commentary on Psalms 51–100*, Hermeneia, Minneapolis: Fortress.

———— (2011), *Psalms 3: A Commentary on Psalms 101–150*, Hermeneia, Minneapolis: Fortress.

Hertzberg, H. W. (1964), *1, 2 Samuel*, OTL, London: SCM.

House, P. R. (1990), *The Unity of the Twelve*, Sheffield: Almond.

———— (1995), *1,2 Kings*, NAC, Nashville: Holman.

Houston, J. (1989), *Prayer: The Transforming Friendship*, Oxford: Lion.

Howard Jr., D. M. (2005), 'The Psalms and Current Study', in D. G. Firth and P. S. Johnston (eds.), *Interpreting the Psalms*, Leicester: Apollos, 23–40.

Jacobson, R. A. (2004), *Many Are Saying: The Function of Direct Discourse in the Hebrew Psalter*, London: T. & T. Clark.

Jenson, P. P. (2008), *Obadiah, Jonah, Micah: A Theological Commentary*, LHB/OTS, New York: T. & T. Clark.

Jeremias, J. (1967), *The Prayers of Jesus*, London: SCM.

Jobes, K. H. (2014), *1, 2, and 3 John*, ZECNT, Grand Rapids: Zondervan.

Johnston, P. S., and D. G. Firth (2005), *Interpreting the Psalms*, Leicester: Apollos.

Johnstone, W. B. (1986), 'Guilt and Atonement: The Theme of 1 and 2 Chronicles', in J. D. Martin and P. R. Davies (eds.), *A Word in Season: Essays in Honour of William McKane*, JSOTSup 42, Sheffield: JSOT Press, 113–138.

Jung, K. N. (1990), 'Prayer in the Psalms', in D. A. Carson (ed.), *Teach Us to Pray: Prayer in the Bible and the World*, Grand Rapids: Baker, 35–57.

Keener, C. S. (2012), *Acts: An Exegetical Commentary*, vol. 1: *Introduction and 1:1–2:47*, Grand Rapids, Baker.

Keller, T. J. (2014), *Prayer: Experiencing Awe and Intimacy with God*, New York: Dutton.

Kelly, D. F. (1990), 'Prayer and Union with Christ', *SBET* 8.2: 109–127.

Kidner, D. (1973), *Psalms 1–72*, TOTC, Leicester: Inter-Varsity Press.

Knohl, I. (1988), 'The Conception of God and Cult in the Priestly Torah and in the Holiness School', PhD diss., Jerusalem: Hebrew University of Jerusalem.

Köstenberger, A. J. (2004), *John*, BECNT, Grand Rapids: Baker.

———— (2008), *Father, Son and Spirit: The Trinity in John's Gospel*, NSBT: Nottingham: Apollos; Downers Grove: InterVarsity Press.

Köstenberger, A. J., and T. R. Schreiner (eds.) (2005), *Women in the Church: An Analysis and Application of 1 Timothy 2:9–15*, Grand Rapids: Baker.

Kraus, H.-J. (1993a), *Psalms 1–59*, CC, Minneapolis: Fortress.
—— (1993b), *Psalms 60–150*, CC, Minneapolis: Fortress.
Leithart, P. J. (2006), *1 & 2 Kings*, BTCB, Grand Rapids: Brazos.
Lenski, R. C. H. (1946), *The Interpretation of St. Luke's Gospel*, Minneapolis: Augsburg.
Levine, B. A. (1993), *Numbers 1–20: A New Translation*, AB, New York: Doubleday.
Lincoln, A. T. (1990), *Ephesians*, WBC, Waco: Word.
—— (2001), 'God's Name, Jesus' Name, and Prayer in the Fourth Gospel', in R. N. Longenecker (ed.), *Into God's Presence: Prayer in the New Testament*, Grand Rapids: Eerdmans, 155–180.
Lloyd-Jones, D. M. (2000), *The Assurance of Our Salvation: Exploring the Depth of Jesus' Prayer for His Own: Studies in John 17*, Wheaton: Crossway.
Longenecker, R. N. (ed.) (2001), *Into God's Presence: Prayer in the New Testament*, Grand Rapids: Eerdmans.
Longman III, T. (1999), *Daniel*, NIVAC, Grand Rapids, Zondervan.
—— (2012), *Job*, BECOT, Grand Rapids: Baker.
Lovelace, R. F. (1979), *The Dynamics of Spiritual Life*, Downers Grove: InterVarsity Press.
McCarter, K. (1980), *1 Samuel*, AB, New York: Doubleday.
McConville, J. G. (1992), '1 Kings 8:46–53 and the Deuteronomic Hope', *VT* 42.1: 67–79.
—— (1993a), *Grace in the End*, Grand Rapids: Zondervan.
—— (1993b), *Judgment and Promise*, Leicester: Apollos.
McKeown, J. (2008), *Genesis*, THOTC, Grand Rapids: Eerdmans.
Marshall, I. H. (1978), *The Gospel of Luke*, NIGTC: Grand Rapids: Eerdmans.
—— (2001), 'Jesus – Example and Teacher of Prayer in the Synoptics', in R. N. Longenecker (ed.), *Into God's Presence: Prayer in the New Testament*, Grand Rapids: Eerdmans, 113–131.
Martin, R. P. (1988), *James*, WBC, Waco: Word.
Metzger, J. A. (2010), 'God as F(r)iend? Reading Luke 11:5–13 & 18:1–8 with a Hermeneutic of Suffering', *HBT* 32: 33–57.
Milgrom, J. (1991), *Leviticus 1–16*, AB, New York: Doubleday.
Miller Jr., P. D. (1994), *They Cried to the Lord: The Form and Theology of Biblical Prayer*, Minneapolis: Fortress.
Miller, P. E. (2009), *A Praying Life*, Carol Stream, Ill.: NavPress.
Mitchell, D. C. (1997), *Message of the Psalter: An Eschatological Programme in the Book of Psalms*, JSOTSup 252, Sheffield: JSOT Press.

————— (2006), 'Lord, Remember David: G. H. Wilson and the Message of the Psalter', *VT* 56.4: 526–548.

Moo, D. J. (1996), *The Epistle to the Romans*, NICNT, Grand Rapids: Eerdmans.

————— (2008), *The Letters to Colossians and Philemon*, NIGTC, Grand Rapids: Eerdmans.

Morris, L. (1992), *The Gospel According to Matthew*, Leicester: Apollos.

————— (1995), *The Gospel According to John*, NICNT: Grand Rapids: Eerdmans.

Motyer, J. A. (1959), *Revelation of the Divine Name*, London: Tyndale.

————— (1999), *Isaiah*, TOTC, Leicester: Inter-Varsity Press.

Mounce, R. H. (1997), *The Book of Revelation*, NICNT, Grand Rapids: Eerdmans.

Mowinckel, S. (1962), *The Psalms as Israel's Worship*, repr., Grand Rapids: Eerdmans, 2004.

Ng, E. Y. L. (1990), 'Prayer in Revelation', in D. A. Carson (ed.), *Teach Us to Pray: Prayer in the Bible and the World*, Grand Rapids: Baker, 119–135.

O'Brien, P. T. (1973), 'Prayer in Luke-Acts', *TynB* 24: 111–127.

————— (1977), *Introductory Thanksgivings in the Letters of Paul*, NTS, Leiden: Brill.

————— (1982), *Colossians–Philemon*, WBC, Waco: Word.

————— (1991), *Philippians*, NIGTC, Grand Rapids: Eerdmans.

————— (1999), *The Letter to the Ephesians*, PNTC, Leicester: Apollos.

————— (2010), *Hebrews*, PNTC, Grand Rapids: Eerdmans; Nottingham: Apollos.

O'Donnell, D. S. (2013), *Matthew: All Authority in Heaven and on Earth*, PTW, Wheaton: Crossway.

Olson, D. T. (1996), *Numbers*, Interpretation, Louisville: Westminster John Knox.

Parry, R. A. (2010), *Lamentations*, THOTC, Grand Rapids: Eerdmans.

Peterson, D. G. (1990a), 'Prayer in the General Epistles', in D. A. Carson (ed.), *Teach Us to Pray: Prayer in the Bible and the World*, Grand Rapids: Baker, 102–118.

————— (1990b), 'Prayer in Paul's Writings', in D. A. Carson (ed.), *Teach Us to Pray: Prayer in the Bible and the World*, Grand Rapids: Baker, 84–101.

————— (2009), *The Acts of the Apostles*, PNTC, Grand Rapids: Eerdmans; Nottingham: Apollos.

Petterson, A. R. (2015), *Haggai, Zechariah, Malachi*, AOTC, Nottingham: Apollos; Downers Grove: InterVarsity Press.

Philip, W. (2015), *Why We Pray*, Wheaton: Crossway; Nottingham: Inter-Varsity Press.

Pitkänen, P. M. A. (2012), *Joshua*, AOTC, Nottingham: Apollos; Downers Grove: InterVarsity Press.

Pritchard, J. B. (1969), *Ancient Near Eastern Texts Relating to the Old Testament*, Princeton: Princeton University Press.

Provan, I. M. (1995), *1 & 2 Kings*, NIBC, Peabody, Mass.: Hendrickson.

Rad, G. von (1972), *Genesis*, OTL, London: SCM.

Reif, S. C. (1993), *Judaism and Hebrew Prayer*, Cambridge: Cambridge University Press.

Reventlow, H. G. (1986), *Gebet im Alten Testament*, Stuttgart: Kohlhammer.

Ross, A. (1997), 'šēm', in *NIDOTTE* 5: 147–151.

Ryle, J. C. (1998), *Practical Religion*, Edinburgh: Banner of Truth.

Sarkissian, M. J. (2009), *Before God: The Biblical Doctrine of Prayer*, Maitland: Xulon.

Sawyer, J. F. A. (1980), 'Types of Prayer in the Old Testament: Some Semantic Observations on Hitpallell, Hithannen etc.', *Semitics* 7: 131–143.

Schaefer, K. (2001), *Berit Olam Studies in Hebrew Narrative and Poetry: Psalms*, Collegeville, Minn.: Liturgical Press.

Schnabel, E. J. (2012), *Acts*, ZECNT, Grand Rapids: Zondervan.

Schreiner, T. R. (1998), *Romans*, BECNT, Grand Rapids: Baker.

Seitz, C. R. (2001), 'Prayer in the Old Testament or Hebrew Bible', in R. N. Longenecker (ed.), *Into God's Presence: Prayer in the New Testament*, Grand Rapids: Eerdmans, 3–22.

Sweeney, M. A. (2007), *1 & 2 Kings*, OTL, Atlanta: Westminster John Knox.

Talmon, S. (1978), 'The Emergence of Institutionalised Prayer in Israel in the Light of the Qumran Literature', in M. Delcor (ed.), *Qumran: sa piété, sa théologie et son milieu*, Paris: Duculot, 265–284.

Thiselton, A. C. (2001), *1 Corinthians*, NIGTC, Grand Rapids: Eerdmans.

Thompson, J. A. (1980), *Jeremiah*, NICOT, Grand Rapids: Eerdmans.

Thompson, M. E. W. (1996), *I Have Heard Your Prayer: The Old Testament and Prayer*, Peterborough: Epworth.

Towner, P. H. (2006), *1, 2 Timothy, Titus*, NICNT, Grand Rapids: Eerdmans.

Turner, M. M. B. (1990), 'Prayer in the Gospels and Acts', in D. A. Carson (ed.), *Teach Us to Pray: Prayer in the Bible and the World*, Grand Rapids: Baker, 58–83.

Verhoef, P. A. (1997), 'Prayer', in *NIDOTTE* 4: 1060–1066.

Walton, J. H. (2006), *Ancient Near Eastern Thought and the Old Testament*, Grand Rapids: Baker; Nottingham: Apollos.

——— (2011), *Genesis*, NIVAC, Grand Rapids: Zondervan.

Webb, B. G. (2012), *Judges*, NICOT, Grand Rapids: Eerdmans.

Wenham, G. J. (1979), *Leviticus*, NICOT, Grand Rapids: Eerdmans.

Westermann, C. (1980), *The Psalms: Structure, Content, Message*, Kitchener, Ont.: Augsburg Fortress Canada.

——— (1981), *Praise and Lament in the Psalms*, Atlanta: Westminster John Knox.

——— (1982), *Elements of Old Testament Theology*, Atlanta: John Knox.

Westermann, C. (1987), *Genesis 1–11*, CC, Minneapolis: Fortress.

Williamson, H. G. M. (1977), 'Eschatology in Chronicles', *TynB* 28: 115–154.

——— (1985), *Ezra-Nehemiah*, WBC, Waco: Word.

Wilson, G. H. (1985), *The Editing of the Hebrew Psalter*, SBLDS 85, Atlanta: Society of Biblical Literature Press.

——— (2002), *Psalms*, NIVAC, Grand Rapids: Zondervan.

Wilson, I. (1995), *Out of the Midst of the Fire: Divine Presence in Deuteronomy*, SBLDS 151, Atlanta: Society of Biblical Literature Press.

Winter, B. W. (2001), *After Paul Left Corinth*, Grand Rapids: Eerdmans.

Witherington III, B. (2007), *Letters and Homilies for Jewish Christians: A Socio-Rhetorical Commentary on Hebrews, James and Jude*, Downers Grove: InterVarsity Press; Nottingham: Apollos.

Woodhouse, J. (2008), *1 Samuel: Looking for a Leader*, PTW, Wheaton: Crossway.

Woudstra, M. (1981), *Joshua*, NICOT, Grand Raids: Eerdmans.

Wray Beal, L. M. (2014), *1 & 2 Kings*, AOTC, Nottingham: Apollos; Downers Grove: InterVarsity Press.

Wright, N. T. (1997), *The Lord and His Prayer*, Grand Rapids: Eerdmans.

——— (2001), 'The Lord's Prayer as a Paradigm of Christian Prayer', in R. N. Longenecker (ed.), *Into God's Presence: Prayer in the New Testament*, Grand Rapids: Eerdmans, 132–154.

Zimmerli, W. T. (1978), *Old Testament Theology in Outline*, Edinburgh: T. & T. Clark.

Index of authors

Allen, L. C., 76
Alter, R., 52
Arnold, C. E., 204
Ash, C. J., 108, 109, 115, 142
Athanasius, 140

Baker, D. W., 20
Balentine, S. E., 20, 31, 37, 109
Baltzer, K., 122
Barrett, C. K., 179, 182
Bauckham, R. J., 225, 227
Baumgartner, W. L., 76
Beale, G. K., 30, 227
Blenkinsopp, J., 71
Block, D. I., 42, 116
Boice, J. M., 182
Boling, R. G., 46, 49
Bonhoeffer, D., 140, 143
Bruce, F. F., 102, 179
Bruckner, J. K., 101
Brueggemann, W., 81
Bruner, F. D., 171
Butler, T. C., 50

Calvin, J., 17, 18, 20, 21, 28
Carson, D. A., 16, 171, 172, 179,
    182, 201, 205
Chester, T., 16, 20, 223, 225, 229
Childs, B. S., 72, 163
Clements, R. E., 16, 20, 31, 47,
Clines, D. J. A., 109
Clowney, E. P., 16, 20, 22
Collins, J. J., 118
Crump, D. M., 167, 172, 175, 176,
    177, 178, 179, 193
Cumerford, B., 91

Davids, P. H., 220, 222, 225
Davis, D. R., 51, 54, 58, 63
Dillard, R. B., 94, 131
Dozemann, T. B., 34

Ellingworth, P., 217

Farris, S., 168
Finkel, A., 167
Firth, D. G., 54, 57, 155
France, R. T., 171, 173, 174
Fredericks, D.C., 108
Futato, M. D., 138

Garrett, D. A., 94
Gerstenberger, E. S., 139
Goldingay, J., 151
Goldsworthy, G., 16, 20, 28
Gordon, R. P., 54
Grant, J. A., 164
Green, D., 164
Green, J. B., 194
Greenberg, M., 37, 45
Gregg, R. C., 140
Gundry, R. H., 176
Gunkel, H., 139, 140
Gunn, D. M., 57

Hallesby, O., 16
Harrison, R. K., 81
Hertzberg, H. W., 54
Hobbs, T. R. 64
Hossfeld, F.-L., 138, 147, 152, 153,
    154, 164
House, P. R., 60, 62, 91, 95
Houston, J., 231

Howard Jr., D. M., 155

Jacobson, R. A., 140, 141
Jacobson, R. A., 152
Jenson, P. P., 98
Jobes, K. H., 226
Johnston, P. S., 155
Johnstone, W. B., 37, 126
Jung, K. N., 139

Keener, C. S., 192, 199
Keller, T. J., 16, 19, 27
Kidner, D., 157
Knohl, I., 36, 37
Köstenberger, A. J., 179, 182, 211
Kraus, H.-J., 138, 147

Leithart, P. J., 60
Lenski, R. C. H., 178
Levine, B. A., 40
Lincoln, A. T., 176, 204
Lloyd-Jones, M., 182, 205, 234
Longenecker, R. N., 16
Longman III, T., 113, 119
Lovelace, R. F., 232, 233, 235, 236

McCarter, K., 52
McConville, J. G., 61, 62, 76
McKeown, J., 20
Marshall, I. H., 172, 178
Martin, R. P., 220
Metzger, J. A., 178
Milgrom, J., 36, 37
Miller Jr., P. D., 16, 22, 28, 31, 33, 147
Miller, P. E., 16, 236
Mitchell, D. C., 164, 165
Moo, D. J., 202, 207
Morris, L., 174, 179
Motyer, J. A., 20, 71, 72
Mounce, R. H., 227
Mowinckel, S., 139

Ng, E. Y. L., 226

O'Brien, P. T., 167, 168, 183, 191, 201, 204, 205, 206, 208, 214, 217, 218
O'Donnell, D. S., 172, 174
Olson, D. T., 40

Parry, R. A., 85
Peskett, H., 20
Peterson, D. G., 37, 192, 195, 201, 217
Petterson, A. R., 105
Philip, W., 16
Pitkänen, P. M. A., 46
Pritchard, J. B., 29
Provan, I. M., 63

Rad, G. von., 20
Ross, A., 22
Ryle, J. C., 231

Schaefer, K., 143
Schnabel, E. J., 192
Schreiner, T. R., 202, 210, 211
Seitz, C. R., 28, 42, 100
Sweeney, M. A., 62

Tanner, B. L., 149
Thiselton, A. C., 212
Thompson, J. A., 81
Thompson, M. E. W., 19, 61, 126
Towner, P. H., 211
Turner, M. M. B., 167, 168, 173, 183, 185

Verhoef, P. A., 20, 27

Walton, J. H., 20, 36
Webb, B. G., 48,
Wenham, G. J., 20, 37
Westermann, C., 20, 139, 155, 156
Williamson, H. G. M., 121, 127, 128

Wilson, G. H., 138, 144, 145, 163, 164
Wilson, I., 61
Winter, B. W., 212
Witherington III, B., 219
Woodhouse, J., 52, 140
Woudstra, M., 46

Wray Beal, L. M., 64
Wright, E., 46
Wright, N. T., 172, 173

Zenger, E., 138, 147, 152, 153, 154, 164

Index of Scripture references

OLD TESTAMENT

Genesis
1 – 11 *21*
3 *29, 54*
3:8–10 *28*
3:15 *21, 22, 27, 179*
4 *19, 20, 21, 30, 54*
4:25 *21*
4:25–26 *20, 21, 27,*
  29
4:26 *17, 22, 27*
5 *20*
12 *21, 27*
12:8 *22*
12:8–20 *31*
13:4 *22*
17:18 *31*
18 *19, 40, 92*
18:22–23 *19*
20:4–7 *31*
21:33 *22, 23*
22 *21*
24:11–12 *31*
24:26–27 *31*
25 *21*
25:21 *32*
26:24 *23*
26:25 *22*
28:22 *32*
32 *32*
32:9–12 *32*
38 *21*
43:14 *33*
48:15–16 *33*

48:20 *33*
49 – 50 *21*

Exodus
2:23–25 *33*
3:13–14 *20*
3:13–16 *172*
5:22 *33*
5:22–23 *33–34*
6:1–8 *34*
6:2 *34*
6:3 *20*
17 *34, 35*
17:4–7 *34–35*
32 *33, 34, 35, 37, 41*
32 – 34 *149*
32:11–13 *35*
32:30–34 *35–36*
32:33–34 *36*

Leviticus
1:4 *37*
16:21 *37*
26 *61*

Numbers
11 – 14 *38*
11:1–2 *38*
11:4–9 *38*
11:11–15 *38*
11:12 *39*
12 *39*
12:8 *145*
12:8–10 *39*
14 *39*

14:11–12 *39–40*
14:13 *39*
14:13–20 *40*
16:22 *40*
27:16–17 *40*

Deuteronomy
3:23–26 *41*
4 *61*
4:5–8 *42*
4:7 *58*
4:7–8 *42*
4:34 *58*
7:1–3 *122*
9:25–29 *41*
9:26 *58*
10:21 *58*
11:8 *122*
23:6 *122*
26:18 *58*
28 *61*
30 *42, 72, 120, 124,*
  126
30:1–5 *42*
32 *54*
33:29 *58*

Joshua
5:13–15 *47*
7 *45*
7:6–9 *45*
7:9 *46*
7:10–14 *46*
7:14 *47*
9:14 *46*

Joshua (*cont.*)
10 *46*
10:12–14 *46–47*
24:7 *47*

Judges
1:1–2 *47*
3:9 *48*
3:15 *48*
4:3 *48*
5 *49*
5:31 *49*
6:6–7 *48*
6:36–40 *49*
10 *48*
10:10 *48*
10:11–14 *48*
10:13 *50*
10:13–14 *48*
13:8–9 *50*
15:18 *50*
16:28–30 *50*
20 *50*
20:18–21 *51*
20:23 – 28 *51*
21:2–3 *52*

1 Samuel
1 *52*
1:11–12 *52*
1:12 *52*
2 *52, 54, 168*
2:1–10 *52, 53*
2:27–36 *54*
6 *55*
6:19 *56*
7 *55*
7:4 *55*
7:5 *56*
8:1–5 *57*
8:6–8 *55*
12 *55*
12:6–17 *55*
12:18 *55*

12:23–25 *56*
14 *56*
14:36 *56*
15:10–11 *57*
16 *57*
23:1–5 *57*
28 *56*
28:7 *56*
30:6 *57*
30:7–10 *57*

2 Samuel
2:1–2 *57*
2:1–7 *57*
2:4 *57*
5:19 *57*
7 *59*
7:13 *58*
7:18 *58*
7:18–29 *58, 127*
7:22–24 *58*
7:25 *58*
7:28–29 *58*
12:16 *58*
21:1 *58*
24:10 *130*

1 Kings
2:6 *60*
2:9 *60*
3 *59*
3:1–15 *59*
3:6–9 *59–60*
3:8 *130*
3:11–15 *60*
3:16–28 *60*
4:29–34 *60*
6 *131*
7:8 *60*
8 *60, 61, 63, 131*
8:15 *61*
8:20 *61*
8:21 *61*
8:23 *61*

8:24–25 *61*
8:27–30 *61*
8:31 *61*
8:40 *61*
8:41–43 *62*
8:47–61 *62*
8:48 *61*
8:52–54 *62*
8:53 *61*
8:56 *61*
8:60 *62*
8:66 *61*
11:1–8 *60*
17:20–24 *62*
17:24 *62*
18:24 *22, 23*
18:36–37 *23, 62, 63*
19:3 *63*
19:4 *62, 63*
19:10 *63*
19:14 *63*

2 Kings
1 *56*
3 *133*
4:32–37 *63*
5:11 *22, 23*
6:15–19 *63*
14:25 *97*
19 *64*
19:10 *64*
19:14–19 *64*
19:34 *64*
19:35 *64*
20 *64*
20:2–3 *64*
20:5–6 *65*
20:10 *65*
21:16 *122*

1 Chronicles
1 *20*
1 – 9 *126*

4:10 *126*
5:20 *126*
16 *127*
16:1–7 *25*
16:8 *22, 25*
16:15–18 *25*
16:35–36 *127*
17:16 *128*
17:16–27 *126–127, 28*
21 *129*
21:16–17 *129–130*
29:10–19 *127, 28–129*

2 Chronicles
1 *130*
1:8–10 *130*
3 *131*
6 *130*
6:19–40 *131–133*
13 *133*
13:14–15 *133*
14 *133*
14:11–12 *133*
18:30–31 *133*
20:6–12 *134*
30:18–20 *134*
30:27 *135*
32:20–21 *135*
32:24–25 *135*
33:10–13 *135*
33:18–19 *136*

Ezra
8 *120*
8:21–23 *120*
9:5–9 *121*
9:10–15 *121–122*

Nehemiah
1:4–11 *122–123*
2:3–4 *123*
4:9 *123*
5:19 *123*
9 *124*

9:6 *125*
9:7–8 *125*
9:9–12 *125*
9:13–21 *125*
9:22–25 *125*
9:26–31 *125*
9:32–38 *125*
9:36 *125*
13 *124, 125*
13:14 *123*
13:22 *123*
13:29 *123, 124*
13:31 *123*

Job
1:21 *54*
5:11 *54*
7 *108*
7:7–21 *109*
10:2 *109*
10:2–22 *109–111*
10:3 *109*
10:8–9 *109*
10:11 *109*
10:12 *109*
12:4 *111*
13:18 – 14:22 *111*
13:20–26 *111–112*
14:3–6 *112*
14:13–17 *112*
15:4 *113*
17:4 *113*
21:14–15 *113*
22:26–27 *113*
23 *113*
23:16–17 *113*
27:9–10 *113*
30 *113*
30:19–23 *114*
33:23–26 *114*
36:7 *54*
38:1 *114*
38:4–6 *54*
40:3–5 *114*

42:1–6 *114–115*
42:8 *115*

Psalms
1 *138, 141*
2 *24, 54, 138, 141,
    142, 193*
2 – 41 *164*
3 *141, 142*
3 – 7 *138*
3 – 8 *138*
3:1–2 *141*
8 *109*
9 – 10 *138*
12 – 13 *138*
13 *22*
15 – 17 *138*
17 *22, 138, 143,
    143–144, 147*
17:1 *145*
17:3 *145*
17:8 *145*
17:13–14 *145*
18 *156*
19 *138*
19:12–14 *138*
20 *138*
20:9 *138*
21 – 22 *138*
22 *189*
25 – 26 *138*
28 *138*
30 – 31 *138*
34:13–17 *224*
35 *138*
37 *157*
37:39–40 *157*
38 *138*
41:13 *164*
42 – 43 *138*
42 – 72 *164*
44 *156*
44:1–3 *156*
44:23–26 *156–157*

Psalms (*cont.*)
50:15 *71*
51 *138, 157, 161*
51:1–2 *158*
51:3–4 *158*
51:5–6 *158*
51:7–9 *158*
51:10–12 *158*
51:12 *159*
51:13 *159*
51:13–17 *159*
51:18–19 *159*
54 – 57 *138*
55:17 *117*
59 *138*
61 *138*
63 – 64 *138*
69 – 71 *138*
72:19 *164*
73 *159, 161, 162*
73 – 89 *164*
73:1 *159*
73:2–16 *159*
73:16–17 *160*
73:18–28 *160*
79:6 *22, 25*
80:18 *22, 25*
84 *138*
86 *138, 143, 145–147, 147, 151*
86:2 *147*
86:9 *152*
86:9–10 *147*
86:11–13 *147*
86:14 *147*
86:17 *147*
89:52 *164*
90 *138, 143, 147–148, 149, 155*
90 – 106 *164*
90:11 *149*
90:12 *149*
90:15–17 *149*
95 *155*

95:6–7 *155*
99:6 *22*
101 *153*
102 *138, 143, 147, 149–151, 152, 153*
102:1–2 *151*
102:1–10 *149*
102:4–6 *151*
102:12–13 *152*
102:14 *151*
102:15 *152*
102:16–17 *153*
102:17 *151*
102:18–22 *153*
102:24 *153*
102:24–25 *151–152*
103 *153*
105:1 *22, 25*
106:48 *164*
107 – 150 *164*
109 *138*
116:4 *22*
116 *26*
116:1–4 *26*
116:12–13 *26*
116:17 *26*
120 *138*
123 *161*
123:2b *161*
130 *138*
139 *161, 163*
139 – 143 *138*
139:1–4 *162*
139:15–16 *162*
139:17–22 *162*
139:23–24 *163*
142 *138, 143, 153–154*
146 – 150 *164*

Proverbs
15:8 *107*
15:29 *107*

28:9 *107*

Ecclesiastes
5:2 *108*
5:2 *171*

Isaiah
1:15 *67, 68, 70*
1:19 *122*
6 *68*
6:8–10 *80*
11:1–16 *68*
11:4–5 *213*
12 *68*
12:3 *23*
12:4 *22*
16:12 *67*
25:1–2 *68–69*
26 *69*
26:1–7 *69*
26:8–13 *69*
26:14–15 *70*
26:16–18 *70*
26:19–21 *70*
31:1–2 *71*
35:1–6 *177*
36 –39 *71*
37:16–20 *71*
38:2–3 *71*
39:8 *71*
41:25 *22, 24*
42:1 *24–25*
59:1–3 *67*
55 *71*
55:6–7 *71*
55:8–11 *71*
55:12–13 *72*
59:17 *213*
62:6–7 *72*
63:15–19 *72–73*
63:15 – 64:12 *72*
64:1–12 *73–74*
64:7 *22*

64:7–8 *72*
65:24 *74, 106*

Jeremiah
3:4 *75*
3:4–5 *74*
3:5 *75*
3:19–20 *75*
7:16 *75*
10:25 *22, 24*
11:9–12 *75*
11:18–20 *77*
11:18–23 *76*
12:1–6 *76, 77*
12:1–12 *77*
12:2 *77*
14 *88*
14:9–22 *76*
14:19–22 *82, 82–83*
15:10 *78*
15:10–14 *76, 78*
15:14 *78*
15:15–18 *78*
15:15 – 21 *76*
15:19–21 *79*
17:14–18 *76, 79–80*
18:18–23 *76, 80*
20 *80*
20:7–13 *76, 80–81*
20:14–18 *76, 81,*
  81–82
31:31–34 *172*
31:34 *179*
32 *83*
32:16–25 *83*
42 *84*
42:1–6 *84*

Lamentations
1:20–22 *85*
2 *86*
2:20–22 *86*
3:55 *22*
3:40–48 *86–87*

3:55–66 *87–88*
5:1–22 *88–89*

Ezekiel
1 *116*
4:14 *89, 90*
9:8 *89, 90*
11:13 *90*
20:49 *90*
36:21–23 *172*
36:37–38 *90–91*
39:7 *172*

Daniel
1 – 6 *117*
2:17–18 *116*
4:1–2 *117*
4:34 *117*
6 *117*
6:10 *117*
9 *117, 121*
9:4 *118*
9:5–7 *118*
9:8–15 *118–119*
9:16–19 *119–120*

Hosea
8:1–3 *92*
8:2 *92*

Joel
1:19–20 *94*
2:12 *95*
2:17 *94*
2:30–32 *95*
2:32 *22, 24, 26,*
  106, 194, 196

Amos
7:2–9 *92–93*

Jonah
1 *96, 97*
1:5–6 *96*

1:14 *96*
2 *97, 100*
2:1 *97*
2:2 *98*
2:3–4 *98–99*
2:5–6 *99*
2:7 *99*
2:7–9 *99*
2:8 *99*
2:9 *99*
3 *96, 97*
3:1–10 *96*
3:4 *97*
4 *98*
4:1–2 *100*
4:1–3 *97*

Micah
7 *175*
7:18–20 *93*

Habakkuk
1:2 *101*
1:3–4 *101*
1:5–11 *102*
1:12–2:1 *102*
3 *102*
3:1 *138*
3:2 *102*
3:13 *102*
3:15 *102*
3:16–19 *103*

Zephaniah
1:6–7 *103*
3:9 *22, 24,*
  104

Zechariah
13:9 *22, 24*
7:12–14 *104*
8:20–23 *104*
10:6 *104*
13:9 *105*

Zechariah (*cont.*)
14:4 *175*

Malachi
2:13 *105*
2:5 *105*
3:16–18 *105*

NEW TESTAMENT

Matthew
5:12 *171*
5:46 *171*
6:1–2 *171*
6:4–6 *171*
6:5–8 *171*
6:5–15 *171*
6:9–13 *172*
6:16 *171*
6:18 *171*
7:6 *174*
7:7–11 *171, 173, 174, 177*
9:36–38 *187*
11:25–26 *187*
14:23 *185*
17:14–21 *176*
18:15–18 *174*
18:19–20 *174*
21:18–22 *175*
21:21 *175*
21:22 *175*
24:15–20 *175*
26 *237*
26:36–46 *187*
27:46 *189*
27:50 *189*

Mark
1:35 *185*
6:46 *185*
9:24 *176*
9:28–29 *176*
14:32–42 *187*

15:34 *189*
15:37 *189*

Luke
1:10–11 *168*
1:50–55 *168–169*
1:68–75 *169*
2:29–32 *169*
2:36–38 *170*
2:37 *170*
3:21–22 *186*
4:40 *222*
4:42 *185*
5:15–16 *185*
6:12–13 *186*
6:27–28 *177*
9:18 *185*
9:28–29 *186*
10:1 *185*
10:2 *239*
10:21 *187*
11 *173, 177, 238*
11:5–13 *177–178*
15 *183*
18 *184, 185*
18:1 *184*
18:2–8 *184*
18:9–14 *184–185*
22:31–32 *188*
22:39–46 *188*
23:33–34 *189*
23:46 *189*

John
4:34 *179*
4:43 *179*
5:17 *179*
10:25 *179*
10:37 *179*
11 *197*
11:41–44 *186*
12:27–28 *188*
14:8–14 *178*
14:10 *179*

15 *180*
15:11 *180*
15:16 *180*
15:24 *179*
16 *180*
16:23–27 *180*
16:24 *180*
17 *180*
17:1–5 *181*
17:6–8 *181*
17:9 *181–182*
17:11–13 *181–182*
17:17–18 *181–182*
17:20–23 *182*
17:24–26 *182–183*

Acts
1 *191*
1:8 *195, 199*
1:12–14 *191*
1:24–26 *192*
2 *26*
2:17–21 *26*
2:21 *194*
2:42 *192*
4:24–28 *193*
4:29–30 *193*
4:31 *194*
5 *239*
6 *194*
6:1–4 *194*
7 *195*
7:59–60 *195*
8:14–17 *196*
8:18–24 *196*
9 *196*
9:11 *196*
9:14 *194*
9:21 *194*
9:40 *197*
10:1–5 *197*
10:9 *197*
12 *198*
12:5 *198*

12:12 *198*
13 *198*
13:1–3 *198*
14:23 *198*
16:25–26 *198*
20 – 21 *199*
20:36–38 *199*
21:5–6 *199*
28:8 *199*

Romans
1:8–14 *202*
5:2 *214*
5:11 *214*
8 *209*
8:15 *17*
8:15 *209*
8:16 *17*
8:23–25 *210*
8:26 *17, 209*
9 – 11 *26*
10:1 *202*
10:12–13 *26*
10:14–17 *17, 28*
11 *234*
12 *210*
12:9–13 *210*
12:12 *214*
14:1 *222*
15:30–33 *212*

1 Corinthians
1 *211*
7:30 *214*
11:3–16 *211*

2 Corinthians
1 *203*
1:11 *213*
6:10 *214*
12:7–10 *208*

Galatians
4:27 *214*

Ephesians
1 *205*
1:15–22 *239*
1:15–23 *203*
1:18–19 *205*
1:22–23 *204, 206*
1:23 *205*
3:14–15 *239*
3:14–21 *204*
3:18–19 *239*
6 *213*
6:14–18 *213*
6:18–20 *213*

Philippians
1:3–6 *206*
1:9–11 *206*
1:18 *214*
2:17 *214*
4 *214*
4:4–7 *214*

Colossians
1:3–5 *206–207*
1:9–12 *207*
1:9–14 *206–207*
1:13–14 *207*
1:24 *214*
4 *215, 239*
4:2–4 *214*
4:3–4 *213*
4:12 *215, 237*

1 Thessalonians
1:2–3 *207*
5:16–18 *215*

2 Thessalonians
1:11–12 *207*
3:1–2 *213*

1 Timothy
2 *210*

2:1–4 *210–211*
2:3 *211*
2:4 *211*
2:8 *210–211*

2 Timothy
1:3 *208*
2:9 *221*

Philemon
4–6 *208*

Hebrews
1 – 4 *218*
1:10–12 *217*
4 *217*
4:16 *217*
7:25 *217*
7:25 *217*
5:7 *218*
7:23–25 *218 –219*
13:18–19 *219*

James
1 *222*
1:5–6 *239*
1:5–8 *220*
1:6 *220*
1:7 *220*
1:8 *220*
4 *220*
4:2–4 *221*
4:7–10 *221*
5 *221, 223*
5:10 *221*
5:13–18 *221*
5:15 *222*
5:16 *222, 223*
5:17 *223*
5:19–20 *223*

1 Peter
3:7 *224*
3:12 *224*

1 Peter (*cont.*)
4 *224*
4:7 *224*
5:7 *10*

1 John
1:8–10 *225*
1:9 *239*
5:9 *226*
5:13–17 *225–226,*
 226
5:14 *226*

3 John
1–4 *226*

Jude
20–21 *224–225*

Revelation
5:8 *30*
5:8–10 *226–227*
8:3–4 *30*
6 *227*
6:9–11 *227*

6:10 *30*
8 *228*
8:3–5 *228*
9 *30*
15:3–4 *228*
19 – 22 *228*
19:1–3 *228*
19:6–8 *228*
21 – 22 *229*
21:22–25 *229*
22:3–5 *229*
22:17 *230*
22:20 *17, 230*

Titles in this series:

1 *Possessed by God*, David Peterson
2 *God's Unfaithful Wife*, Raymond C. Ortlund Jr.
3 *Jesus and the Logic of History*, Paul W. Barnett
4 *Hear, My Son*, Daniel J. Estes
5 *Original Sin*, Henri Blocher
6 *Now Choose Life*, J. Gary Millar
7 *Neither Poverty Nor Riches*, Craig L. Blomberg
8 *Slave of Christ*, Murray J. Harris
9 *Christ, Our Righteousness*, Mark A. Seifrid
10 *Five Festal Garments*, Barry G. Webb
11 *Salvation to the Ends of the Earth*, Andreas J. Köstenberger
   and Peter T. O'Brien
12 *Now My Eyes Have Seen You*, Robert S. Fyall
13 *Thanksgiving*, David W. Pao
14 *From Every People and Nation*, J. Daniel Hays
15 *Dominion and Dynasty*, Stephen G. Dempster
16 *Hearing God's Words*, Peter Adam
17 *The Temple and the Church's Mission*, G. K. Beale
18 *The Cross from a Distance*, Peter G. Bolt
19 *Contagious Holiness*, Craig L. Blomberg
20 *Shepherds After My Own Heart*, Timothy S. Laniak
21 *A Clear and Present Word*, Mark D. Thompson
22 *Adopted into God's Family*, Trevor J. Burke
23 *Sealed with an Oath*, Paul R. Williamson
24 *Father, Son and Spirit*, Andreas J. Köstenberger and
   Scott R. Swain
25 *God the Peacemaker*, Graham A. Cole
26 *A Gracious and Compassionate God*, Daniel C. Timmer
27 *The Acts of the Risen Lord Jesus*, Alan J. Thompson
28 *The God Who Makes Himself Known*, W. Ross Blackburn
29 *A Mouth Full of Fire*, Andrew G. Shead
30 *The God Who Became Human*, Graham A. Cole
31 *Paul and the Law*, Brian S. Rosner
32 *With the Clouds of Heaven*, James M. Hamilton Jr.
33 *Covenant and Commandment*, Bradley G. Green
34 *Bound for the Promised Land*, Oren R. Martin

35 *'Return to Me'*, Mark J. Boda
36 *Identity and Idolatry*, Richard Lints
37 *Who Shall Ascend the Mountain of the Lord?*, L. Michael Morales
38 *Calling on the Name of the Lord*, J. Gary Millar

An index of Scripture references for all the volumes may be found at
http://www.thegospelcoalition.org/resources/nsbt